Five Ways to Make
Architecture Political

Five Ways to Make Architecture Political

An Introduction to the Politics of Design Practice

Albena Yaneva

BLOOMSBURY VISUAL ARTS
LONDON • NEW YORK • OXFORD • NEW DELHI • SYDNEY

BLOOMSBURY VISUAL ARTS
Bloomsbury Publishing Plc
50 Bedford Square, London, WC1B 3DP, UK
1385 Broadway, New York, NY 10018, USA
29 Earlsfort Terrace, Dublin 2, Ireland

BLOOMSBURY, BLOOMSBURY VISUAL ARTS and the Diana logo
are trademarks of Bloomsbury Publishing Plc

First published by Bloomsbury Academic 2017
This edition published 2018
Reprinted 2021

Copyright © Albena Yaneva, 2017

Albena Yaneva has asserted her right under the Copyright, Designs and
Patents Act, 1988, to be identified as Author of this work.

For legal purposes the Acknowledgements on p. ix constitute an extension
of this copyright page.

Cover design: Eleanor Rose
Cover image © New Street Station, Birmingham: photograph © AZPML

All rights reserved. No part of this publication may be reproduced or
transmitted in any form or by any means, electronic or mechanical,
including photocopying, recording, or any information storage or retrieval
system, without prior permission in writing from the publishers.

Bloomsbury Publishing Plc does not have any control over, or responsibility for,
any third-party websites referred to or in this book. All internet addresses given
in this book were correct at the time of going to press. The author and publisher regret
any inconvenience caused if addresses have changed or sites have ceased to exist,
but can accept no responsibility for any such changes.

A catalogue record for this book is available from the British Library.

Library of Congress Cataloging-in-Publication Data
A catalog record for this book is available from the Library of Congress.

ISBN: HB: 978-1-4742-5235-5
PB: 978-1-3500-8971-6
ePDF: 978-1-4742-5237-9
ePub: 978-1-4742-5236-2

Typeset by Integra Software Services Pvt. Ltd.

To find out more about our authors and books visit www.bloomsbury.com
and sign up for our newsletters.

For Martin

Contents

List of Figures		viii
Acknowledgements		ix
Introduction		1
1	Architecture and Politics	15
2	How to Study Ecology of Practice	33
3	Political Objects: The First Way of Becoming Political	53
4	Experiments in Practice: The Second Way of Becoming Political	75
5	The Multiple Natures of a City: The Third Way of Becoming Political	91
6	Sites of Politics: The Fourth Way of Becoming Political	109
7	Urban Publics: The Fifth Way of Becoming Political	133
Conclusion		159
Glossary		167
References		171
Index		183

List of Figures

I.1	Still from *Misleading Innocence* (Tracing What a Bridge Can Do)	3
I.2	Image of bridge	3
2.1	The namBa HIPS building, Osaka	35
2.2	Architects at work in the office of Takamatsu	39
2.3	The practice of Takamatsu, Takeda, Kyoto	40
3.1	The Benzie building, Manchester School of Arts	54
3.2	The Benzie building, section, Feldon Clegg Bradlet Studios	55
3.3	The Benzie building, interplay of different disciplines, Feldon Clegg Bradlet Studios	56
3.4	The Benzie building atrium/vertical gallery, ground floor	57
3.5	The Benzie building atrium/vertical gallery, staircase	58
3.6	Lecture theatre in Benzie building	70
4.1	Birmingham train station, location	78
4.2	The Gateway building, steel façade	78
4.3	Identified glare areas affected by redesign	81
4.4	West façade of the Gateway building	86
5.1	Image of the Birmingham New Street Station, concept design of the station envelope	94
5.2	The Birmingham New Street, the construction site	100
5.3	Layers of Movement, public presentation, Redevelopment of New Street Station, Birmingham, April 2008	102
5.4	Construction site, July 2012	106
6.1	The fresco room, the old Jesuit theatre of the *Alte Aula* in Vienna	115
6.2	The 'surprises' of the fresco, the *Alte Aula* in Vienna	117
6.3	Bolshoi theatre in Moscow	120
7.1	Vertical display of models of the CCTV tower, OMA, Rotterdam	140
7.2	Rem Koolhaas presents a project in OMA, Rotterdam	145
7.3	The public at the presentation of Andrés Perea in Madrid, video snapshot	149
7.4	The Marina Bay Sands, Singapore, Courtesy of Safdie Architects	151
7.5	Mosche Safdie draws, Courtesy of Safdie Architects	152

Acknowledgements

I began writing this book a long time ago. As early as 2002 I had ideas about exploring the connections between politics and architecture in an unconventional way. However, the motivation for studying further many empirical cases as a part of the book sparkled in discussions with my 13-year-old son Martin when he started asking questions: 'What is politics? How is it done? Is it all about equality and rights, votes and petitions?' As easy as it is for a mother to silence him by a brief 'Yes', these questions demand long answers. Luckily, the questions piled up and gradually revolved around architectural issues of all sorts as Martin was 'forced' to visit architectural landmarks during his holidays: buildings of Koolhaas, Siza, Foster, Hadid, Gehry, Zaera-Polo and others. Just like his interest in politics tangled with curiosity in design, the book developed as an inquiry on the political dimensions of architecture. My attempts to keep the flame of his curiosity subsequently developed into a thinking of how to respond to similar questions to our 20-year-old students who wish to understand how politics relates to the mundane objects of our lives, to the arrangement of a classroom, to the narrowness of the pavements, the security belt in our cars, to the height of the bridge we cross every day, to the faint shape of iconic skyscraper. This book 'narrates' extensive answers to these simple questions.

Research on the book was generously supported by a grant from the British Academy to study architectural presentations as a form of political action (BA award SG50346), a grant from the Graham Foundation of Advanced Studies and small research grants from the University of Manchester. Two visiting professorship appointments – at the Princeton School of Architecture (2013) and the Parsons School of Design in New York (2015) – provided further opportunities for research and discussions around the empirical materials and ideas of the book. An invitation to lecture at the Canadian Centre of Architecture (CCA) in Montreal in 2014 offered a chance to discuss further ideas related to the pre-release of the CCA documentary *Misleading Innocence;* this event inspired and informed back the book. An invitation at the Strelka, Institute for Media, Architecture and Design, in Moscow was a chance to practice my long forgotten Russian, and to study the amazing case of the renovation of Bolshoi theatre. I lectured at many other places in the world; various questions asked at these lectures found place in the book as arguments or empirical stories. However, my most sincere and most vivid critics were at home, in Manchester. I am greatly indebted to my colleagues and intellectual friends from the Manchester Architecture Research Centre for their generous comments and support all along the work on the book: Isabelle Doucet, Lukasz Stanek, Leandro Minuchin, Ray Lucas, Alan Lewis, Deljana Iossifova and Amy Hanley. My PhD students – Paul Gottschling, Jeremy Lecomte, Ahlam Sharif, Athena Moustaka, Yu Yoshii and Garrett Wolf – listened to the empirical stories and arguments presented in this book and helped me to make them better. My husband Svet and my younger son Christian (not-yet-interested in questions of politics and design) were both endlessly patient. Martin's impatience grew bigger. I dedicate this book to him, hoping he will read it soon.

Introduction

What is left from the classic parables of architecture and social control?

What is the best story we tell to illustrate the political effects of architecture and building technologies? How can we better demonstrate how buildings get endowed with authority and become mechanisms of control and domination? As classic example, the panopticon prison developed by Jeremy Bentham better exemplifies the social effects of buildings. Like other prisons, the 'Penitentiary Panopticon' relied on the isolation of the prisoners in solitary cells and on discipline through work. Yet, what set the Benthamite panopticon apart was the inspection principle that implied the governor located in a central tower of the prison to spend his time overseeing the prisoners and their guards. This hierarchy was inscribed in the prison structure in a way that the prison building became a mechanism for controlling human behaviour and exercising power. Concealment, oversight and eavesdropping made the 'omnipresence of the governor' possible and hence, the 'omnipresence of power'. Architecture helped to generate and stabilize social order.

Another classic parable of architecture's power to control and generate order revolves around the bridges of Robert Moses built in the 1920s. The political philosopher Langdon Winner published a provocative article titled 'Do artefacts Have Politics?' in 1980. He argued that artefacts and material-spatial arrangements embody social relations and power; infrastructure and buildings can contain political properties and can be interpreted in political language. The low overpasses on the bridges of Long Island designed by Moses play as a key example for Winner's argument. The height of the bridges, he argued, was not randomly chosen; they were deliberately built with a height of 8.5 feet so as to make impossible the presence of buses on the parkways; this specific design filtered and limited access of racial minorities and low-income groups to Jones Beach – the acclaimed park of Moses. The highways and bridges he built favoured the use of automobile over the development of mass transit and presented a way of engineering relationships among people. As 'certain technologies *in themselves* have political properties' (Winner 1980: 122), artefacts and material arrangements can influence the way we exercise power and the very experience of citizenship. That is the reason why, as advocated by Winner, we need to pay more attention to the characteristics of objects and we should raise awareness for designers that the material arrangements they produce could be a way of settling an issue in a particular community. The message of Winner to architects and planners also reads: built environment contains explicit or implicit political purposes; we should recognize the political dimensions in the shape of buildings and urban infrastructure; architecture contains a potential for ordering human activities.

Winner's argument triggered lots of debates in the fields of technology studies, urban studies and political theory; and activated controversies among urban practitioners, policymakers and political scientists. A recent documentary produced at the Canadian Centre of Architecture, *Misleading Innocence: Tracing what a bridge can do*, by Francesco Garutti presents a re-enactment of the debate between social constructivists and Actor-Network-Theory (ANT) scholars as a result of Langdon Winner's publication in the 1980s. The bridge is portrayed in this film as a much more complex material and social artefact than the bridge pictured by Winner. Tracing simultaneously a discursive layer by the means of interviews with protagonists in this scholarly debate along with a visual layer, the documentary recollects the multidimensionality and the versatile agency of the bridge.

As the documentary unfolds, we are convinced that Winner's interpretation presents a very anaemic version of technology, as only the height of the bridge is discussed, 8.5 feet is the height of the parkways, whereas the height of a bus is 12 feet. There is no mention of materiality, shape, construction, technological innovations or users; nor is there a mention of natural forces and how they happen to be channelled in a specifically shaped artefact – the 'low bridge'. On the other side, only one type of politics is discussed – racial discrimination. Winner reduces politics to racial politics, and the complexity of the bridge to its height. Placing the bridge's height and racism into an equation of causal explanation, Winner reproduces the divide between politics and infrastructure. However, a bridge is neither simply material nor is it merely political; it can only be understood as the intersection and the balance of a range of forces, from the political to the natural, from the real to the metaphorical. The documentary shows its materiality with a series of close-ups (Figure I.1). We witness its different dimensions. We see the bridge technology in action. We watch this artefact being used, failing and being repaired. So, we witness the agency of a very complex object, which is brought out visually by illustration of its various dimensions and the many different actors* that gather around it and maintain it on a daily basis. We observe the failure of the artefact and so we have a much more complex understanding of both technology and politics. It is not any longer possible to sustain the divide between infrastructure and politics and to reduce the technology of low bridges to racial politics. We rather focus our efforts on understanding the bridge manifestations and the wider cultures of the built environment.

The documentary also reminds us that a bridge never exists without builders, construction and maintenance workers, planners, policemen, senators, engineers and traffic controllers. It is simplistic indeed to just mention one actor related to it – Moses and one dimension only of the bridge – its height (as per Winner's interpretation). The documentary brings a much larger crowd of actors around the bridge; an entire network. They all interact with it. They gather around this bridge and speak about it, but also on behalf of it. The bridge witnessed here cinematographically becomes a much more hybrid artefact because we pay attention to what it does, not just to what it is or what it means. The film reveals the bridge as an object that is far from static. It also advocates a research approach that states: if

Figure I.1 Still from *Misleading Innocence* (Tracing What a Bridge Can Do) © Canadian Centre for Architecture.

Figure I.2 Image of bridge. © Louis Minutoli.

we follow the processes of design, of contestation, of daily use, of maintenance, we can gain unique access to architecture and urban infrastructure.

The key question of Winner is 'Do artefacts have politics?' Or in other words, these are questions that read: 'What is an artefact?' 'What does it mean to have low passageways?' Yet, none of these questions are the questions we should be asking. They trap all interpretations of buildings and infrastructure in metaphysics of essence. Instead, we should question how design becomes political: 'What does the bridge do?' 'Where and how?' 'How and where?' 'What are its modalities of actions?' 'How does it connect or disconnect, and how does it produce political effects?' 'How, when, to what extent and under what circumstances can design become political or generate political relations?' In other words, the question is not whether the bridge *embodies* racial politics, it is about what it does and how it performs politics in various situations: in the process of design, contestation, renovation and use, accident control and traffic management.

The film turns the bridge into a political site; politics here is generated by the artefact as it acts and connects with many other things* in a network. It reaffirms that 'design can have political effects but must not be reduced to a given politics' (Barry 2001). It also illustrates the *unfolding* of the political (Domínguez and Fogué 2015) as opposed to the traditional foucauldian understanding of the micro-technologies of disciplinary institutions that enable design to operate at a subpolitical level as enfolding, inscribing power relations in material arrangements, artefacts, technologies and buildings (Fouclault 1975). The bridge is political to the degree to which it becomes a site of contestation and not because it symbolizes state politics or ideologies. If we follow the course of the events that make the bridge connect with engineers, architects, politicians, contractors, citizens, journalists, traffic controllers, repair workers and so on; if we are able to trace the many unpredictable alliances that all those protagonists with variable ontologies and disagreeing voices can shape together while moving according to different times and spaces, we will be able to witness the political. *Here* is the political; not in the artefact itself, but in the way it acts and connects to other objects and people in a related way. It is *in* the various manifestations of the bridge, *in* the many unpredictable alliances traced among the different protagonists in bridge design and maintenance, *in* the course of the events that make architects connect with planners and New Yorkers, *in* the process of accounting for its transformations.

Where is the political?

The classic examples of the Panopticon prison and the bridges of Moses remind us of the long relationship between architecture and politics. Existing attempts to connect architecture and politics typically strive to reveal the politics behind design or the design techniques disguised as politics. In the existing scholarship, architecture is considered as important factor in the construction of nationalist imaginaries (Tafuri 1976; Lefebvre 1991; Vale 1992; Boyer 1994; Mitchell 1994; Edelman 1995; Leach 1999; Huyssen 2003). Buildings can act as 'socially classifying devices' (King 2010) and can become powerful metaphors for social relations (Markus 1993; Sennett, 1994; Dovey 1999). Architecture's relation to politics is commonly understood in the light of traditional foundational theories of politics related to ideology, state, nation, government, policies and activism. These realities are foundational in the sense that we tend to start with them before proceeding to justify and explain everything in architecture within their terms. Politics is a separate domain of action with its own logics, institutions and practices; it is *outside* of architecture's remit and far from the architectural objects and processes. Standing aloof from the world of architecture, it can explain it by the token of often linear, uninterrupted or mediated* causal relation: politics is projected on, mirrored, reflected or embedded in built form, city plans, urban artefacts and thus comes to explain the shape of buildings and urban infrastructure.

Political philosophy has witnessed a rapid development in the last twenty years. Yet, the field of architecture is only slowly catching up with it. In the 1990s, Beck argued that there is a displacement of politics (Beck 1992, 1999). That is, political scientists look for politics in the wrong places as political action now often takes place *next to* or *across* institutionalized political orders. He suggested that in order to regain a handle on political dynamics and on the agenda for institutional renewal, political scientists should engage in studying the 'subpolitical' processes that take place outside the domain of formal politics. At the time marked by the displacement of politics, the crisis of legitimation of party-based and national politics, to accept that buildings and architectural projects can miraculously legitimize or embody power, is a form of anachronism; to assume that the simple participation of users in design is sufficient for democratic design is to indulge into facile politization. Party politics and decision making of elected representatives alone cannot uphold the classical-modernist order of politics. Citizens seek multiple forms of representations and thus the ordering of politics that allocates the authority of legitimate decision-making to elected representatives is challenged. Design, I argue in this book, can help us to reimagine the forms of political representation and reinvent the sites of political action. If politics in its conventional form amounts in the activities of political parties and the state, the 'political' is understood as the area of openness of new sites and new sights, of difference, of new objects, of events (Barry 2001). Design matters politically as it holds the unfolding capacity 'to propose and open up the possibility of novel forms of action and thought' (Domínguez and Fogué 2015: 148). The 'political' is the ontological condition of politics and of being together in general; it is performed on many sites related to design, construction and renovation practices; it is enacted by architectural visuals, design experiments, material arrangements and urban artefacts.

A number of authors, including DeVries (2007), Barry (2001) and Latour (2004a, 2005a), illustrated that politics is not foundational; it is no longer to be found in the big concepts of 'domination', 'inequalities', 'power struggles' 'elections', and 'revolutions' and cannot be limited to citizens, elections, votes, petitions, ideologies and institutionalized conflicts. If politics is a-foundational, irreductivist; this means that there is no prepared and defined ground on which it rests, and to which it can be easily reduced; nor can it become a ground for explaining the cultural realities of arts, architecture and music. This irreductivist political thought is still very new for architectural discourses; its insights can cast architecture in both a new light and a new language. If politics is not a base outside of architecture's remit that can be used to explain architecture, how can we scrutinize and conceptualize the political dimensions of buildings and cities? Here is my answer: the *locus* of political action has shifted. The 'political', I claim, can be explored and generated at the level of design and architectural practice, it can be seen as integral to many features of building, planning, construction and renovation processes; it *emerges* and can be witnessed as we trace the transformation of objects, sites, urban publics and the multiple realities of a city.

Taking inspiration from the irreductivist approach to politics, the book explores the different ways architecture can be political. It argues for the necessity to engage with the world of architecture making and to commit to the possibility of grasping the underlying political dimensions of the built environment, its objects, institutions, actors, objectivity and networks. Studies that focus on architecture and politics are abundant. Studies that focus on the becoming political of architectural objects (drawings, plans, codes, regulations, infrastructures) are very scarce. Two studies in particular deserve mentioning here. Following planning practice techniques in the Netherlands, Gomart and Hajer (2003) trace how design drawings circulate, how the plan for the *Hoeksche Waard*, an island south of Rotterdam, becomes a robust political plan and how the traditional architectural techniques get modified to tentatively construct this plan as political. Moore and Wilson (2013) study the politics of building codes in American projects and argue that architecture, social justice and urban ecologies are 'co-constructed'. They influence each other in-their-making. Moore and Wilson advocate the need for a broader, irreductivist, pragmatist interpretation of architectural production. Drawing on insights from these two studies, from recent debates in the field of Political Philosophy and Science and Technology Studies (STS) and in particular debates on object-oriented politics (Latour and Weibel 2005), agency and material citizenship (Marres 2012), the book offers conceptual and methodological tools for describing the various political modalities of architecture. It invites political scientists to explore the possibilities of *other ways* of doing politics – architectural, designerly, urbanely ways; while design practitioners are encouraged to build awareness of the inherent relational valence of architecture that could inspire a more political kind of practice.

In the traditional understanding of politics, the political question is about 'who participates in design, in urban experiments and policy?' 'Is it a small group of technocrats, or all those affected by urban practices and policies?' A different way of phrasing the political question in design would be to focus on the relations and urban norms, the groupings and associations, the agency and the scenarios of use, the politics deployed *in* the performance* of buildings, in urban technologies, *in* design, construction and planning practices. Thus the question is no longer who acts, decides, chooses, participates and represents, and whether this participation follows democratic procedures, but rather *how* specific capacities to act are performed through design and urban practice. How does design 'engage' people? How do different design, construction and renovation practices transform human experiences and affect human trajectories? By human, I mean both the makers (designers, planners, builders, renovators and craftsmen) and the dwellers (the inhabitants, the passers-by, the random visitors and the larger groupings of neighbours, communities and citizens). How do the various experiences and performances coexist? Instead of focusing on who acts, it is necessary to turn out attention to the practices that shift the trajectories of things and persons; the political emerges as a phenomenon that could be grasped at the level of design and urban practice. It is critical to direct out sights to the settings, arrangements and objects, which allow humans to grow endowed with specific qualities; to get transformed. The political sites.

The escape from perspective

Architectural theory often embraces an understanding of buildings that would assume that buildings have an objective reality 'out there' while a number of subjective perspectives *to* that building are being expressed, compared, weighted and reconciled. This interpretation, termed as 'perspectival flexibility' (Daston 1992), implies the divergence of individual perspectives and viewpoints. This would infer an understanding of the architectural object as scrutinized by the subjectivity of individual idiosyncratic perspectives and evaluated according to the different interests of stakeholders. Architecture studies share the view that apart from generating physical reality design has *a meaning* for many other actors (users, planners, citizen groups) and designers should attend to what these other actors and entities experience in design process. Designers have *a perspective*, and every design project holds this perspective; that is, they attribute meaning to what they believe a building stands for. They acknowledge also *the perspectives of others*, their points of view to the objective reality of built forms. In a perspectivalism view, every architectural project exemplifies an interpretation of the world we live in. Architectural scholars believe that studying perspectives of all these various participants in design, without excluding the participation of the users (Till 1998; Hill 2003; Blundell et al. 2005; Cupers 2013), is a way of attending to the nature of buildings and urban reality. Yet, by entering the realm of *meaning* the built reality is left out. In a paradoxical way, in the world of meaning nobody is in touch with the reality, but everybody interprets it. In a perspectival understanding, the interpretations of buildings will vary while the built form will stay untouched and will recede behind the different subjective readings.

My ambition here is to take a step away from the dominant perspectivalism in architectural and design theory, and to rather foreground the practicalities, materialities and events of buildings; to trace the complex processes of transformation, inhabitation, renovation and presentation of buildings. If instead of bracketing the practices, in which a building is handled, we rather foreground the practices of design making, renovation and dwelling that appear so visible in the material practices of the actors, in their disagreements, in their alliances; if the actions of urban practitioners (designers, planners, renovators, constructors) are foregrounded, buildings-in-design and buildings-in-use will cease to be passive objects that can be understood, interpreted or perceived from the point of view of seemingly endless series of perspectives. The analysis would escape perspective. If we take this step, the buildings discussed here will not be seen any longer as political symbols or embodiments of big political forces; they will rather become a part of what is done in design, renovation, presentation and dwelling practices. Following processes of designing, experimenting, presenting and renovating, experiencing buildings will place the analysis within the 'aperspectival objectivity' (Daston 1992; Daston and Galison 2007) of built form, which holds the ethos of interchangeable observer as the variability is located in the object itself. The chief source of variability shifts from the many viewpoints and variable subjectivities (in the perspectival view) to the multiple reality of the built object. In this view, the building itself comes into being with the practices in which it is manipulated; the accounts presented in this book will tell us what buildings *do* in practice to all those who relate to them. And since the object of manipulation tends to differ from one practice to another, reality multiplies. The architects, the planners, the renovators, the crowds, the technologies, the visuals: all of them are more than one. More than singular. More than unique. This triggers the question of how they are related. That is, a political question.

The method

The study of the political dimension of architecture presented in this book is inspired by a pragmatist philosophy that implies a realist understanding of architecture and design practices. It relies on symmetrical understanding of nature and culture taken in their multiplicity; a perspective where no prioritization of a privileged point of view is taken. That is, an ANT approach to architecture inspired by the tradition of STS. STS 'flourished' in the 1980s in the aftermath of the structuralism wave, with the writings of Bruno Latour, Michel Callon, Madeleine Akrich, Michael Lynch, Peter Galison and others, and generated new concepts and methodologies for the understanding of the social*. In the past decade STS, and in particular ANT, gained critical acclaim among researchers in the fields of design and architecture studies, in cultural geography and material culture studies. ANT is a method of social inquiry used to overcome simplistic dichotomies such as nature/culture, materiality/meaning and subject/object (Latour 2005b). Taking this method into the field of architecture would imply investigating the architectural cultures and practices of designers rather than their theories and ideologies (Callon 1996; Yaneva 2005). ANT allows reporting what architects, designers, engineers and dwellers *do* – their daily routines, individual moves and collective groupings – in spite of their interests and theories, thus constantly prioritizing the pragmatic content of actions, not of discourses. Architects are to be studied not because they are important with their theories, values and ideologies (an approach advocated by critical theory) and not in opposition with architecture, but because they make possible the existence of numerous objects, buildings and artefacts, instruments and theories that constitute architecture and the built environment. This method helps circumventing both traditional sociological approaches that rely solely on social contextualization of the working environment of architectural firms (Blau 1984) and anthropology-informed approaches that treat all products of architectural design as socially constructed (Cuff 1992).

An ANT-inspired approach to architecture assumes: first, that the divide between the 'subjective' and 'objective' is abandoned. Objects are often grasped in architectural scholarship in two different ways: either through their intrinsic materiality (that would define them as material, real, objective and factual) or through their more 'symbolic' aspects (that would define them as social, subjective and lived). ANT helps us escape this modernist division. Suggesting that matter is absorbed into meaning, that it is *in* the world, architectural research could engage in analysis of how materiality from one side and politics from the other are to coalesce.

Second, drawing on ANT, we could do justice to the many material dimensions of things without limiting them in advance to pure material properties or to social symbols. Matter is much too multidimensional, much too active, complex, surprising and counterintuitive to be represented in stabilized artefacts and static institutions. A second advantage of an ANT perspective is that it offers a fuller view of these dimensions and makes us embrace a complex conglomerate of many surprising agencies that are rarely taken into account. Such descriptions would reveal the unpredictable attachments to non-humans* both in the processes of making and experiencing buildings; and that is what makes them so materially interesting.

Third, instead of looking for explanations outside the field of architecture, an ANT perspective will consider context as a variable; that is, as something moving, evolving and changing along with the various objects and practices. Context is made of the many dimensions that impinge at every stage on the development of a project, at every stage of experience. And this is the third advantage of an ANT perspective to architecture. Instead of analysing the impact of external factors on architecture, such as market forces, class divisions, economic constraints, social conventions or politics, we should attempt to grasp the performance of different types of matters, objects, technological settings and institutions. ANT gives us one more tool, with which to follow the painstaking ways humans interact with objects and environments and shape dynamic architectural cultures at different scales.

The number of architects and architectural theorists interested in ANT today is sheer. It is impossible to describe ANT in the abstract because it is grounded on empirical case studies; we can only understand the approach if we have a sense of those case studies (Law 2007). There is confusion among ANT scholars regarding ANT's status as theory. ANT is not a theory, argued John Law, because it is descriptive rather than foundational in explanatory terms. He claimed: 'it is a toolkit for telling interesting stories... about how relations assemble' (Law 2007). By following and accounting networks in different empirical cases, new implicit theories (with a small 't') emerge: new theories about the nature of markets (Callon and Muniesa 2005; MacKenzie 2009); about human body (Pasveer and Akrich 1996; Mol 2002), about scientific facts and truth (Latour and Woolgar 1979), about engineering design (Law 1987, 2002). As those 'interesting stories' unfold, we find implicit theories that come right from the actors' worlds and are told with their native words. The use of an ANT methodology does not lead to the generation of one foundational theory, but inevitably generates many new implicit theories that are better suited to explain the actors' world-building activities. Mobilizing ANT allows us to study 'architecture in the making'; it provides new tools for tracing the becoming political of architectural objects and settings.

To understand how design can be political, I will tell a number of stories, which will lead me to unearth a palette of implicit theories about the political (with very small 't' and 'p'). I will examine how politics *transpires* in design and planning offices, on construction and renovation locales, in public presentations. These are sites (often) unrelated to the traditional *loci* of political action, sites where both the architectural and the political are performed and can be enacted. Analysing and scrutinizing these sites is in the core of this study. Guided by a series of 'how' questions, I will take the reader to the heart of these places and will trace empirical accounts of various sets of practices and design techniques, which have political effects. I will follow how architects participate in world-makings and how they manipulate reality by means of various tools in the course of design practice. I will describe how images and models travel outside the architect's office, how they are modified, juggled, revised, retouched and negotiated, how they ignite the formation of different publics, trigger reactions and affect communities; how these visuals become political sites. The argument here is not that politics has no relevant connection to architecture and architectural analysis. Politics and architecture are abstract constructs; as such they cannot explain each other. Yet, at the level of the practice, at the level of making, both the political and the architectural get decomposed to myriad of small elements; fluid and unstable, fragile and composite. The political emerges as an underlying dimension of architectural practices that can only be grasped by following *how* they unfold.

The ANT-inspired accounts (McLean and Hassard 2004) of the political dimensions of design, renovation or inhabitation presented here all bear three similar features. First, the accounts include all the participants in architecture – single and collective, human and non-human – encountered in the different observations and limit themselves to the time spans of the studies. The actors in the stories were selected on the basis of the number of traces they left and the ways they found to intensify their presence: they manifested themselves *in situ*, they participated actively in different processes, their names appeared in interviews and informal conversations with the participants in design, as well as in textual and visual documentation; they invaded the design, building and renovation sites, the visuals of architects and builders, the archives and the programme documents of clients; they made difference, they triggered effects. That is how they emerged as the 'relevant' actors to be included in the ANT-inspired stories of the becoming political of architecture. Second, the observations embrace heterogeneous data collected throughout the different studies by treating symmetrically human actors and non-humans (buildings' layers, frescos, material arrangements, design sketches, glare, atria, stairs and presentational models). This is also achieved by identifying situations in which non-humans talk back to humans instead of following only the activities of those usually delegated* to talk on their behalf. Third, the accounts *deploy* the actors as networks, instead of merely describing them ethnographically, or unveiling in a critical fashion, what is behind architectural objects – the political forces at work. To deploy means to account with meticulousness the performances of the entire collectives* of humans and non-humans instead of relating action merely to a particular agent, or explaining it with enduring historical structures and systems.

Using ANT as 'a very crude method *to learn from the actors* without imposing on them an a priori definition of their world building capacities' (Latour 1999b: 20), I attempt to overcome the one-sided interpretation of buildings as heavily relying on the human subjects being central, with little room for non-humans. In my particular rendering of ANT here, I follow the slow transformations of buildings-to-be, buildings-in-use, buildings-in-renovation, buildings-in-becoming. The common denominator of all the empirical case studies, of all ANT accounts, is that they all tell a story of the emergence of the political. However, they tell it in different ways: by following different types of connections among the participants in design; by recalling different orderings of reality; by tracing different circuits of elements that are glued together to make the political.

My ambition is not to offer any classificatory schemes for distinguishing good from bad architecture, politically well sound or unsound design; no general rules of method are to be instated. Instead, engaging in an ANT-inspired enquiry of architectural practice, I will propose specific tools for working in and upon particular situations where the political can emerge in order to know these better. Attending to the specificity of different design worlds, I will endeavour to make my empirical accounts as detailed as possible so as to be able to make difference, to interfere. Situating the analysis at the level of architecture making I wish to inspire practitioners to a more political kind of practice, to enthuse new ways of making difference.

Structure of the book

The book is framed as seven chapters that can be read alone or in sequence. Each of them seeks to open a different kind of conceptual window onto the politics of architecture through a specific lens: the objects, the practice, the design experiments, the sites, the urban publics, the city. Furthermore, they are empirically grounded in ethnographic accounts complemented by archival sources, media reports and in-depth interviews with the participants in design. These accounts are not exemplar case studies that aim at showcasing (in a normative or illustrative way) how in general architectural practice could be and should be political. They rather present more objective, anthropological snapshots of ordinary practice demonstrating how architecture *happens* to be political.

The book begins with an overview of the long tradition of contextualism and reflective foundational thought that dominates architectural theory and engages in discussion of how the traditional understandings of politics and architecture can be rethought. I propose a step forward in materializing the insight that the focus of politics mostly played within 'the political domain' of parties and ideologies is now to be shifted to new, designerly or urbanely locations (Chapter 1). As a new approach, the ANT-informed ethnography helps us to produce interpretations of the political dimensions of architectural practice that will be radically different from the interpretations generated by the practitioners. Defined broadly as a trans-disciplinary endeavour to trace the intrinsic logic of design, design 'from within', this method enables researchers to engage in intense dialogue with the worlds of design makers (Chapter 2). Its main facets are its symmetric attention to human and non-human participants in design, and the infra-reflexive, multi-sited and multi-temporal engagement with the world. The new ethnographies pay close attention to materials and ontology and thus contribute to situating the relevance and the limits of knowledge practices related to design without engaging in critique but rather in what we call, following Deleuze, *immanent critique*; situated within the very field of practice, it allows to make difference, it is inherently political.

There are, I suggest here, five ways of engaging in an informed enquiry into the different ways architectural design can be political. First, objects and material arrangements mediate everyday human relationships and make possible political and social life. Architecture becomes political through the connected agency of all these objects and artefacts (Chapter 3). Second, we should scrutinize design practice as a complex ecology involving actors with variable ontologies; politics is enacted through the work of designers, renovators and builders and in the many daily experiments in design (Chapter 4). Unpacking design practice is the second way to make architecture political. Third, architecture becomes political by grasping the multiple realities of a city. As the city cannot be removed from the practices that sustain it, its reality is multiple. It becomes something that is manipulated and enacted in design and construction. Different enactments entail different political ontologies (Chapter 5). Forth, to understand how design can be political we should examine *how* politics happens on sites where buildings are actively transmuted while recalcitrantly acting back, 'surprising' and resisting transformation. Tracing the sites of renovation is another way for architecture to emerge as political (Chapter 6). Fifth, in architectural presentations a number of persuasive techniques and material tactics are mobilized by architects and planners in a quasi-martial quest to ignite the formation of groupings that can better grasp the variability of architectural objects. Architecture becomes political through fostering participation and engagement; design publics emerge (Chapter 7). That is another way for architecture to become political.

There is little awareness of politics at the level of the architectural practice. As Jeremy Till notes, 'architecture exists in denial about the political implications of the processes and products of practice' (2005: 34). Therefore, it is important to situate the analysis at the level of architecture making by directing the enquiry to the practice as it intends to inspire practitioners to a more political kind of design. If we trace the course of the events* that make a work of architecture connect with other works, with design objects, arrangements and human participants in design; if we are able to account the many trajectories and unpredictable groupings that all those protagonists with variable ontologies, and sometimes-discordant voices, can shape, we will be able to grasp the political. Just like the low bridges of Moses, buildings such as the Benzie Art School in Manchester (Chapter 3), Bolshoi theatre in Moscow (Chapter 6), the New Street Train Station in Birmingham (Chapter 5), the *Alte Aula* in Vienna (Chapter 6), the Marina Bay integrated resort in Singapore, the Whitney Museum of American Art in NYC and the *Palacio de Congresos* in Leon (Chapter 7) can become political sites; a glare experimentation can become a site where cosmopolitical arrangements are negotiated (Chapter 4). None of them embodies directly big politics related to governments or ideologies; yet *another* type of politics is performed on these sites: politics with small 'p' generated by artefacts, visuals, material arrangements, settings and humans as they connect with each other and with other constituents of the architectural and urban networks.

Design happens differently in different practices, cultures, contexts and political climates; architectural projects have distinct dynamics in the cities discussed in this book. However, engaging in analysis of these culturalistic differences will not lead us towards a better understanding of design. To provide slow ethnographic accounts of the political dimensions of architecture would mean to avoid falling into the trap of easy and quick culturalism. Yet, how can we *trace* a project in Singapore, UK, Spain, Austria, the United States or Russia without embracing the culturalistic discourses of urban difference? Of context that stays and endures. The danger is that when we talk about *different* cities we often refer to local treatments of the universal. We assume that there is a unique, non-situated urban nature, which makes all cities have common features: infrastructure, markets, transport networks, city authorities. Culture is taken as variable, relative, situated. This makes us *compare* cities *in* the UK with cities *in* Spain, cities *in* the South with cities *in* the North. By deciding not to compare cities in different contexts and therefore to reduce the differences to contextual specificities, by choosing not to compare architects and therefore to explain dissimilarities with individual idiosyncrasies and variations, this book will test the traditional preconception of the unity of urban nature versus the diversity of cultures. To understand these cities, I account for what is specific for Manchester, Moscow, Birmingham, Vienna, Singapore, Boston, New York, Madrid or Leon. To understand a project of Koolhaas or a project of Safdie, I analyse their architectural practices and design approaches, not their backgrounds and styles. Culture appears here as an ontological quality, not as an attribute. That is, a step aside from simplistic comparisons. This is a move towards depicting design as a pertinent ethnographic object; the urban – as describable, accountable, alive.

1

Architecture and Politics

Architecture and politics: Asymmetric ontologies

Architecture is not solely an artistic practice concerned with aesthetic form and semiotics. Instead, it is a cultural form that has long-standing and close links with dominant political and economic interests. Architecture and politics are commonly understood as two separate domains of activities with their own logics, institutions and practices. Existing attempts to connect architecture and politics typically strive to reveal the politics behind design or the design techniques disguised as politics. Architecture and politics often stand on the two sides of a reflecting surface; put in relationship of influence, dependence, interlocution, projection or determinism. When it comes to architecture's relation to politics, the latter is still understood in the light of traditional foundational theories of politics related to ideology, state, nation, government, policies and activism. These realities are foundational in the sense that they are commonly used to justify and explain everything in architecture. Architecture is often tackled as a form of political intervention, or as a reflection, enhancement or mediation of political regimes. Governments and political decisions are considered as important factors impacting architecture and built forms, and influencing styles, master plans, city shapes and forms of activating the urban. Related in a mirror-fashion, on the one side we place power, political shifts and domination, while on the other architectural form, styles and architects. Yet, this is an asymmetrical equation: politics appears as a separate domain of reality that can be used as a specific type of causality to account for aspects of architecture. The domain of architecture is given a solidity, durability and consistency that it cannot hold by itself. Some of the most common asymmetric projections and ontologies read: 'Architecture reflects politics and can produce political effects', 'Architects are agents of power', 'Architectural styles mirror political shifts', 'Politics is imprinted on cities', 'Architecture helps the construction of identities' and 'Building types embody politics'.

Architecture reflects politics and can produce political effects

As well as being shaped by bureaucratically codified state regulations, architecture is also fundamentally conditioned by the broader political-economic context in which it is commissioned, designed and understood. Therefore, architecture is rarely immune to the social, historical, economic and political contexts of the society in which it is designed and implemented. For most scholars and practitioners, architecture generally denotes, exemplifies, represents and performs political, social and economic functions (Sandler 2004: 6). A traditional representational logic of understanding space and built environment would imply to position buildings as symbols of reliance and admiration between the state and its citizens. Lefebvre advocated the acknowledgement of both the physical and symbolic elements of space as well as the ideology, which stands behind its production. He asked, 'What is an ideology without a space which it describes, whose vocabulary and links it makes use of, and whose code it embodies?' (Lefebvre 1991: 44). 'Representation of space' (Lefebvre 1991) refers to institutionalized conceptions of space inscribed within urban planning procedure; it denotes physical spaces to which social meanings have been imputed and is contested by different groups (Lefebvre 1991: 38–46 and *passim*). Inspired by this representational agenda, architectural historians and theories have for long connected built form to wider visions about the nature of the state citizen relationship. Rooted in Marxism, this reflectionist view assumes that every work of architecture will reflect the society that has produced it. Architecture is believed to have the extraordinary potential to embed political and civic values – 'to turn fraught geopolitical "space" into the unified "place" of nationhood, as much through its entrenched social, symbolic, and ceremonial values, as by the cultural and social values that inform its appearance' (Freschi 2007: 32). Architecture is expected to play a role in the cementing of norms of civility and difference and in the spatial disciplining of citizenship.

Architecture is both configured by power and is a resource for power. As Kim Dovey put it, 'The design of built form is intrinsically linked to issues of power: it is the imagination and negotiation of future worlds. The invention of the future will always be contentious and places will always mediate power relations' (1999: 7). Attempting to avoid economic determinism and a vulgar reflection theory, architectural critics engaged in discussions of the complex mediating role of architecture in contemporary societies and its key role in shaping political discourses. Following a Marxist way of thinking, to make architecture is seen as a powerful way to shape social and economic relationships, to construct knowledge, to build visions. 'To make architecture is to map the world in some way, to intervene, to signify: it is a political act' (Dutton and Mann 2000: 117). Architecture, then, as discourse, practice and form operates at the intersection of power, relations of production, culture and representation. It is considered as being instrumental to the construction of our identities and our differences. It is also located at the political centre of a transforming global capitalism. Scholars inspired by the Cultural Political Economy (CPE) approach argue that we should not sustain the illusion of the political-economic disinterest of architecture within the architectural field. It is precisely architecture's status as a rich semiotic form that gives it much of the distinctiveness and social resonance that explains its continued centrality to political and economic projects. CPE authors framed architecture as one expression of the embedding of 'economic imaginaries' (Jessop 2004) and connect architects and their designs to the interests of states and markets while at the same time taking seriously the specificities of the architectural field. This interpretation assumes that there is a political-economic foundation that regulates the built environment. The role of architecture is reduced to the one of providing a culturalized frame within which economic and political transformations are embedded.

Placing architectural discourse and the social practice of producing architecture within the global transformations of the political economy and culture would create the expectations that architecture should reconstruct a new social project (Dutton and Mann 1996). Since the modernist movement, architectural theorists believed that architecture can cure social ills. Yet, to better analyse architecture's political role in society in the present period, in order to understand architecture's specific role in mediating the relationship between economic development and the ideological order, it is important to maintain a theoretical distinction between form and content, to analyse their interpenetration and to view them operating in a particular dialectical relationship, argued Dutton and Mann (2000); the effect from their separation had been damaging to architectural theory. Thus, this view takes for granted that form has political significance and it always carries political meaning; it is produced out of political conditions and by the same token it has political effects and consequences. This understanding outlines the importance to find out what specific mediations actually occur and what political effects can actually be produced through formal interventions on specific political terrains.

Architects are agents of power

It is generally agreed that professionals have a critical role in the diffusion and adoption of institutions and political ideas. Architects play an important role in understanding the way form is wedded to formal power; the discourses of architects are crucial for state politics. Architects seek social change through formal gestures and engage more and more in producing social effects. As a result, architectural autonomy becomes an illusion (Till 2009). Star architects play a critical role in legitimizing power, and in consolidating the cultural and financial credibility of administrations (Ponzini 2011). In their attempts to consolidate political agendas, cities strive today for signature architecture, sometimes with little regard to their urban context, their size and role in the global market, the democratic decision-making process and the urban effects.

The level of heteronomy is far greater in countries whose enforced hierarchies have a stronger bearing on architectural practice. To demonstrate this, Serhat Ünaldi (2013) studied the modern city centre of Bangkok and analysed how architects cope with traditional power structures in Thailand, torn as they are between the autonomy ascribed to their profession by architectural discourse and the practical heteronomy of their work. Drawing on a series of interviews with professionals, he argues that external forces have an impact on the work in Bangkok. These forces are both contextual (constraints set by the client, the budget, the social functions of building, the specifics of a particular site and the involvement of other building specialists) and generic (formal laws and regulations, institutional interests, state ideologies, cultural taboos and general social and political conditions). If contextual forces constitute a variable, creating a condition, which might be termed practical heteronomy, the limitations and provisions set by generic forces cannot be negotiated. However, it is at the level of structural heteronomy, argued Ünaldi, where architects face local socio-economic and political conditions to which they cannot but submit themselves.

Political climates can influence the visions of architects. In a recent account about the Italian social movement Autonomia, Pier Vittorio Aureli examined how the post-1968 political events and the rethinking of Marxist theory by intellectuals like Mario Tronti influenced a variety of that era's architectural projects and writings, including Manfredo Tafuri's critique of architectural ideology, architect Aldo Rossi's reinvention of categories in his book *The Architecture of the City*, as well as Rossi's 1962 government centre for Turin (Aureli 2008). The influences behind the political visions of architects can be related to specific technologies and experiences engrained in the politics of their time. Examining the epistemological and philosophical consequences of the aerial vision on Le Corbusier's architecture, Adnan Morshed (2002) argued that the mode of looking from above affected considerably his design strategies and the aerial experience had an impact on his thinking. From the airplane, Le Corbusier saw only geography without political boundaries and, consequently, imagined an architectural programme that internalized all sorts of divisive lines, and even that of the horizon. This aerial experience did engender a radical turning point in his urbanism as through the aerial vision twentieth-century urban planners sought to fulfil the modernist dream of transforming the city into an object of knowledge and a governable space. This implied seeing the city through a privileged point in the sky and a kind of politicized aerial reconnaissance to reprogramme the existing city through an artificial terrain of infrastructures. It articulated a megalomaniac vision that globalized capitalist society should function across political, cultural and ethnic boundaries.

Thus, architects are not just artists engaged in design. Their capacity to position their buildings makes them important political actors (Jones 2006). Today's architects actively engage in promoting and even shaping urban planning policies as we can witness this in cases of major urban developments in the UK (Charney 2007; Kaika 2010, 2011), China (Broudehoux 2010) or Australia (Dovey 2002). Architects' discourses frequently reveal many tensions between culture, politics, power and identity. Architects and designers are considered as important agents of political change even though today we are past the modernist tradition that demanded that architects had something meaningful to say about society. Keen to please the client, the public and the authorities, contemporary architects are rarely subversive, and that is what makes them so significantly different from the generation of great modernists. Today's designers, famously argued Maria Kaika (2015), are like trains, they go on rails and they 'follow the tracks and trajectories laid down for them by capital investment'. The model of the heroic architect who opposed authority and public norms has been replaced by the opportunistic one who is afraid of 'derailing'.

Recent studies also suggested that today's design should have more transformative and critical power. Designers in contemporary societies can act as important political agents (Berglund 2013; Thorpe 2014); design can play a crucial role in shaping urban space and activism as a way of promoting urban change. The political aim is to use design for collective benefit and thus design activism emerges as a way to make the world a better place (Berglund 2013). Designers might contribute to protests and acts of resistance of broader social movements, beyond simply designing banners or props and beyond unknowingly creating products or buildings that are later enrolled in social movements, argued Thorpe (2014). The material and visual nature of design suggests that in some cases design activism can help articulate and express claims for transformational change: with the aid of design, people could be encouraged to think and behave differently. Some authors went as far as to argue for the importance of designers to affiliate closely with progressive political organizations and social movements to test architecture's mediating potential. Architects, they suggested, should 'strive for a critical and strategic practice of architecture that tries to reorient subjectivities and affirm the oppositional cultures of social movements' (Dutton and Mann 2000: 128). These ideas are part of a new cultural phenomenon: a concept of design as able to solve the world's problems and, therefore, as inherently activist, transformative.

Architectural styles mirror political shifts

Architectural styles are conceptualized not only as means to show cultural shifts in taste, as mere architectural aesthetics; they also serve as deeper indicators of changes in state authority, strategies of administration and the relationship between citizen and state (Holston 1989; Sennett 1994; Rabinow 1995). Thus, political change spawns different architectural styles that echo respective political climates. Reflecting on the interrelation between architecture and politics, Mary McLeod argued that architectural movements are connected to governmental currents and economic shifts. She claimed that if the reassessment of modernism occurred in a tight economy, which encouraged reflection and criticism, postmodernism began to flourish in the boom economy of the early 1980s (McLeod 1989). If art forms can be seen as reflecting market pressure, architecture's forms differ from other forms of art such as music and painting by the expenses they entail. Architecture depends 'on the sources of finance and power extends to nearly every facet of the design process: choice of site, program, budget, materials and production schedules. These economic and utilitarian parameters ordinarily limit architecture's transgressive and transformative power, but they also inscribe areas for potential social action. In other words, architecture's production processes imply possibilities of institutional change itself, here, architecture's connection to politics appears more direct than that of other arts' (McLeod 1989: 682). Thus, the assumption is that as architecture is intrinsically joined to political and economic structures by virtue of its production, its forms and its meanings expressed as specific styles and movements can be considered as cultural objects that carry political resonances. Similarly, responding to a new and radically different political and economic order the recent rise of the Mafia Baroque style in Eastern Europe highlighted public concern over corruption, organized crime and dissatisfaction with post-socialist urbanization (Holleran 2014). Seen as a badly orchestrated attempt at postmodernist architecture, this style met the opposition of planners and architects who found themselves increasingly excluded and beholden to clients who they both distrusted and disapproved of as decision makers.

An architectural style mirrors politics for it expresses a vision; visions are constrained by larger economic, demographic and historical forces. Engaging in political history of architecture, Daniel Immerwahr (2007) showed that by favouring a programme of tropical modernist architecture for its prestige buildings in Lagos and British New Town style for its housing estates there, the government of Nigeria sought to demonstrate both its independence from European culture and its ability to perform the functions of a modern state. Yet Lagosians shaped a different city from below. Policymakers in independent Nigeria had a bifurcated architectural vision for Lagos: they favoured tropical modernism, a bold hybrid idiom, as the official style of government offices and major downtown buildings while at the same time preferring by-the-book copies of European residences for government housing estates (Immerwahr 2007). The inhabitants of Lagos, by contrast, responded to the demands of low wages and a burgeoning workforce by favouring built forms that allowed them to maintain a complex informal economy and to keep alive some aspects of indigenous building traditions. Immerwahr demonstrated that styles can express conflicting and differing visions; these visions for postcolonial Lagos informed policies and actions around prestige architecture, housing estates and shantytowns.

Politics is imprinted on cities

A classic example of this asymmetrical projection is the divided cities. The literature on Berlin, Nicosia, Jerusalem, Mosdar and Belfast is abundant (Pullan 2011; Calame and Charlesworth 2016). Architecture organizes power in divided cities. In Nicosia, for instance, the connection between political power and the architectural processes allowed for the contextualization of divisiveness that has dominated the architectural forms in Northern Cyprus and in particular government buildings built after 1974 (Gurdalli and Koldas 2015).

Capital cities are largely discussed in the literature on politics and architecture. A capital city plays an important role in how politics as ideology is represented by and expressed in architecture and city plans. In the traditional interpretation, the physical plans of capitals are commonly treated as political tools, equal to governmental policies. Drawing on the analysis of Jerusalem, Nitzan-Shiftan (2005) showed how architecture became a technique for executing politics in the urban landscape of the city and how the professional knowledge that was invested in this technique played an important role in the cultural campaign to legitimate Israeli rule over Jerusalem. It also intervened in the politics of space of a city the visual image of which was for a long time geared towards religious sentiments and tourist industry.

Moreover, architecture is used to rebrand cities and strengthen their image. Studies in architecture and urban planning have examined how emblematic architectural projects manage to attract public attention, reinforce the singularity of cities and provide recognizable iconic images. Architecture plays an important role with regard to urban regeneration strategies in providing 'a culturalized frame within which economic transformation is embedded' (Jones 2009: 2519). This happens either as part of culture-led regeneration strategies or strategies aimed at rebranding cities or urban quarters (Evans 2003; del Cerro Santamaria 2007; Kaika 2010). In their attempt to shape cities in their way, political regimes eagerly attract new investments in the built environment to demonstrate power and might. A considerable body of work in cultural geography has focused on the nature of the icon (Sklair 2006, 2010), the practices of global architects (McNeill 2008; Faulconbridge 2009; Ren 2011) and also the struggles and conflicts surrounding the implementation of these architectural projects (Dixon 2010) and their social and economic impact. Beyond merely providing an aesthetic spectacle, these architectural projects are deeply political. In Paul Jones' words, 'Corporate and state actors and institutions mobilize architecture as one way of making political-economic strategies socially meaningful' (Jones 2009: 2520). An example of this is the revitalization of Melbourne's riverscape studied by Sandercock and Dovey (2002). Tracing the relationship between planning and democracy, they explained the revitalization with global competition, local politics, urban design transformations and broader demographic changes. They argued that this development had become inextricably implicated in processes of place marketing and city imaging, in the service of which architectural and urban design imagery came to play an increasingly important role. The method of financing projects planning in Melbourne no longer aspired to comprehensiveness, consultation or equity and stood at odds with the standards of participatory democracy exacerbated by the intercity competition for flexible capital investment.

Architecture helps the construction of identities

A vast number of architectural scholars have outlined the links between architecture and the construction of nationalist imaginaries, including Boyer (1994), Edelman (1995), Huyssen (2003), Lefebvre (1991), Mitchell (1994), Tafuri (1976) and Vale (1992). Buildings and space have an important role in the social construction of national identity (Delanty and Jones 2002). The built environment is forced to express, clarify or reinforce diverse kinds of identities (Vale 1999: 396). Landmark architectural projects such as that at the Ground Zero site provide one significant way in which collective identities can be represented materially (Jones 2009). In this case, architecture served as an important cultural expression of collective identities, with states often using landmark buildings to reflect 'their' national identity and to supplement the historical narrative of collective memory. Tracing the critical discourse analysis of texts that accompanied the design and construction of the Israeli Supreme Court, Yacobi illustrated how this building reflects – and thus strengthens the hegemonic interpretations of Israeli social and cultural reality (Yacobi 2004). He argued that the building's significance lies within the array of social power relations that create them and outlines the important role of architecture in the construction of national identity. Placing architecture at the centre of a history of state formation, the sociologist Virág Molnár (2013) demonstrated how architecture was politically mobilized in the service of social change, first in socialist modernization programmes and then in the post-socialist transition in Hungary and East Germany. She claimed that our understanding of political regimes must include an analysis of the 'transformation of the built environment'. Architecture is in this interpretation a cultural practice whereby the state is 'both materially produced and represented' (Molnár 2013: 9). It can provide a useful and wide-ranging field of inquiry that can inform global studies of state formation.

Building types embody politics

Architecture as *expression* of politics is also exemplified by a number of building types. Building forms are seen as metaphors for social relations (Markus 1993; Sennett 1994; Dovey 1999). While assessing architecture's role in rendering social and economic strategies meaningful, an informed understanding of building types is crucial. Two architectural theorists in particular have made seminal contributions to the sociology of building types, namely Anthony King (1980, 2004, 2010) and Thomas Markus (1993). Following King (2010: 29), we can understand building types 'as socially classifying devices, providing us with insights into how social formations are organized, both spatially and temporally, and with reference to institutions and social relationship'.

Large-scale socially significant buildings are seen as the most visible emblems of urbanization and important symbols of economic and political power. Buildings are used in place-making strategies and the reimagining of cities; they reorder urban space and locate economic functions in the urban realm. Buildings confirm the existence of new economic or political regimes. Cultural buildings have been often put into service of politics and have acted as vehicles for diffusing ideology. So were, for instance, the theatres in Mussolini's Italy (Berezin 1991), where a number of factors, the high organizational disorder of the Italian theatre, a pre-existing legal framework and a ready army of state bureaucrats, all made a space for the regime to enter. So was Bolshoi theatre in Moscow – for seventy years Soviet politics was performed on its stage and this contributed to the symbolic power of Russian nation's most political theatre (Sporton 2006). Thus, theatres served as places where fascist or communist ideology was disseminated, 'staged' and reproduced.

Yet, the architecture of power and authority is more prominent in the official buildings of the state, such as parliament architecture (Goodsell 1988). The question of how to design the spaces for public assembly is a question that requires re-imagining the possibilities for public expression and political togetherness. The design and use of parliament buildings is thought as part of a process of social construction of nations that can privilege particular forms of embodied citizenship. Different parliament buildings, for instance, the Scottish Parliament and the National Assembly of Wales debating chambers, exemplify different notions of citizenship developed in the two countries. Attempts to reimagine a more inclusive national/regional identity in this context have been in tension with attempts to fashion new symbolic buildings (Hastings and Thomas 2005). Conceptualizing national identity should be expressed through the construction of new environments, in which, among other facets, the need for explicit consideration of embodiment emerges.

State and parliament buildings are important in their prominent task of representing and expressing power. If we wish to get insights into political regime's ideological agenda, we should scrutinize how they decorate what they build as the specific decorative programmes in public buildings play an important role in constructing national imaginaries, and are representative of ideologies. Freschi's analysis of the New Constitutional Court in Johannesburg demonstrated that the decorations of the Court represent in a powerful way the national imaginary of 'unity in diversity' in contemporary South Africa. He convincingly argued that 'in buildings it is easy to conceal political subtext under the mantle of function: ornament, in effect, becomes "naturalized" as part of the fabric of the building' (Freschi 2007: 31). Architectural ornament has the overwhelming potential of being inherently politicized: either through the appearance of the actual structure or through the elaboration of the façade and some user-oriented aspects of the building. The decorative programme reiterates the symbolical meaning of buildings. The return of the ornament in contemporary architecture, argued Antoine Picon (2013), is directly to be linked with political issues in contemporary societies. Ornaments are inherently political, not simply aesthetic, as they convey vital information about the destination of buildings, the rank of the owners and by so doing they participate in the expression of social values, hierarchies and order; ornamented buildings can have a greater contribution to collective values.

Architecture megaprojects such as Olympic stadia form another typical example of how architecture reveals power structures and reproduces hegemony. The connection between political leaders and monumental architecture is not new (Kostof 1991). Historically, power seekers have relied on spectacular events to legitimize their rulership by distracting, appeasing and controlling the masses. The spectacle provided by the built environment enhances power by offering extraordinary visibility of the state and an appealing material embodiment of political agency. A notable example for this is the Beijing Olympics where architecture played a central role in the spectacularization of Beijing's urban environment and became part of the theatrics of power used by the regime to reassert its legitimacy as China's sole leader. However, as much as architecture can embody power and make it visible, it can also obscure and conceal power relationships (Broudehoux 2010). The new architectural developments in Chinese cities present an illuminating example of how megaprojects can similarly act as a camouflage to mask the growth of autocratic corporate power and contribute to the reproduction of the established order by concealing the perpetuation of domination and legitimizing the interests of property developers. The tendency to privilege megaprojects and to remove these governmental architectural initiatives from the normal channels of democratic scrutiny is a disturbing feature of contemporary urban development (Sandercock and Dovey 2002). Very often large-scale projects and spectacular developments are used to compensate for the absence of democratic politics (Ponzini 2011). Tracing the development of Saadiyat Island megaproject in Abu Dhabi, supposed to host a number of iconic buildings of star architects, Ponzini demonstrated that while the media fostered successfully the image of a contemporary global capital city open to Western culture and business, matching global objectives with local identities has proven difficult. Designed as Western-style luxury suburbia, the island excluded lower income dwellers and reinforced the alienating effect of high culture.

For a building 'to be noticed and testify to the grandeur of its sponsor, it has to be conspicuous and carry a strong aesthetic presence, using size, form and outward appearance to imprint a compelling and memorable image upon collective consciousness' (Broudehoux 2010: 57). As monuments of grandeur and opulence, iconic buildings link to civic and national pride and could be inscribed in the public imagery as landmarks. Politicians and city governments have come to recognize that impressive and innovative architecture designed by leading star architects may positively contribute to the exposure of their cities. The most notable example of monumental iconic type of buildings is the skyscraper, and as such it provides access to the colossal ambitions of power seekers. Skyscrapers are regarded as the ultimate symbols of capitalism and embody global power. They became important as urban signifiers after the 1970s when European societies embarked in 'new urban economy', a moment when societies became organized not around industrial activity, but around the strength of the financial sector, global capital and information flows, corporate power, mass tourism and the consumption of services (Harvey 1989). Skyscrapers, argued Maria Kaika, are temples of private capital; form follows power. Guaranteed by the symbolic authority of their patron, these buildings acted as guarantors for the continuation in time of the patrons' name and fame (Kaika and Thielen 2006; Kaika 2010). They became sought-after business locations and were etched in the public imagery as 'landmarks' and 'icons' (Jencks 2005; Sklair 2005, 2006; Kaika 2011).

Recently, tall buildings formed an important part of an extensive programme of regeneration that is supposed to change dramatically London's skyline (Kaika 2010, 2011). These latest debates illustrate how global architects commissioned to design tall buildings in London after 2000 contributed to legitimizing the mayoral ambitions of Ken Livingstone 'to reach for the sky' (Charney 2007: 195). Retracing the debate and analysing its framing, Charney showed how in order to relegate long-lasting opposition to tall buildings, the mayor chose to draw attention to design and architecture as the lingua franca of the tall-building discourse. By stressing the role of iconic design produced by global architects, it was possible to convince the public that tall buildings were justifiable because of their aesthetic qualities. These debates indicate that tall buildings play a major role in the development of cities today.

Similarly, the office tower appears in the literature as another powerful building type that represents economic-political imaginaries and exemplifies how buildings can act as 'socially classifying devices' (King 2010: 92). Grubbauer (2014) argued that the interest in the spectacle of megaprojects has obstructed our view of architecture's role in urban restructuring. She argued for the importance to direct our attention to everyday buildings, which have been often disregarded. More attention is to be paid to the fundamental way in which architecture is able to embody and refer to social and economic functions without necessarily being spectacular. Grubbauer studied the office towers in Vienna to demonstrate that this building type discursively and visually anchors the new economic imaginaries in built environment. That is a view inspired by the CPE trend: the visibility and plausibility of a new economic regime and social imaginary can be enhanced if they are discursively connected to and visually represented by buildings in urban space.

Exploring further how starchitecture and cultural megaprojects change the landscape of cities, another spectacular building type – museums and galleries as cultural institutions – comes in the limelight. Scholarly explanations for the popularity of iconic architecture often propose a 'neo-liberal thesis' that points to global political economic trends and the advancement of a market logic into the governance of cities. Surprisingly, very little attention has been given to the primary clients of iconic architecture, and these public institutions do play an important role as independent players within cities that interact with but are not determined by the larger global forces of neo-liberalism. To explain the affinity between public institutions and iconic architecture, Matt Patterson (2012) studied two examples in Ontario: The Royal Ontario Museum and the Art Gallery of Ontario. These organizations, he argued, depend primarily on establishing 'public legitimacy', which allows them to attract the outside support and donations necessary to sustain themselves. Iconic architecture is seen as a strategy of building public legitimacy in an era of neo-liberalism.

Embracing a similar understanding of buildings as representing systems of authority and control leads to the analysis of some less glamorous typologies, like the bunker or the mosque. Often understood as a static mass of concrete, the bunker is a container of people and objects, a structure whose inherent materiality is fixed in solid state that can rarely be made vibrant (Bartolini 2015). The recent interest in bunkers is linked to the ongoing reappraisal of post-war modernist architecture and its relationship not only to the violence of the Second World War but also to the secrecy and passive aggression of the Cold War. While the bunker promises security and control in the form of refuge, it is also a sign of the deadly power that requires reinforced shelter. John Beck (2011) argued that 'the solidity of the reinforced bunker invokes both the power of the weapons it is intended to repel and something of the folly of the attempt to seek any sort of shelter from them. As such, the bunker is both a sign of industrialized warfare and of there being no escape from it.' As a symbol, the bunker embodies violence either achieved or promised. It is a highly ambivalent building type; attractive and repulsive by the same token. Another politically ambivalent type is the mosque. It could be read as a highly contested 'representational space' by Muslim and non-Muslim urban residents (DeHanas and Pieri 2011). Following contestation surrounding mosque buildings in Birmingham, Richard Gale (2004) assessed how urban planning processes condense and mediate the relations between social groups and argued that the mosque gets ascribed different meanings by the various groups concerned by this type.

All these understandings of the relationship between architecture and politics assume a dichotomy between the world of the politics and the material and technical world of buildings. Moreover, they accept buildings and built form as static, immutable and they lend themselves to the asymmetrical representational regime by simply exemplifying and embodying a number of political values, meanings and norms. Although the analysis has shifted towards understanding of what can be achieved through creating connections between these two realms, the analytical power of the underlying differentiation between politics and architecture is still strong. In some of these analyses, the interrelation of architecture and politics leads to the emergence of new political dimensions with a degree of complexity that surpasses anything that could be achieved within either one of them. Yet, while the two realms interact and fruitful couplings might arise, the underlying dichotomy is rarely questioned by architectural theorists. The ontology of the design worlds remains unaffected; their logic and inherent dynamics remain unexplored. Moreover, buildings, materials and settings are far from being static, immobile anchor points for memories and identities, for city branding and ideology; they are active according to the logic of their own realm (Brand 1994). They are rarely perceived at once for their aesthetic qualities; their impact rather occurs gradually through use and repeated interactions with the built. As a result, the relationship between politics and architecture is more complex, including both spatial configurations and figurative dimensions as equally important in the analysis of production and reception of architecture.

Towards a symmetric ontology of architecture

If politics is not reflected on architecture, what orderings can architecture bring about? Are there other ways of 'doing' politics when architecture is involved? Two significant emergent tendencies in the recent literature slightly deviate from the common analytical patterns of architectural contextualism and reflectionist thinking reproducing the asymmetry: First, the direction of projection between architecture and politics is not simple, unidirectional, always causal; but it varies and becomes mediated. Architecture is not just produced, it is 'co-produced'. This signals a move towards a more dynamic understanding of architectural production. Second, the field of politics is not completely isolated and completely ignorant to developments in the field of urban studies and architectural history and theory. A recent trend in political theory has acknowledged that 'Stuff matters for politics'.

Not reflection, but co-production

Featuring buildings as stages of political, cultural or social acts renders them static. A different understanding of architecture would require tackling buildings and physical spaces as part and parcel of the dramatization of politics, as vigorous setting to re-establish links and connections among various actors. Recent studies of parliament buildings began acknowledging buildings as complicit in the staging of politics; buildings are rendered active, and this draws attention to their dramaturgical and compositional role (Filmer 2013). Going beyond a simplistic representational analysis of parliamentary buildings, these studies argued for the importance to trace the bodily inhabitation of traditionally political buildings. Parliaments were tackled as stenographic multisensory spaces for performing democracy (Puwar 2010). Tracing the building experience of the Westminster parliament building, Puwar explored how ritual and performance are enacted in the arrangement and rearrangement of bodies in occupation of the buildings, furniture, walls, statues and artistic iconography. Drawing on the dual nature of parliaments as living museums and working environments, the researchers adopt the role of situated *flâneurs,* wandering around in these buildings, experiencing them. While parliamentary buildings largely facilitate the reproduction of established modes of political performance, they remain vulnerable to being performed differently (Filmer 2013). Political space is co-produced by buildings and the bodies and actions that perform them.

A similar more pragmatist understanding of another traditionally iconic typology, the stadium, suggests that instead of contemplating the iconicity of the stadium building (Church and Penny 2013), we can provide a different view on the changing nature of the stadia by analysing how the process of stadium relocation involves the emergence of new spaces that have implications for the power relations between stadium owners, managers and sport supporters. These authors also advocated the need to trace the mutual co-production of power relations and spaces. As a result of such a co-construction, that new stadia would involve equally profit-driven and technologically managed sites as well as signifiers of cultural importance linked to naming and memorialization in the new spaces to encourage a sense of attachment and collective identity amongst supporters.

Recent studies in archaeology of architecture also argued for the importance of co-production. In this field, the built environment is traditionally seen as the passive by-product of interconnected environmental, cultural, social and economic factors and there is a long tradition of understanding the architecture of societies from prehistory to the present by reading architecture as a social document. Recent studies of the relationship between architecture and power emphasized the ongoing reciprocal development of architecture and power through time (Moore 1996; Maran et al. 2006), and argued about the importance to investigate how spatial practices of power shape the nature of politics. A notable example of this trend is the work of Cameron Monroe (2010), who, using space syntax methodology, argued that the architectural design of Dahomean royal palaces played a crucial role in fostering political order in West Africa during the Atlantic era. He demonstrated how the overall complexity of palace spaces, the architectural patterns and the inclusion of internal walls to demarcate the spaces facilitated elevated levels of control over Dahomean bureaucratic élite and accentuated distance between the king and his officials in the late eighteenth century. As a result, the architectural control over those navigating these spaces increased dramatically. Instead of serving as static symbols of power, the royal palace sites were rather used to promulgate social and political order in a period defined by political and economic instability and contributed to increasing the inter-élite hierarchy over time. Following a similar explicitly spatial approach to politics in complex societies, Innocent Pikirayi (2013) showed convincingly that within the Zimbabwe culture, stone architecture was not a mere reflection of the existing power of elites; rather, the process of creating architecture was also one of creating elite power. In his analysis, stonewalling is actively implicated in the development, enactment and negotiation of power. Drawing on this specific relationship between stonewalling, nature and authority, the ruling elites skilfully manipulated architecture to entrench their authority.

Stuff matters for politics

Recently, political sciences started growing the realization that both the formal sense of political institutions and the less formal sense of public debate can be changed because of its relationship to material things and non-humans that is so often denied in traditional political theories. At the same time, philosophers like Bruno Latour and Isabelle Stengers, and recent developments in the STS strongly advocated an object-oriented understanding of politics (Latour and Weibel 2005). Architecture was seen not just as a translation of visions of power into physical realities, but also as an important vehicle to make power durable (Mukerji 1997). Following this inspiration, a number of geographers, political scientists and STS scholars started sketching in their works a materialistic theory of politics that attempts to replace the foundational concepts of 'nature', 'culture' and 'politics' and, by implication, collateral concepts like 'economy', 'society' and so on; they engaged in rematerializing political phenomena. Baunn and Whatmore suggested taking seriously stuff and materiality in politics (2010). A number of seminal studies acknowledged the constitutive nature of material processes and entities in social and political life: Andrew Barry argued for material controversies (2001), and material politics (2013), while Noortje Marres advocated the role of material participation for democratic processes and signalled the formation of material publics (2012). All these studies outlined the importance for rematerializing the political in (other) ways that would challenge some of our conventional partitions between 'the politics' and other spheres of activity.

Using the conceptual resources of relationality and its material semiotics on one hand, and the emerging notion of 'thing' politics on the other, some geography scholars engaged in tracing dynamically urban spaces to attend to a different view on urban politics as relational. An exemplar of this trend comes from the work of Escobar (2014), who followed the refurbishment of the public space of Trafalgar Square, and its material and political dimensions. She dissected its accomplishment and its contestation as a material process of placing and displacing all sorts of human and non-human objects. In scrutinizing this more-than-human materiality, a wider politics of difference and displacement can be fleshed out. Even the pigeons, denoted Escobar, have been active participants in the performative and material configuration of Trafalgar Square, rather than merely having an instrumental or marginal role in its refurbishment. Leandro Minuchin put forward an original understanding of relational politics; construction is for him a constitutive element of urban politics as it activates 'the capacity of interrelated material interventions to disentangle the established associations between places and practices, forms and function' (Minuchin 2012: 915). Developing further the notion of articulation, he pointed to the emergence of a type of politics that stems from prefigurative tactics far from established institutional politics and the articulation of governance (Minuchin 2016). This holds also an empirical proposal to unpack the variable sets of configurations of actors and substances that populate a given terrain and could be deployed in situations of construction. The relational accounts of power in urban design presented by Escobar and construction processes presented by Minuchin are quite revealing of how power is made and unmade relationally and how it is accumulated.

Drawing on the important role of the built environment as a mediating agent, constructing and reconstructing power relations, some recent studies in political theory started acknowledging the importance of space for the performance of politics. They argued that physicality matters to democracy as physical forms affect political action. Yet, these authors limited themselves to analyses of the traditional sites of political action, such as public squares for gatherings and demonstrations, and parliamentary, state buildings and assemblies. They argued that even at the time when entire revolutions are coordinated and cheered via Facebook and Twitter in a digital world, democracy depends on the availability of physical public space – parks, squares and other public areas (Parkinson 2012). The performance of democratic roles is limited or constrained by such factors as availability of public spaces for democratic behaviour, their design and the changing nature of the ownership of spaces. Design enables democratic performance by enhancing or limiting democratic values and behaviour; good urban design becomes a condition for democracy. Certain kinds of spaces encourage encounters and others not (Gieryn 2002); proximity inspires interaction and the development of community; propinquity is a condition for social formations (Buchli 2013). Walls present barriers for expression of rights and freedom, they limit certain actions and facilitate small range of other actions; the removal of physical walls makes people put up psychological and communicative barriers. Urban artefacts encourage encounters and 'breaks' by making people stop, sit and take in their surroundings (Sennett 2002). Thus, space is not a neutral, passive and inert backstage of political actions; it rather has an impact on political efficacy by virtue of physically preventing or mandating certain actions, encouraging certain kinds of behaviours rather than others and triggering a sense of identification or recognition.

Architectural sites of the political: An irreductivist view

Yet, in spite of these recent developments, the dominant view in the literature presented here shows that architectural theorists have repeatedly and spectacularly succeeded in purifying the concepts of architecture and politics. The architectural literature has preciously preserved the modernist roots of official architectural scholarship and, in particular, the dualist split between people and things, assuming a free-standing material world of architecture and infrastructure, created, fabricated, built, governed, mastered and controlled by powerful humans (designers, architects, planners, renovators, builders, politicians, decision makers). The overall ontological vision here is an asymmetric dualism between the world as knowable, buildable and controllable, and humans as genuine agents of creativity. The key questions are 'who acts', 'who decides' and how this is reflected on built form and urban fabrics. As the agency is often placed on the side of politics, the dichotomy architecture/politics sustains its asymmetric dualist ontology: politics is made by powerful men who act and institutions who decide on political matters, while architecture is a passive cold material world of buildings and infrastructures; a subject of decisions. Politics is a distant reality situated outside of architecture's remit that is brought to explain architecture. There is a two-level schema. At the ground level, we find the usual cases on materials, software and issues of building science. At a meta-level, we find people, typically politicians, reflecting on what should be done at the ground level, and a set of conventionally political institutions that support that. This dualist ontology has an impact both on our imaginations and on our understanding of architectural production. Architecture appears in this interpretation as an immutable form, where power is actively working to project and imprint itself on buildings.

However, in practice architects and planners themselves fail to exemplify this ontology. Recent ethnographies of architectural design have demonstrated that architects at work are far from 'deciding' or simply following a plan made by others, far from mastering materials through knowledge and skills and far from controlling the world through the channelling of forces and energies in built form (Houdart and Minato 2009; Yaneva 2009a, b; Loukissas 2012), just like in their laboratories the scientists are far from dominating their materials through knowledge (Latour and Woolgar 1979; Galison 1997; Knorr-Cetina 1999). Instead, designers engage in rather symmetrical open-ended and performative dances of agency, experimenting with materials and shapes, testing options, developing scenarios, cutting foam, scaling models, struggling with instruments, and trying software, finding out what the building-to-be will do in different circumstances and responding to what emerges in a process of mangling (Pickering 1995). These dances of agency are just as much what models, sketches, pixels and parametric algorithms do, as what designers do. The studies of architecture in the making help us to step outside the moralized space of human uniqueness and forget the classic tales on star architects, design creativity and groundbreaking ideas (Yaneva 2009b). Making or using buildings delineates a realm of non-modern artefacts, artefacts that remind us of our ontological condition rather than veiling it from us. In the process of making, the material world of design is not a passive substrate awaiting the firm hand of human agency; instead, it talks back to the designers, it makes them act, turn, dance, run and interact with others and the things at hand with a different pace of speed. Designing architects are densely intertwined with their environment, rather than aiming at a dualist separation from it; they bear enigmatic attachment to models, software and sketches; they live in dense material milieus crowded with visuals, instruments and samples; and they battle with a foldable time that runs at different speeds according to project intensities and design deadlines. Architecture happens in a network of actors that all contribute to the complex process of making and building, a network where everything 'acts'.

Instead of echoing back the dualism between people and things, politics and architecture, might it be possible to go in a different way? Architecture provides numerous empirical examples in support of different ways of acting in the world that do not feature a dualist separation and that support open-ended becoming. If we follow design in the making, people in the process of strolling in buildings and interacting with them, we might suddenly start to think about the world in non-dualist terms and, more importantly, we might grasp that there are an indefinite number of ways to stage a non-dualist ontology. When we follow design processes, tracing the performative and fluid dance of agency in design and use, architectural objects appear less as reflections, mirroring power and political shifts. The need to explain architecture becomes less significant as this dynamic view allows a symmetrical treatment of the shaping of the architectural and the political. Following design-in-the-making and architecture-in-use requires a radical rethinking of the ontological and epistemological basis of architectural studies, questioning the modernist roots of official architectural scholarship and challenging the hegemony of ontological dualism in design practice, architectural thought and representation.

It is not surprising to see that architectural studies guided by mainstream social sciences tackle architecture, on the one hand, and politics, on the other, to identify and characterize the different formulas of relationship between them, presuming that they are all stabilized entities, fixed, defined and determined. The ANT methodological offer is different: to study what is normally an exception for architecture theory and is often tackled by anthropologists – the unstable states of the architectural and the political in order to describe what happens in these extreme situations of volatility. Following 'the making of …' design visuals, architectural presentations, building renovation, publics and city images, we can account the variable ontology of entities that are shaped in an intermediary, non-stabilized state of the world. Only then can we witness moments in which the network has neither the complete status of an object, nor that of a subject; moments where new forms of objectivity and subjectivity emerge, where meaning and materiality are negotiated; here the political and the architectural are brought in the same analytical view and reshuffled together in a symmetric ontology. To capture this process, I will analyse different sites of design, renovation, construction and dwelling, which will exemplify unstable non-modern ways of organizing the world. Seized on these sites, the buildings discussed in this book will never be static, complete, immutable, sharp in form. They will rather appear as ontological theatres, staging dances of agency with their designers, renovators, builders and inhabitants, thus taking the ontological vision seriously and resisting fixed form. This implies a symmetric distribution of agency: instead of imposing human plans from the outset, designers and dwellers will tune their plans in the light of what the buildings do and make them do.

The sites presented here will be reminiscent to the settings of scientific experiments, extensively studied in the literature of science studies. It has been argued that the setting of a scientific experiment or a medical intervention can act as a mediator* through which the object investigated gains capacities it did not have before (Stengers and Prygogine 1988; Pickering 1992; Stengers 1993; Galison 1997). The settings perform capacities. The good experimental set-up, and by extrapolation, the good design, is not one which is neutral but one which deforms, constrains and enables in thought-provoking ways. In a good experiment, the setting is not invisible and passive; it is rather present and active. Isabelle Stengers defined a good experiment as an occasion for sudden reversals, unexpected results. The aim is not to reduce the influence of the setting, but to construct an influential setting which deforms the phenomenon in an interesting way. To interest someone to something, for Stengers, means to construct an arrangement in which a thing (an object, an apparatus, an idea) might become capable of concerning the makers, and even intervening in their lives, eventually transforming them (Stengers 1993). Similarly, both dwellers and makers of material settings in architecture should be transformed by what occurs. In the light of this perspective, buildings could be analysed as mediators, as active forms, which do not simply host, accommodate or contain, but rather transform and fabricate new capacities in those who pass through them. This transformative aspect of the settings of design, construction or dwelling has a political valence. It is precisely *that* political dimension that I wish to explore here. The philosophy of scientific experimentation urges us to develop another definition of politics: what does a setting (practice, form, site, material arrangement, built form) *do* to those who are engaged in it? The sites of design, construction, renovation and dwelling are often not recognized as political but involve emergent practices that lead to groupings and regroupings, to new alliances, and even to collective deliberation on public problems, and, as such, could become politically important. The argument here is: architecture plays an active role in 'doing politics' as the political emerges on these sites and in various shapes and settings. Doing politics is no longer a procedural attempt to reach a good decision or to achieve the perfect 'consensus' that will be further embedded, translated and projected in urban form. Doing politics is rather a substantive move to 'materially refigure' and transfigure the practices, reshape the connections and redistribute the agency in a slow and relationally efficient way.

2

How to Study Ecology of Practice

The past decade has seen a renewal of attention towards the practice of architecture and we have witnessed its evolution from the *Architects and Firms* of Judith Blau (1984) and *The Story of Practice* of Dana Cuff (1992) to recent studies of architectural and engineering practices based on multi-sited ethnographies. This trend has shifted our focus from architecture as meaning to architecture as process, from the lives of those who inhabit the cities to the life of material entities such as buildings, streets, urban artefacts, images, scale models and simulations. Cultural geographers, anthropologists, sociologists and science studies scholars have engaged in path-breaking research that aims at deciphering practices of design, use and inhabitation, their scalar and ontological specificities, and their political outreach.

Reality is exported from architectural practices not in the form of big theories, visions, manifestos, but rather in the shape of scale models, renderings, videos and drawings. If we study the fabrication and circulation of these objects, we will be able to gain access to the ontology, that is, to what that belongs to the real. That is, a versatile and multisided reality that does not precede the mundane process of design making but is rather shaped *within* these practices. Therefore, to study the practical course of design means to be simultaneously involved in the particular type of politics related to design making. The term politics here underlines this active mode, this process of shaping, fabricating, inventing and assembling, and the fact that its character is both open and contested. Politics is enacted through the work of designers, builders, their repertoire of actions, drawing practices, consultations with stakeholders, risk-taking and negotiations. The realities produced by architects and designers are political, because other variations possibly exist and may be enacted.

In this book, I reckon that to grasp the political dimension of design, one should study design practice. Here, I will scrutinize design practice as a complex ecology involving actors with variable ontologies, scales and politics. 'Ecology' means in this context an alternative to modernization and emancipation (Latour 1998). To view architecture as an 'ecology of practice' means to redefine the complicated forms of associations between all its beings: habits, skills, buildings, sites, city regulations, designer's equipment, clients, institutions, models, images, urban visions and landscapes. 'Ecology' dissolves boundaries and redistributes agency. It is not a naturalizing metaphor, but rather a politically sensitive concept to capture and understand contemporary design practice. The analysis will be based on materials from ethnographic research conducted in the practices of Mosche Safdie in Boston (Chapter 7), Rem Koolhaas in Rotterdam (Chapter 7), Alejandro Zaera-Polo in London (Chapters 4 and 5), Rudolf Prohazka in Vienna (Chapter 6) and Andrés Perea in Madrid (Chapter 7). To explain how ethnography matters for architectural research, I will visit a building (as I will also do in Chapter 3), and I will travel at a longer distance to faraway Japan, and back in time, back to the 1980s when Japanese postmodernism and machinic architecture were trending. I will tell two different stories of this visit narrated by two distinct epistemological figures: the hasty sightseer and the slow ethnographer. I will further engage in discussion of architectural ethnography, its pitfalls, challenges and key steps of ethnographic analysis, as well as its importance for understanding the politics of architectural practices. Architectural ethnography requires a radical rethinking of the ontological (how we grasp reality) and epistemological (how we get to know what we know) basis of architectural studies, questioning the modernist roots of official architectural scholarship. Its main facets are infra-reflexivity, multi-temporality, sensory engagement with the world and political commitment.

Slow and quick: Epistemology at two speeds

In the 1980s, Félix Guattari met the Japanese architect, Shin Takamatsu, then visited Japan and engaged in dialogue with him. A short and somehow forgotten piece – 'Les Machines de Shin Takamatsu' – published in the journal *Chimères* in 1994 bears witness to his fascination with the concept of machine in Takamatsu's architecture. Recollecting Guattari's encounter with Japanese architecture, I have become equally fascinated by the architect who inspired his thinking. I grew eager to witness and empirically recount different ways of exploring machinic architecture.

The summer of 2010. Following Guattari, I visit Takamatsu's office in Kyoto. I stroll the streets of different Japanese cities to find his buildings and engage in an exploration of the ontology of presence of architectural machines.

Osaka. A hot day in the summer of 2010. Wandering around downtown Osaka to find the iconic Kirin Plaza building of Takamatsu, a strange machinic building catches my attention. The air conditioners look tempting, and here I begin strolling through the building with a different pace of speed; I experience it. Later, I discover, I had actually experienced a Takamatsu building. This is the recently built namBa HIPS building – an entertainment complex poised to become Osaka's newest landmark (Figure 2.1). At 280 feet tall, the building houses a variety of entertainment facilities with separate floors for golf, beauty salons and restaurants. Integrated into an exterior wall of the building is the Yabafo – Japan's first building-mounted free-fall amusement ride. It is seen as the building's main attraction. From 240 feet up, the ride provides passengers with a panoramic view of the city before dropping them down the side of the building at a top speed of 50 miles per hour.

There are two ways of exploring this building, which correspond to two epistemological positions. The first one is the quick one, the one of the hasty sightseer whose perception of a building will not be better than the one of a racing car driver travelling across the fields and seeing but only the flitting landscapes. She will visit

Figure 2.1 The namBa HIPS building, Osaka (photo by the author).

the building once, will take pictures and produce a quick theory by connecting it with meanings, memories and stories related to the building's design; these stories will then be connected to key concepts in architectural theory and history. Or she will visit the office of Takamatsu for a day, yes only a day! She will undertake an interview with the star-architect from the 1980s; she will take pictures of the models in his office and enjoy a chat with the younger designers. She will then go back home and reconnect the materials from the quick visits with the contextual materials on machinic architecture and Japanese postmodernism.

The second epistemological position is a painstaking one. The slow ethnographer visits the building every day, trying to understand its ontology by experiencing it, keeping her diary carefully, trying to recognize words and movements in a strange environment. The slow ethnographer will be able to see and experience a building differently. She will move about, within and without, and through repeated visits, she will let the building gradually yield itself to her in various lights, speeds and intensities, and in connection with changing moods, crowds of people and flows of things. Or else, another type of slow ethnography will consist in visiting the office of Takamatsu and witnessing the daily process of design through interviews and ethnographic conversations with all designers; following the process slowly as it unfolds, trying to witness and make sense of the agency of scale models and drawings, and the networks of humans and non-humans deployed in design venture.

Quick, quicker …

An instantaneous experience of this building is impossible. The hasty sightseer will flee through the building, take a picture and hope that the image will provide her with the possibility of coming back and slowly discovering all those features that the swift moment of perception hampered her from seeing. But she never comes back. She believes that she has seen the building all at once, and this belief relies on the assumption that buildings occupy space, and reach us from various points in space as a single simultaneous perception. When she takes a picture of it, she believes that the building is *on* the picture, trapped there, solid, motionless, *in* there. Passing quickly by the building, she can have an impression of it, but hardly an experience of it. When she takes a picture, the building becomes an aesthetic object – a static one.

She has some knowledge about Takamatsu, having earlier read different accounts of his architecture, and archives from the 1980s. She conducts the interview mobilizing this knowledge. She makes specific assumptions when setting the questions. She strolls around the office and takes pictures. She sets up the tape recorder: chats in English; silence; chats in Japanese; silence. Her expectations are met. She gets what she anticipated; but isn't that already said in other publications? Yes. The answers of Takamatsu are predictable. They do not add anything new to the writings of Guattari. In the formal setting of a dark conference room, bordered by solemnly displayed scale models and waiting to be photographed, Takamatsu rather stubbornly repeats the existing discourse. Nothing new; nothing unexpected. Our hasty sightseer is now a hasty visitor of an architectural practice in the Takeda suburb of Kyoto. Going home she will become a hasty writer and will produce a quick account of this visit that relies on causalities, on symbolic interpretations and confirmed discursive expectations.

Embracing the position of a hasty sightseer, she goes back home with an image of a part of the building totality and an interview that confirmed all expectations. Such a swift and partial perception will inevitably limit any theory of it as well. Its interpretation will be analytical and one-sided. Her aesthetic theory will rely on rigid conceptualizations based on principles and ideas (styles, languages, functions, typologies) that are framed outside of direct aesthetic experience. It will be expressed in strict categories of symbols and meanings. The classifications will set limits to perception. The experience of the hasty sightseer is reminiscent of that of an archaeologist who will quickly disentangle the multiple and intricate structures of Takamatsu's design philosophy, of Japanese architecture from the 1980s, of Guattari's concept of architectural machines and will swiftly recollect them through operations of exhumation, identification, classification – rather than slowly excavating intricate meaning from materiality. The hasty sightseer never allows herself the time to become a slow ethnographer. That is why she will begin to replace the missing experience of the building with unrelated notions coming from other worlds – the world of theory, the background of the architect, the society, the period. Her interpretations will arbitrarily define the random equivalent relationships between the building, on one side, and the interpretations produced after it was built, on the other. This will situate the building in much larger circuits of meta-symbols, societies and cultures.

Slowing down

A slow exploration of the architectural presence of the namBa HIPS building in Osaka makes me experience accidentally its machinic effects. Accounting the namBa HIPS building ethnographically leads me to engage in cartography of architectural presence, relying on the trajectories, the events and the happenings in this building. Here, am I, a slow ethnographer (Stengers 2011). When I engage in a day-to-day ethnography of the building, keeping my precious diary to hand, I engage in a continuously unfolding process of cumulative interactions; instead of discovering a part of it 'at once', I gradually witness the building growing in front of me and with me. Experiencing the building is complex; its qualities are rich and form a spectrum that can hardly be put into rigid categories. I account for the play of light on a building with the constant change of shadows, intensities and colours and shifting reflections. A building is never immobile or still in perception. It can be perceived only in a cumulative series of interactions. There is a continuous building up of the architectural object. I visit the namBa HIPS building many times and I describe what I see. I interact with it and with the other people inhabiting the building and keep a diary of these interactions. I practice a form of 'site-writing' – a term coined by Jane Rendell. That is, a form of writing that happens between words and things, between writing and speaking, between one place and another; 'it is a two-way inscription, dreamed and remembered, of sites written and writings sited' (Rendell 2010: 151). Inspired by Rendell, and taking the concept outside the field of art criticism, this form of writing involves a double movement to and fro between inside and outside, between the researcher and the work of architecture and suspends what might be a purely subjective judgement. The building cannot make an instantaneous impression on me. It is through a continuous process of interactions that it becomes possible to introduce enriching and defining elements of the machinic nature of namBa HIPS.

As an ethnographer who strolls in the building and wanders around it, I extract speeds from the building. Not meanings. These speeds are not given once and forever. They could not happen on their own. Hidden in steel and glass, wood and concrete, slick and bold surfaces, they conceal in the thresholds, they spy from the corners, they sleep in the shadows of darker and lighter colours. The contrast of materials, colours and textures can awaken them and activate their energies. Diverse means are employed to sense the building gaining rhythm: ruptures of symmetry, discontinuous segments, decentred forms fitted together, a vertical slit where the Yabafo structure is placed as part of the façade, the steeply inclined back part of the building as opposed to a flat and open façade. An abyss-like void opens to the sky when Yabafo has moved down, thus inviting the blue Osaka sky to enter the building. I stroll again. If it is all steel, then aluminium would be the material that will make the dark and light grey steel vibrate and produce intensities. In order to obtain this effect of rupture, crossed by diverse transversal elements, the symmetries are systematically derived from the two circles of the façade slot, which become semicircles when the movement of the Yabafo traverses the building. I witness the pulsations of the façade machine, the vibrations; the subsequent openings of the sky destabilizing the dimensions and forms anticipated by ordinary perception. The slit remains the focus, the attractor of subjectivity. 'The becoming machine' can only be obtained, as Guattari argued, through the crossing of a threshold, in the course of which an effect of faciality [*visagéité*] will seize the building in order to make it live, in an animal-animist, vegetal-cosmic manner (Guattari 1994: 136). The faciality is expressed through the many repetitions of the Yabafo – as a pulsating, virulent machinic core – and different intensities are produced. What matters is the constant succession of slow and fast, fast and slow; that is what makes the building dynamic. What runs with a great speed, then gradually slows down; what runs with a slow cadence, then suddenly speeds up.

Experiencing this Takamatsu building and its 'becoming machine', I stroll in the building and I follow the people who walk around every day. I do not ask the questions: What does this big machine-like structure stand for? What does it mean? I just stroll; I follow the circuits; I lend myself to the different intensities of the building rhythms. Nothing is really neutral nor passive. There is something vital, and powerful. The colours, the materials do not say anything either. I witness only speeds; slow and fast, fast and slow. I do not question the meaning. Taken by the fine circuits of this machinic entity, making me immerse into different intensities of flows, speeding up and slowing down, slowing down and speeding up, I just ask: 'How does this building work?' 'What does it do?' 'How and where?' 'Who sets it in motion?' 'In what cases?' 'What are its modalities of action?'

If the hasty sightseer relies on existing past or recent archives of the building, she can quickly connect to a history of events and meanings; as a slow ethnographer I rely on the diagram of the building as a configuration of forces and fields of energies that shape the way that I experience it. The machine-like building does not symbolize anything. The movement does not mean anything. The setting in which I am strolling while writing these lines does not say anything. It works. What makes it work is the network of light grey metal modules that set disjunctions, outline colour contrasts and speeds and the reversible game of transformations, of reactions, of inversions, of inductions, of slowing down and speeding up; the moving core of Yabafo includes the disjunctions and distributes the connections. That is, a strange life circulating in the building, a vital force. Speeds. Not meanings. That is what we get from the building.

Races of pace, speeds, accelerations, intensities, a twinge of new velocity, turns, degrees of swiftness. Speeds flow from all the materials used by Takamatsu: metal, aluminium, decorative tubes and steel brooches, parallel bars, metallic adornments and glass. Takamatsu extracts the speeds from the contrast of materials, from their different surfaces and colour shades.

Back to the practice of Takamatsu, we know what questions to pose. Asking an architect 'Why do you do this?' has no meaning, no importance. We should rather ask: 'How do you do this?' and 'How does this building work?' His discourses might turn around issues of meaning and symbols, as they did in the hasty visit of the office, but while designing he will be experiencing different speeds and moves (Figures 2.2 and 2.3). When projecting and sketching a movement, Takamatsu speeds up and slows down and he wants this to happen in the different successions of dark grey and light grey metal surfaces of the building-to-be. Just like the visitors strolling in the building and wandering around it, the architect is to extract those speeds from the building in the process of drawing and designing it (Yaneva 2005). They are not given once and forever. They could not happen on their own. While working with the speeds, he does not express or symbolize anything; he simply immerses into the tempo of design and adjusts its different rhythms with engineers, contractors and investors.

The slow ethnographer can gain an experience of the building that will be the product of her continuous and cumulative interactions with its world. It is this rich

Figure 2.2 Architects at work in the office of Takamatsu (photo by the author).

Figure 2.3 The practice of Takamatsu, Takeda, Kyoto (photo by the author).

experience of the vast range of the building qualities that will form the core of her interpretations; this should be the only foundation for architectural theory. A building experience should be expressed slowly in adjectives that will narrate the physical conditions of its perception; the large spectrum of building qualities cannot be recounted in a rigid repertoire of categories and fast concepts. Historical and cultural information will throw light on the building, but will not substitute the understanding of the architectural object in its own qualities and relations. Its interpretation will derive from the world of a building that 'opens to interpretation' because of its own activities, from its immediate presence.

Exploring the namBa HIPS architectural presence as a slow ethnographer, I find out different spatial and temporal parameters that are able to generate properties and inform differently about the intensities produced. Experiencing slowly the building would mean following a series of events, internal resonances and movements. We can find in its organization different spatio-temporal dynamisms, confrontations of spaces, flights of time, syntheses of speeds, directions and rhythms. The namBa HIPS building appears as a field composed of differential relationships that define each other reciprocally in a network; there is a distribution of singularities, of differences, of intensities, of trajectories. The building is not immobile. It does not express anything. It works, and its meanings vary according to the distribution of properties manifested in its process of working.

Judging a complex object like the namBa HIPS building as an aesthetic and static object would require the hasty sightseer to embrace an authoritative way of speaking on behalf of established principles and reference to the works of other leading architects, of other buildings, of this style or period, of architectural theory. Such a way of interpreting the building relies on quick images taken by the hasty sightseer and fast interviews, archives and accounts. It will treat it in its rigid aesthetic form and will have a limiting direct response in perception. When we say a building expresses Japanese culture or embodies politics, we rather think about a stable form that would reify subjective meanings.

The slow ethnographer engages instead in an inquiry into the architectural presence of the building that can only be understood in meticulous studies of the specific works of architecture. The object of the ethnographer is far from being stable; it appears rather as a dynamic map of all the trajectories and events it triggers; and it changes according to different speeds. The epistemological practice will rely on the posture of the slow ethnographer, where presence and immediacy are crucial. That is, a process of creative and immediate engagement with the present that will make us immerse in assembling and reassembling all human and non-human ingredients that a building is made of.

This type of research epistemology will lead us towards a better understanding of the architectural work – its qualities, forces and events; its different materials and textures – the noises, the accidents, the runners traversing it; the dramas in its premises. As witnessed here in the short story of the ethnographer, the apprehension of the machinic nature of the namBa HIPS building grows from the architectural object as it enters into the experience of slow observation by interaction with her own knowledge and sensitivity. Thus, experiencing and describing an object does not derive from objective standards nor is it the outcome of purely subjective impressions and feelings. When conducted in an architectural practice, slow ethnography helps us to witness the difficulties and the unpredictable turns in the process of its design and invention (Yaneva 2009b). It opens the inquiry to situations where subjective and objective are again not stable but multiple and changing; a situation where all distributions are possible.

What is architectural ethnography?

The interest in the world of architecture led me to engage in slow ethnography as early as 2001 when I entered the practice of Rem Koolhaas, the Office for Metropolitan Architecture in Rotterdam (OMA). As an anthropologist trained by Bruno Latour, I engaged in studying the activities and beliefs of the tribe of architects and designers; their cultures, their exoticism, their strange obsession with time, novelty and innovation; their enigmatic attachments to models, sketches and drawing software; and the extraordinary inconsistency in how they define themselves and their practices. Questioning what matters to architects and what truly defines their world, I engaged in a pragmatist re-description of the socio-material dimensions of design. Thirteen years later I keep on referring to the OMA ethnography in my lectures; my architecture students keep on asking questions in refrain: 'What does an ethnographer do?' 'What is ethnographic data?' 'What do we gain from embracing the position of symmetric anthropologist?' 'How can symmetric anthropology provide a different foundation of architectural theory?' 'How is an ANT-informed ethnography of architectural design different than other approaches?' While this chapter does not pretend in any way to engage in an extensive discussion of architectural ethnography, I will provide answers to these questions by advocating the ANT-inspired approach as being a fruitful alternative to a critical theory-based perspective to design.

Whenever I happened to present results from my ethnographies of OMA (Yaneva 2009a, b) over the last years, I always had someone in the room telling me: 'Oh.., I know Rem, I met him once, … and it is not *like this* that design happens at OMA …'. Such kind of reactions always make the life of a design anthropologist harder than the one of a historian, who will rely on silent archival sources, and whose *dramatis personae* will never 'resurrect' from the archives to confront her in a lecture theatre objecting to the way they have been depicted. Yes, historians are lucky; they rarely meet their subjects of research. Ethnographers, meanwhile, run the risk of objection, disagreement and doubt as practitioners presented in ethnography retain their singularity. This requirement situates the anthropologist.

Such an approach aims at unpacking the 'ecology of design practice' from which architectural knowledge evolves, rather than focusing on one particular participant in design. It is inspired and informed by 'the symmetric anthropology' advocated by Bruno Latour in *We have Never been Modern* (1991). Here symmetric holds the status of requirement: that is, to require the ability to describe and compare without having to recognize any intrinsic obstacles to this comparison. Symmetric anthropology can be a highly productive approach when it puts our own practices to the test of symmetry, because in doing so it openly clashes with our claims to be different, rational and objective. Symmetric anthropology attempts, at its own risk, to represent designers and their so-called 'modern' practices in a way that is distinct from the way that practitioners will present themselves (Stengers 2010a). Hence, all objections are welcome. Any design anthropologist would be happy to hear that designers disagree with the way they have been depicted. And so was I.

From products to stories of practice

For a long time architectural scholarship had focused on the products: buildings and places. In the 1980s, the field of architecture witnessed a shifting scholarly interest from products to practice. Architectural practice became an object of interest as scholars focused on the internal organizational life of small- and large-scale firms studied as bureaucratic organizations that have hierarchy, formalized rules and specific ideologies. The attention was directed to the specific correlations between firm ideology, office structure and design quality (Blau 1976). These studies were inspired by a sociological perspective, based on quantitative methods, and used to understand the social underpinning of design and architectural production (Blau 1984). It was assumed that the social context has an impact on the characteristics of the work setting of the firms and the quality of the architectural work.

Yet, the research shift from architecture as organizational structure towards architecture as a process necessitated a move from quantitative to qualitative methodologies. Inspired by anthropological methods, Donald Schön engaged in pioneering research of designing architects with a focus on architectural education. His concept of 'reflection-in-action' (1983) made a revolution in design anthropology in founding a new epistemology of practice taking as its point of departure the competence and artistry already embedded in skilful practice. Design progresses, argued Schön, as architects reframe problems and engage in a reflective conversation with the materials and shapes of the situation. While Schön followed designers at work in the architectural studios, Dana Cuff (1992) approached the internal life of architectural firms and based her findings on painstaking ethnographic observation of US practices in the San Francisco area. Up to that moment studies of architectural practices from the inside were non-existent. Cuff's approach was more informed by anthropology rather than traditional quantitative sociology. Deflating the myth of the autonomous architect-hero, Cuff argued that all buildings, all products of architectural design are collectively and socially constructed through negotiations among architects and an array of contributors: clients, politicians, planners, bankers, engineers, civic groups and corporate executives. According to her, architectural practice is shaped 'through constant interactions among interested parties, from which the documents for a future building emerges' (Cuff 1992: 3). The term practice is central here; professional practice is understood as the customary performance of professional activities based on commonplace experience as they evolve and weave webs of meaning among a group of participants; this forms the very basis of architectural culture. As Cuff argues, 'If we are to offer a sound advice about how architectural practice *ought* to function, we must know more about how it functions now' (Cuff 1992: 6). Digging deeply into the significance of the daily professional lives of architects, their situated actions and meanings, Cuff's work offered a better understanding of architectural practice and her ethnography shed light on the culture of designing architects.

From the stories of practice to network-oriented ethnographies

If for Cuff architectural practice emerges through constant social interactions among interested parties, the most recent ethnographic wave of studies tackles architecture as a collective process of negotiation widely shared with a variety of non-human entities. Crucially, this research reorientation occurred simultaneously in the fields of cultural geography and science studies. Architecture became a new terrain for STS-trained anthropologists as early as 2000, who following a programmatic article of Michel Callon (1996) engaged in tracing design in the making (Yaneva 2005, 2009a; Houdart and Minato 2009). In the words of the geographers Jacobs and Merriman, to speak of 'practising architectures' attends to the ways in which architectures – and their inhabitation and consumption – refract contemporary theoretical ideas about performance, place and embodiment, from the everyday spaces of events to the ephemeral. Here architecture is 'understood not simply as an accomplishment (or artefact) of human doing, but as an on-going process of holding together' (Jacobs and Merriman 2011: 212). While STS-informed research focused on architecture as embedded in complex networks of design practice, geographers provided interpretations of architecture as embedded in the practice of inhabitation, dwelling within and interacting with the 'living body' of a building or a performative urban environment.

Both groups of scholars shared the assumption that architecture cannot be reduced to a static frame of symbolic meaning (Latour and Yaneva 2008); that a deeper understanding of architecture can be gained by studying ordinary unfolding courses of action in design, use, inhabitation, maintenance, reuse and urban contestation. While the focus on the iconic and symbolic dominates the architectural literature, process-oriented geographers and anthropologists of architecture judged a focus on representation as insufficient in its potential to do justice to the complexity of architectural processes. The contemplative attitude to architecture effectively risked 'paralysing' its objects of study. Embracing an understanding of architecture as something 'more than "just" representation' (Lees 2001: 53), geographers tackled the ways in which space, performance and event are shaped in the process of use, inhabitation and evaluation of buildings and urban spaces. Bringing into view the often-overlooked work of maintenance that is central to sustaining architectures of all kinds (Graham and Thrift 2007), they studied the interactions of bodies and everyday practices in designed urban environments (Degen et al. 2010), and they engaged in unravelling the mundane 'life of buildings' that appeared in their accounts as being reminiscent to 'living bodies' (Jacobs et al. 2007; Strebel 2011) sustained in the everyday social practices of inhabitants, concierges and experts of various kinds.

In their articulation of a mode of processual inquiry into the life of buildings, geographers took much inspiration from STS (and in particular from the work of Bruno Latour), which, transformed by the influence of socio-cultural anthropology, resulted in extensive ethnographic studies of scientific and technological processes. The city had by then already been thrust into the STS limelight, notably in the lens of ANT (Latour and Hermant 1996). Architectural design became an epistemological territory of exploration for STS-trained anthropologists like myself and some colleagues. Rather than profiling architects and their 'tribes' as professional groups, our writings traced the materialization of design operations and the socio-material complexity of design outlining anthropologically the routines, actions and transactions of all participants in design in compound spatial settings. Furthermore, this added to the list of non-human entities, turning our gaze to architectural renderings (Houdart 2008), scale models (Yaneva 2005), city plans (Zitouni 2010), simulations (Loukissas 2012), maps (Nadaï and Labussière 2013), computer-generated images (Rose et al. 2014), urban artefacts (Doucet 2015) and more recently the objects of urban planning (Rydin and Tate 2016). Thus, reintroduction of the ethnographic methods into architecture, twenty years after the pioneering work of Dana Cuff, has furthered the importance of studying the texture of the ordinary life of designers, dwellers, engineers and maintainers, and has inspired an interest in the politics of practice.

In their pragmatist studies, both geographers and anthropologists relied on the assumption that architecture is collective but it is shared with a variety of non-humans. It is not a social construction, as argued by Dana Cuff, but rather a composition of many heterogeneous elements, an assemblage. Engaging in a careful study of all participants in design and dwelling, human and non-human, skilfully connecting discursive and non-discursive layers of information and interpreting them, these recent studies engaged in unpacking the ecology of architectural practice. The ANT-inspired architectural ethnographies, which I will term here 'new ethnographies', follow the principles of no hierarchy, attention to the detail, symmetry: noticing what happens between humans and non-humans, undivided attention to words and the gestural and non-verbal language.

My ethnographic work is part of this tradition. The new ethnographies we developed denote an approach that pays specific attention to the texture of ordinary life of designers and generate 'thick descriptions' of the knowledge practices of different participants in design. It also points to the introduction of ethnographic methods into architectural scholarship. This development signifies a rapprochement of distinctive disciplinary traditions such as architecture, socio-cultural anthropology and STS (and in particular ANT), which resulted in a number of monographs of architectural practices (Houdart and Minato 2009; Yaneva 2009a, b; Loukissas 2012). This recent trend could be also termed as 'ethnographic turn in architecture' as it is the outcome of several related processes: the emergence of a reflexivity trend among architectural professionals as a key epistemological feature of architectural studies, the growing realization of architecture as a social practice and the social nature of outcomes of architectural production, the tendency to acknowledge the collective nature of design. It would be a mistake to view this development as an emergence of a new methodological fashion, which just like the theoretical ones, have their picks and flare out with time; nor is it a range of new tools that can be appended to conventional architectural research. Instead, as a methodological innovation, the reintroduction of the ethnographic methods into architecture twenty years after the pioneering work of Dana Cuff does hold remarkable potential to investigate new questions. It can contribute to dislodge the certainty of traditional architectural knowledge, the belief placed in the absolute authority of the historical archives and its simplifications by its practitioners reducing, even naturalizing architectural research to the production of critical discourse about practices, yet taking it far from the nitty-gritty realities of design making.

In what follows, I will discuss some distinctive features of the 'new ethnographies of architecture' referring to examples from my own ethnographic fieldworks and the work carried out by colleagues. It is hoped that this reflection can contribute to a more open and flexible framework of ideas and epistemological techniques to approach the political dimension of architectural practice.

Questions of ethnography

'What does an ethnographer do in a design context?' 'What is architectural ethnography?' After my first visit of OMA in a grey November afternoon in 2001, I started an ethnographic observation of the practice. The questions that troubled me through the first weeks were: 'What sources can I use?' 'How do I gain access to them?'

'How do I select them?' 'How do I start making sense of them?' Ethnography is based on a number of sources which include reports of meetings with clients and technicians, reports of visits to sites, long descriptions of the construction of models, working papers, office-made archives, sketchbooks, correspondence of the star architect with clients and with his numerous fans and so on. It is also based on hundreds of photographic documents, which are not commonly used in sociological analyses of the profession, usually based on statistic data and questionnaires (Blau 1976, 1984; Champy 2001). It is also a very different nature of sources than the ones used and presented by architects themselves or their critics, who are more interested in the buildings and their philosophical impact, aesthetic qualities and symbolic meaning or else, in the technological performance of buildings. I found all these materials in the AMO archive, which Rem opened up for me while allowing unlimited access to all other sources in the OMA. The questions that haunted me further were: 'Do I have everything on this project?' 'Will I manage to collect all the sources available?' No, and I know it now. I ended up collecting a number of different sources, none of which was a stable factual body of data like the solid historical archive. Unlike the chronological and dense, extensive and well-documented body of facts contained by the archives, the ethnographic collection of materials is eclectic, random, partial, circumstantial and volatile as ethnographic data are shaped by 'our own constructions of other people's constructions of what they are up to' (Geertz 1973: 10). Having an unrestricted access to a number of volatile and haphazardly collected sources can prompt additional problems too. The problems of time management came first. I spent entire days and nights reading more and more without selecting. Swept away by untold stories of design, open letters to Rem, clients' briefs and hundreds of unpublished sketches and images, I found myself dreamily lost in the AMO archives. I read exotic anecdotes, struggled to decipher words from the architectural jargon, which I encountered for the first time by writing them down in my notebook and trying to pronounce them as if they were to form the ingredients of a mysterious new language. Surrounded by the piles of this archive for nights and days, I felt as though I had awakened in a foreign and exotic culture that seemed only vaguely familiar to me. I felt more determined to get to know it.

Ethnography starts with the tedious collection and exploration of all these disparate sources. They bear witness of the daily process of design, keep precious traces of actions, present unshared quotidian choices and translate outlandish voices. Paraphrasing Clifford Geertz (1973), if we want to understand what architecture is, we should look in the first instance not at its theories or its findings, and certainly not at what its apologists say about it; we should rather look at what design practitioners do. At the level of the methodology, architectural ethnography could include different participants in design and involves formal interviews (some of them took 2–3 hours), informal chats and conversations (usually initiated in the process of discussing an important decision or design move), participant observation (following situated actions in the premises of OMA and outside it), archival research (including the 'home-made' project-based archives in the practice), site visits or tours often alongside with the architects (the 'natives' from the office) or engineers, clients and potential inhabitants of the building. Ethnography typically happens in an architectural practice, but also outside the office – construction sites, planners' headquarters, client's offices, public presentations, participatory public events, architectural exhibits. All these sites have been less investigated than the practice.

From a textbook point of view, doing ethnography is establishing rapport, selecting informants, transcribing texts, taking genealogies, mapping fields, keeping a diary and so on. But what defines ethnography as a form of knowledge 'is the kind of intellectual effort it is: it is an elaborate venture in "thick description"' (Geertz 1973: 6). To illustrate how extraordinary 'thick' ethnographic description can be, this study took two years of participant observation in the office of Koolhaas (2002–2004), three years of additional research and writing and it resulted in two books with overall 400 pages. I used ethnography to understand what it means to design and to unravel the many local arrangements that creativity springs from. I followed designers at work just like the sociologist of science Bruno Latour did in the 1970s, following scientists at work to understand the production of scientific facts (Latour and Woolgar 1979; Latour 1987). To capture and understand OMA's architectural approach, I put aside the existing official interpretations in the architectural scholarship, I focused on the intrinsic logic of design: tracing the ordinary forces and conditions of experience, following the designers in the office, watching the way their actions spread and the way architects make sense of their world-building activities – the routines, the mistakes and the workaday choices. The detour to design experience allowed getting a better understanding of OMA's design and to avoid the passage through the vague notions of society, culture, imagination and creativity, which do not explain anything, but need explanation.

Mainstream social scientists assume that anthropological research consists in observation, *just* observation, and that ethnography is far from being an interpretative activity. They are very wrong about it! Ethnography requires interpretation from the very start. Ethnography is not *simply* about observing and describing. Before we even start the observation, we need to make a number of choices: who to follow, where and how, how often, in what spaces, what type of activities. Confronted with these questions, I used the archives of AMO as a 'shelter' to spend more time answering these questions and reflecting on the number of choices I needed to make. Moreover, additional questions piled up: 'Shall I follow just one project (the Whitney extension) or shall I look at the other projects in the office (the CCTV, the Seattle library, the music hall in Porto and others)?' 'Shall I interview Rem only or all the architects I get the chance to meet and talk to?' 'Shall I follow other participants in design (value engineers, stage designers, museum professional, clients and others)?' As we make this kind of choices, we already make assumptions about the reality we will account ethnographically, we engage in interpretation. For instance, had I decided to follow just Rem, and interview just the star architect, I would have never produced an ethnography of design that would account design as a collective venture of human and non-humans, designers and models, pixels and paint. Yes, ethnography is interpretative from the very start! Right down at the practical level, as we deal with the nitty-gritty realities of tedious operations of design and with all kinds of factual specifics (of how to cut the foam and how to draw an axonometric diagram, how to calculate budgets or where to place the mechanical systems), we are already interpreting, deciphering, explicating, guessing and trying to understand and untangle the different meanings of the design moves that we witness. When we follow participants in design at work, we do not observe simple facts. We are rather faced with a multiplicity of complex operational structures, superimposed spatial layers, conceptual meanders and various rhythms of work knotted into one another; all of them happen at once, most of them look strange to us and occur in a simultaneously cacophonic way; they run with irregular and inexplicit paces. Lost at first, enchanted by the estrangement and virtuosity of a practice whose rhythm we can only hope to fully apprehend, we first try to grasp its tempo, its spirit and soul, and then little by little, we attempt to render, untangle and make sense of it. Doing ethnography is difficult and challenging, precisely because it is a down-to-earth activity: messy, hectic, cacophonic and vertiginous at once.

Taken by the beat of ethnographic observation, I ask myself: 'How shall I capture this rhythm?' I observe, record and analyse what I see, hear and sense and this all happens at the same time. These are not separate self-sufficient operations, but rather knowledge-seeking steps that all occur at once. What I inscribe in my notebooks is not the factual reality of OMA or a solid set of truths about every architectural practice; I only have direct access to *that very small part* of the design process that my informants lead me to discover and understand (mainly architects from the Whitney team and a small number of designers from other projects). Anthropological analysis is not about facts that have never been discovered before or a precious unknown archive that a historian can disclose in search of the genuine factual reality. Nor is anthropological analysis about the reconstruction of a simple reality 'out there'. It is about guessing, presuming and wondering about the web of meaning of the architectural moves we witness; assessing the guesses and assumptions we have; speculating on the numerous statements and hypotheses of the 'natives' on us; and drawing explanatory conclusions from the better guesses and assumptions.

While engaging in ethnography we deal with 'natives', that is the practitioners we follow and whose worlds we describe. As ethnographers we spend a lot of time with them, and we are often tempted to become natives or to look like them. Charmed by the world of architecture, swept away by its conceptual and rhythmic complexity, I learnt with the time that the relationship to the natives is a very delicate one. No matter how much I happened to appreciate the design world I was temporary part of, no matter how much architects enjoyed the presence of a slow ethnographer, no matter how cautiously we managed to build a strong admiration for each other, I knew I should not be seeking to become a native. My enchantment with the architectural profession led me to recurrently wish and dream to become an architect. Yet, had I decided to become an architect, I would have never produced accounts of entities and beings that architects take for granted (such as models, scaling instruments, experiments). This fragile distance allowed me to question and unpack the nature of these non-humans. For instance, Dana Cuff and Yanni Loukissas, who have been trained as architects, managed to maintain their anthropological presence by keeping multiple distances with the research subjects and their practices. At the start I attempted to mimic the natives, but I soon realized that only romantics would seem to find a point in that. Instead what was more important was to be able to converse with the natives, to gain access to their conceptual world, to be able to ask questions that 'no one ever asked before' and to listen for hours to everything they wanted to share with me. In the very first days of my ethnographic observation, I had to ask basic questions such as: 'What is this?' 'How do you go about making a model?' I was scared the natives will take me as an amateur, but nevertheless dared to ask them. They loved this sort of questions! They loved them because they triggered long conversation on the practicalities of design; simple and unpretentious queries allowed the answers to take the shape of rich and extensively narrated eloquent stories. I felt embolden by the dense and meaningful texture of the data I was able to collect by humbly daring to look naïve (not easy for someone trained as a sociologist to do so!). I enjoyed witnessing how my presence in the office made architects to become more reflexive and enticed them to articulate concepts, moves and effects that are usually tacitly shared, but never explicated. It was important to be able to see things from inside out (from the perspective of the designers' own world), not to impose my assumptions of how design should be explained through a number of ready-made explanatory frameworks coming from outside (society, culture, zeitgeist).

The accounts I produced all relied on a depiction of the world of architects. Instead of providing a definition of the big concept of Creativity, we rather gain access to the designers' own understanding of it so that the interpretation of creativity will be entirely 'actor-oriented', practitioners-oriented. Writing anthropologically about design in the making by following the intrinsic logic of design implied the construction of actor-oriented descriptions; they happened to be lengthy so as to present, narrate and decipher all these cumulative findings. I needed to fill more and more pages. Therefore the genre in which to present ethnographic interpretations is the one of the essay or the monograph. Anthropological writing is an interpretation that constructs an extensive reading of what happens along with a detailed presentation of the dense texture of factual reality. A good account of architectural ethnography tells us what specific designers say at a specific time, in a specific place, what they do, what is done to them. If it takes us into the heart of the events, that is how we know it is a good interpretation! The description can sweep us away, and then without knowing it, we will find ourselves in the middle of a sound lab (Loukissas 2012), in the London underground (Vertesi 2008), in the midst of a rendering making in Kuma's offices (Houdart and Minato 2009) or building maintenance in Glasgow (Strebel 2011), or in the midst of a scaling trail in Koolhaas' practice (Yaneva 2009a, b). A good ethnography is not about a neutral recording of events, vignettes and anecdotes; it is about capturing events that gain specificity in their own moments of occurrence and collating them into an engrossing account that will constitute a meaningful story of practice.

Anthropological analysis is microscopic. In an ethnographic account, we can have exceedingly extended descriptions of extremely small matters: how to find a tree on a rendering, how to inspect a model with a model scope, how to find the right models for a specific presentational setting and so on. Follow the pixels on the screens of designers in the office of Kengo Kuma or the foam cutting in the process of model making in the office of Rem Koolhaas and you will witness that by tracing the small operations, gradually and slowly, painstakingly and meticulously, we will be able to confront the 'grand reality' of Creativity commonly tackled by design researchers and architectural historians. Yet, when confronted with it in the obscure and messy contexts of the studio, the model making shop, the sound lab, we can take the capital letters off 'creativity'. By so doing creativity is not any longer a 'big word'; thanks to ethnography it takes a graspable form in an ordinary context. Yet, the question that remains is how to get from a collection of ethnographic miniatures and descriptions of exceedingly infinitesimal design matters to the big concepts of Creativity or Design Innovation. How do we move from microscopic data to macro-concepts and realities, from local truths to general visions? It will be naïve to assume that we can find the essential characteristics of Design Creativity somehow summed up and simplified in OMA. It will be absurd to claim that OMA is a typical architectural practice. Instead, what we find in the practice of Koolhaas in Rotterdam is *OMA's life*; the localized, confined, microscopic and slow study of this life is important on its own. It has its own relevance; not because it will capture the big concept of Creativity in the little manifestations and daily operations of design. That is another misunderstanding I had to cope with: my study was *not* on OMA; design anthropologies do not study studios and offices. They rather study *in* studios and offices as the concepts of Creativity and Invention can best be tackled in confined localities. OMA was never the object of my study; OMA was rather the *locus* of a study on design creativity.

Yet, the question is how the microscopic data we extract from years of ethnographic observation of design practices can help us to reach to macro-concepts and realities. How do we translate the local truths about model-making, scaling, scoping, sketching and reasoning about smart buildings into broader visions of design? Or, in other words, what is the specific connection between descriptive interpretations and theoretical formulations? In the format of ethnographic study, the conditions of theory are rather different: instead of producing abstract regularities and generalizations across the cases ('in design, creativity always happens this way!' or 'foam-cutting is important for every design practice today!'), the specific task of theory here is to produce 'thick' ethnographic descriptions by following the actions and transactions of human and non-human actors in complex spatial settings, and thus to be able to generalize *within* the specific cases. Hence, the role of theory here is to offer a vocabulary in which design actions can be expressed; that is a vocabulary that comes straight from the speech of the natives and is actor-oriented. The anthropological accounts simultaneously describe, interpret and explicate design practice; theory emerges gradually as we learn to draw large conclusions from small but very densely textured ethnographic matters and decode the 'inscribed' meaning of social actions. It helps us to detect, analyse and diagnose what the knowledge obtained demonstrates about the design practice in which it is found (OMA), and beyond that – about design as such.

It is precisely because we wish to get access to the complex specificity and circumstantiality of a phenomenon that we need to conduct long field work and produce protracted descriptions. To study design practice anthropologically requires long-term engagement with mainly qualitative, highly participative and almost obsessively fine-comb ethnographic data extracted in the confined context of a design practice. Yet, only such a study can contribute to giving sensible actuality of the mega concepts of design Creativity and Invention. To write about creativity is to write about particular attempts by particular designers to place these things in some sort of comprehensible meaningful frame. Ethnography does not provide answers, but makes available to us answers that architects and other participants in design have given. Ethnographic analysis is intrinsically incomplete. At the end, there are no conclusions to be reported; there is merely a discussion to be sustained.

The challenges of symmetric anthropology

Studying the practices of architects, we engage in ecology of practice where designers do not address a silent and docile world. Their mode of existence is relational and constraint, not visionary; their avatars do not refer to a more general authority, but to a 'here and now' they fabricate and which makes them possible. Yet, I do not advocate an anthropological approach to the ecology of architectural practice in general, of how, for instance, computational design has changed architectural practice in general, how digital methods will transform architectural research in general. The vocation of architects cannot be defined any longer in terms of 'general purposes' but is inherent to the art of fabricating all sort of material entities: scale models, renderings, simulations. This is a distinctive feature of the new ethnographies. Following Latour we can call all these beings fabricated by architects factish* (Latour 2010a); they may be refereed to 'as real' and endowed, no matter that they are fabricated, with an autonomous existence. Follow a model at the OMA and you can witness the factish. I have chosen the foam model because it exemplifies in a particularly dramatic way the paradoxical mode of existence of all those beings constructed by designers and that exist in a way that affirms their independence with respect to creativity and experimentation. On the one hand, the model is produced as a result of unlimited experimentation and exchange of ideas; on the other hand, it has to respond to constraints and limitations. Once it is generated, it exists with all the characteristics of a real 'actor' endowed with properties; an actor that is enabled to talk on behalf of larger entities. It is also the result of a dense network of practices and their histories. Models, renderings and images are beings that designers fabricate and that fabricate them back as they receive autonomy that the designers do not have. That is, they gain the power of 'factish Gods'. Renderings and models talk back to the creators, they transcend their fabricators; they are irreducible to a critical epistemology usually embraced by architectural theory or to the kind of 'objects' that architecture likes to contrast to 'subjects'. If we trace ethnographically how they are produced, negotiated, fabricated and circulated, we are able to follow simultaneously the co-production of design reality and the designers as professionals.

The new ethnographies of architectural design account for the non-discursive along with the discursive as what architects say and what they do often differs. That is why insiders' accounts and interviews should be coupled with outsiders' observations. However, compared to the ethnography of Dana Cuff (1992), the new ethnographies pay close attention to the spatial settings of action and the ontological status of ethnographic data. These features relate to the specific epistemology that ethnography of current design practices is capable of generating. They are of distinctive nature as they theorize the role of materials in design practice and this makes them different from the social constructivist ethnographies. The assumption is that materials and design objects play a constitutive role in the cognitive activities of architects: architects at OMA think through slicing foam and scale models, Kuma's designers think through computer renderings, Arup engineers think through simulations. This distinctive way of doing architecture is suggested in the medium of thought: the foam, the pixels, the simulation diagrams. Both in Kengo and Koolhaas's case, we do not see the master architect appearing as a powerful creator, as a mythical figure, as genius. Design is distributed across different settings: design meetings, conversations with clients and site visits. The master architect is not as present as he would be in a book produced by his critics that would portray, glorify and praise his architecture. In the new ethnographies, we witness the specificity of Kuma's or Koolhaas's architecture through what constitutes it: the setting, the material, the design trails. On the other hand, the ethnography does not merely capture a portrait of the practice of a certain architect. This is an attempt to describe not so much architects in their working environment (the classic topic of the sociology of architects), but *what* architects at work witness and *what* they experience; the combination of materials, experiments, processes and effects. To capture this, an ANT-informed ethnographic observation is needed.

The new ethnographies also ask what things are: what is a scale model, what is an architectural rendering, what is a computer simulation, as opposed to what the practitioners of design might think them to be. This is a question that has irreducibly ontological character. Holbraad (2009) calls this approach 'ontographic' to indicate the peculiar investment in charting the ontological status of diverse ethnographic data. This understanding is situated in the analytical coordinates in the debates about the relationship between mind and matter, subjects and objects, materiality and culture. The new ethnographies point to a problematic tension in architectural discourses: the phenomena studied by ethnographers appear to posit ontological continuities. Yet, the typical interpretations of architectural theorists and the critical tradition that informs predominantly the current discourses posit ontological separations.

With ANT in hand, we do not unravel meanings. We rather show how things become knowable and new realities are obtained; how architectural reality is exported from the architectural office in the form of objects that carry reality (in the context of this book – political reality). Following ANT's epistemology, we witness and describe the modes of existence of various objects and account for numerous connections that flow out of these streams of experience; we focus on gradually accounting and understanding, like a slow ethnographer, these architectural objects, settings, institutions, practices and working cultures rather than replacing them with the quick concepts of society, culture and politics, like a hasty sightseer. Yet, such an approach does not consist in their simple description. It rather aims at making explicit the performative or pragmatic dimension that connects objects with the practices of their making, with the streams of experiences, with their makers and inhabitants. In what follows, we will tell a number of ethnographic stories based on careful and very slow accounts of connections, actions, individual moves and collective groupings in design and inhabitation. Told in a meticulous and situationist way, these ethnographic accounts will trace pluralities of concrete entities in the specific spaces and times of their coexistence so as to grasp the underlying political dimensions of architecture.

3

Political Objects: The First Way of Becoming Political

Politics of mundane architecture

How can a building, a bridge, a master plan, a key or a chair be political? What does an atrium do? How do material arrangements matter politically? How can the design of a lecture theatre stimulate thinking? How can mundane activities as simple as climbing stairs or taking the elevator have political effects? These ordinary artefacts and environments are commonly discussed in the process of design and planning and widely used in daily practice. To understand their becoming political, we need to embrace a dynamic view. There is no politics *behind* a bridge, *behind* an auditorium or elevator; politics is rather something emergent, something to be witnessed as we interact with, stroll, inhabit and let ourselves being guided by mundane architectural artefacts or infrastructures. Here, we will be ambling *in* spaces, interacting *with* mundane architectural objects, getting lost and finding ourselves, wandering *according to* spatial transition, letting ourselves being steered, transferred and made to connect with others; all this with the help of architecture. That is, a dynamic view that will make all buildings reminiscent to the gull in the work of Etienne Jules Marey (Latour and Yaneva 2008), not static projective surfaces of big politics, but 'birds in a flight', flights that can become 'political'. This is the first way of architecture to be political: by activating the connecting agency of objects and material arrangements.

The example chosen here is a university building. I will explore its dimensions as a political site, its design and material arrangements. The typology discussed here is not among the ones that we usually associate with politics: the state buildings, the iconic skyscrapers, the office towers, the stadia or the megaprojects in big cities (Chapter 1). It is instead a mundane typology used on a day-to-day basis in academia. In this chapter, I will take you for a walk on the campus of the Manchester School of Architecture where I happen to teach, and we will visit together the Benzie building, home of the Manchester School of Arts (MSA) (Figure 3.1). First, I will stroll for a while in the spectacular atrium of the Benzie building and experience its space. Then, I will focus on a number of mundane artefacts and building technologies and I will analyse the specific type of political effects they generate. The narrative strategy of this chapter will imply the use of both an 'I'-narrative form, which I will employ to present my arguments, methodological choices and the steps of the analysis, while the 'we'-narrative form will be used to describe the acts of experiencing the political valence of

Figure 3.1 The Benzie building, Manchester School of Arts, © Hufton & Crow.

spaces, material arrangements and artefacts that the readers will be invited to witness and share with me. The 'we' who symmetrizes does not speak 'for everyone' but rather applies to me and to those who 'join' for the visit of the Benzie building. In other words, the 'we' constituted of me (the author) and you (the readers) is a very concrete 'we'; not the abstract 'we' of an unknown collective.

The making of the Benzie building

The original architecture building, Chatham, was designed by S. G. Besant Roberts of the City Architect's Department, and built between 1966 and 1971. The building was renewed by the architectural practice of FCBStudios and a new part was added to the Chatham building – the Benzie building. The Benzie building opened doors on 19 November 2013 and it was named after Alan Benzie, the outgoing Chair of Governors. The university describes the Benzie building as the home to an impressive vertical gallery, workshops, a roof garden and hybrid studio areas offering flexible space

Figure 3.2 The Benzie building, section © Feldon Clegg Bradlet Studios.

for a range of events from meetings and conferences to product launches and exhibitions (Figure 3.2). The roof terrace, located on the fourth floor, offers a unique new space for events with a capacity of up to 200 people. It is believed that 'the highly visible new vertical gallery space creates a new "Window on the Arts" for the Faculty'.[1] The new building also provides stunning views over the campus and the city of Manchester.

Architect Tom Jarman from FCBStudios explains that from the very start 'the Dean David Crow was in many ways introduced as a catalyst for change and for rethinking the way in which the faculty both related to the outside world, but also internally: how the interactions of the different parts came together, and at the time, it didn't necessarily come together as much as one might hope.' (Interview with Tom Jarman, 11 November 2015). The architects received an interesting brief that 'didn't stipulate in very close terms how that accommodation should be achieved. And yet, instead it proposed *a series of hybrid environments* in which it was possible to imagine a number of types of activities and interactions; it was a deliberately deterritorialised environment' (Interview with Tom Jarman, 11 November 2015) (Figures 3.3). By hybrid, they meant open, flexible and adaptable spaces, which were hard to find in the old building.

The problem with the old building was that previously 'the department was split over two buildings, and people were very hidden in their own little areas – fashion students knew about fashion, embroidery students knew about embroidery, graphics

---

[1] http://manchesterhistory.net/manchester/tours/tour8/area8Apage7.html.

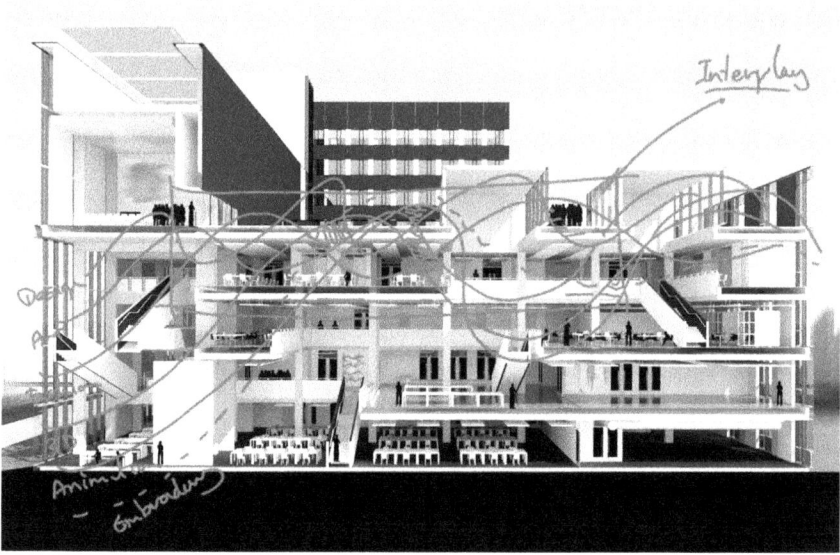

Figure 3.3 The Benzie building, interplay of different disciplines © Feldon Clegg Bradlet Studios.

students knew about graphics, but nobody really knew about each other'.[2] The separations hid the work developed by students and staff as it 'had everything behind doors, everything was within corridors, and it just felt totally wrong. You walked around and you never really saw any work, it was all hidden'.[3] The MSA wanted to develop a more open and hybrid building as they 'have been challenged subsequently in various debates about arts pedagogy'. The new building was supposed to offer flexible and adaptable areas, appropriate for the changing needs of the arts education.

Starting from the ambition to step back from a very traditional model of art education organized in disciplines, FCB architects furthered instead a thinking about how professional artists behave and how they work in multidisciplinary teams, how they learn from each other. As Jarman expounds, 'the whole concept of the building was actually informed from art practice, rather than education' (Interview with Tom Jarman, 11 November 2015). Their approach was all about 'looking at ways of challenging arts education to be more like the practice. So as an example, the interaction between the workshop, the studio and the social spaces was something that needed challenging'.[4] The architects were aware that 'many old school art schools in a way find the idea of this openness problematic. And they worry that there's not enough intensity of focus. But, to worry in the context of this project is misplaced because we

---

[2] Jane McKeating, Director of Studies Department of Design MSA in "Old School, New School, Art School" accessed: http://fcbstudios.com/work/view/manchester-school-ofart?sort=highlights.
[3] Andy Theobald, Partner at FCBStudios, in "Old School, New School, Art School" accessed: http://fcbstudios.com/work/view/manchester-school-ofart?sort=highlights.
[4] John Brooks, Vice Chancellor MMU, "Old School, New School, Art School" accessed: http://fcbstudios.com/work/view/manchester-school-ofart?sort=highlights.

have various rooms that have strong identities, but they assert in a slightly more subtle way' (Interview with Tom Jarman, 11 November 2015). The new building creates a stimulating environment for design and art teaching.

In the official statement of the architects FCBStudios, we read: 'The new building celebrates the interrelation of the various art and design disciplines and encourages 21st-century students to work alongside each other and enjoy the crossover rather than concentrating on the differences.'[5] It allows light deep into the space so that people can work together but also get good natural daylight. Keith Bradley says, 'It's the forefront of where creativity and invention happen, and you know, working in different ways actually will happen, rather than separate in silence.'[6] The main studio building is now totally open and there is a whole world of activity in it. 'It's like a hive, almost like bees

Figure 3.4 The Benzie building atrium/vertical gallery, ground floor © Hufton & Crow.

---

[5] FCBStudios, 2013, http://fcbstudios.com, accessed 24 November 2015.
[6] Keith Bradley, Senior Partner at FCBStudios, "Old School, New School, Art School" accessed: http://fcbstudios.com/work/view/manchester-school-ofart?sort=highlights.

working away.'[7] The space is supposed 'to help the students be more interdisciplinary, to be able to understand how they might work in a team situation, how they might be able to learn from each other and from the different disciplines that they study. They need to be a jack of all trades, and a master of one.'[8]

If Benzie is designed to facilitate collaboration and cooperative working, so is the very first space you find yourself in – the vertical gallery. As soon as we enter the Benzie extension, we look up and we see a huge balconied atrium, the floor plates are gently cascading, filling even the ground floor with a muted, and beautiful, natural light (Figure 3.4). This space is open, visually exciting. Venturing in the opposite direction, and via the lifts to the tower, a further three floors are accessible. Zoned for the architecture school, these floors are unique in layout when compared to the extension.

This building can hardly be explained by the dichotomy form/function or in terms of aesthetic or stylistic patterns. Follow a student as she travels through

Figure 3.5 The Benzie building atrium/vertical gallery, staircase. © Hufton & Crow.

[7] Andy Theobald, Partner at FCBStudios, in "Old School, New School, Art School" accessed: http://fcbstudios.com/work/view/manchester-school-ofart?sort=highlights.
[8] David Crow, Dean MSA, in "Old School, New School, Art School"; accessed: http://fcbstudios.com/work/view/manchester-school-ofart?sort=highlights.

the spectacular new entrance gallery (Figure 3.5) from the cafeteria downstairs holding a coffee in her hands, strolling through circulation and exhibition zones, climbing up the large staircase of the building overlooking skies, studios, exhibits of peer colleagues and meeting different morning crowds. What guides her in space? Is it the programme? Is it something else? There is a whole scenario of use, orchestrated by designers, where a certain pattern of interactions among students and tutors is predicted and it occurs in space. And, as we will be strolling in a university building, how is it that its architecture aids the creation of specific research cultures?

Atrium design: New trends and politics of use

Before we explore the Benzie atrium, let me reflect on what type of space is implied by the atrium typology and what is its politics of use. The atrium is commonly a large open space, often several stories high, covered by transparent or translucent material and usually located immediately beyond the main entrance. In ancient Greek and Roman houses, the atrium served as a particular form of courtyard, as the social centre. It has developed in history as a unique form of architecture (Bednar 1986) with vast design possibilities for creating covered interior spaces that protect dwellers from the climate while still enabling them to enjoy the light, view the open sky and be part of a highly interconnected communicative environment. The need for this kind of space has emerged with the trend towards bringing together researchers traditionally scattered across a university campus and having them work in an interactive environment under one new roof in the hope that sparks will fly. The atrium of contemporary academic buildings combines a range of programmes, fulfilling a key role in the life of many research universities. The open staircases create sight lines between floors, departments and an assortment of activities.

The atrium is the quintessential typology of the trend that shaped the new generation of academic buildings by permitting a great deal of flexibility, for they can be easily reconfigured and subdivided as needed. Yet, for a long time scientific buildings were designed as traditional black-box buildings with segregated spaces. They used to impede interaction among scientists from different disciplines, especially in the natural sciences where protected areas and enclosures kept researchers physically isolated. These types of separations were specific to an archaic model of laboratory design prevalent in the 1950s and 1960s. Most science buildings at that time were designed as big windowless boxes that consisted of inflexible laboratory modules reflecting the hierarchical nature of science. The offices were tucked away in labs, making them inaccessible and inconvenient (Collins 1999). By contrast, the type of 'generic' laboratory pioneered by Louis Kahn's Salk Institute offered wide-open expanses to make for interactions among scientists and to reconnect spaces and flows of people and materials (Galison and Thompson 1999). The use of moveable fixtures and glass windows instead of solid walls brought crowds of scientists to free-float from place to place, intensifying their interactions. By making it possible to share spaces, resources and facilities and by thus promoting knowledge-sharing effectively (Gieryn 1999, 2006), the open lab design let new connections be shaped among scientists from different fields and let new groupings and research communities be assembled architecturally. The design of open sharable spaces for collaborative research affected scientists and had a major influence on their scientific culture.

Just like the spatial and technical flexibility had become an important feature for science buildings and a way to keep up with the rhythm of scientific research, openness, versatility and hybridity are the key features permeating the design of educational buildings in the arts. The studio followed the lab. Its plasticity today is ensured primarily by creating a layout that allows for the reassessment of space and supports a spatial distribution that can accommodate change. The overall spatial qualities of the schools of architecture, the specific material arrangement of the studios, the spatial organization of the programmes, affect the way students learn and interact. It is known that the open studio plan always encourages cross-pollination between different ideas and knowledge. Moussavi's analytic comparison of the Architectural Association (AA) and the Harvard Graduate School of Design (GDS) is very revealing in this regard (2012). The spatial arrangement and pedagogical strategy of the school, she argues, influence the kind of character students take on in the future. The compact layout of the AA and the small spaces create a sense of intimacy as the rooms allow tutorials to be conducted as one-to-one interactions potentially generating greater self-belief and faith in their own projects. In contrast, the GSD has one main space, the Gund Hall, where all of the students work alongside one another, and this results in the discarding of individual projects and creates an atmosphere of collectiveness, encouraging collaborations and shared ideas.

As research in the arts and sciences changes with the pace of contemporary societies, this has impacted the design of all academic buildings. This trend has resulted in art and science pedagogy to be increasingly conditioned by this paramount need for flexibility. In addition, interdisciplinary dialogue is at the heart of every field, which reinforces the challenge to reinvent the spatial geometry and cognitive potential of spaces for collaborative research and networking and to enhance the social performance of academic buildings. Therefore, it is not surprising that the emphasis today is on the atrium as a specific environment conducive to interacting, collaborative thinking and networking, one that gives rise to new collective synergies and partnerships.

A superb execution of the atrium as the 'social heart of a building' could be found at Oxford University's Chemistry Research Laboratory (CRL 2004), built by RMJM to the highest specifications and intended to confirm Oxford chemistry's dominant position within the scientific community. The CRL atrium has an important connecting function, that of bridging the office and research spaces. Its communal meeting space with catering facilities and furniture for social contact is meant to stimulate professional communication and initiate collaborative actions and scientific networking. It offers a motivating environment in which scientists can work irregular hours in a pleasant and functional space commensurate with the communicative aspects of their work. Another example of an open atrium space that furthers the intellectual cross-pollination between different fields is the atrium at the Genomics Institute at Princeton University in New Jersey designed by Viñoly architects. Two perpendicular rectangular building blocks and a curved glass façade enclose a two-story atrium space. As the southern façade is transparent, the atrium space becomes an extension of the exterior. A casual meeting room with a Frank Gehry sculpture staged in the middle of it invites scientists to interact and exchange ideas. The changing light throughout the day and the shadows created by the lattice-like screen of louvers make the atrium a cheerful, appealing space.

The atrium can also serve as an urban knot. Two notable examples of this are the Vontz Center designed by Gehry for the University of Cincinnati considered as 'the most successful laboratory, architecturally, since the Salk' (as quoted in Cohen 2000: 212) and Janelia Farm research campus of the Howard Hughes Medical Institute (HHMI) in Ashburn, Virginia, designed by Viñoly architects considered as another laboratory building comparable to the Salk Institute. They both offer innovative design solutions for collaborative research and feature the inventive potential of an atrium serving as the complex knot of a quasi-urban network. To generate a community of scientists with varied expertise and an interest in interdisciplinary research, the lab organization of Janelia Farm is reminiscent of a city (Bonetta 2003) that has 'streets' and integrates all kinds of facilities (housing, dining, conference, fitness). Frank Gehry also defines his latest science building, the Stata building on the MIT campus as a city with research facilities grouped in 'neighbourhoods'.

Going back to the Benzie building atrium, we will take a closer look at the features of its design, materiality and social use; we will stroll in it and explore its architecture in a dynamic experiential way. Slowing down and following the interactions of other people in these spaces will allow us to explore the ways the atrium can facilitate connectedness, decongest activity, mediate relations, trigger new professional partnerships and improve the social capacity of an academic building. In other words, what is the specificity of an atrium in an art building? How can this space spawn political dimensions that set the new generation of academic buildings radically apart from austere and faceless campus buildings of the past?

Strolling in a vertical gallery

Here we are in the Benzie building. As soon as we enter the door, we find ourselves in the atrium space, and we are immediately taken by the roundabout-like buzz of a number of activities. Bridging interior and exterior and employing different design approaches to create open spaces bathed in natural light, the Benzie atrium invites the creation of new types of connections among academics and students from different art disciplines, and among university people and random visitors (see Figure 3.5). It serves as the 'kind of agitator for the project that enables the variety to manifest within what is otherwise a very gridded and structured building' (Interview with Tom Jarman, 11 November 2015). 'With the reduction in teaching time and the reduction in contact hours', the atrium prevents people 'from staying home in their bedsits and re-engender a studio culture in the absence of dedicated studio space'. So, the programme of action of the atrium is to provide an incentive for academics and students to stay longer on campus rather than work in isolation from home or from the library. Replacing the home office, the library desk, but also the studio space, the atrium offers a unique working environment that allows blending formal and informal patterns of communication, a place where neat material arrangements amalgamate with bits of creative messiness in a vertiginous way. As Tom Jarman explains, FCB architects did not want to make the atrium a 'very heavily working space', as in addition to spaces for hard work, designers needed slack spaces where people can have discussions, meet tutors, plan for lectures and so on. They tried 'not to revert to the usual models of what people term as breakout space because it feels so tokenistic', explains Jarman, and he goes, 'It feels like some slightly flabby bit of corridor outside a lecture space isn't really enough to create a kind of place that you might want to hang out and spend time' (Interview with Tom Jarman, 11 November 2015). That is the reason why the atrium spaces are meant to support work continuing through the day as there are no clear distinctions between working, having a coffee and talking about a project; all these activities happen at once and are part of a continuum called art practice. A continuum that can best be deployed in loose working spaces, where working and comforting activities can be mixed, spaces where work can resume in a slower pace and outside the formal lecture rooms and studios.

Thus, the atrium relies on the assumption that most research breakthroughs start not in isolated spaces (studios, offices or labs) or in formal meetings but rather in casual interactions among colleagues. The attractiveness of a site, along with open, light-filled spaces for work, comfortable meeting spaces, can allow academics to get on with their work and still be well connected with their colleagues while remaining related to the outside world. A successful academic building should have spaces for casual encounters, with the atrium having the main role. As we witness with our example of the Benzie atrium, all aspects of its design and infrastructure stimulate multidisciplinary and team-driven research needed to advance the arts. As the problems confronting the arts today are far too complex to be solved in a traditional artistic environment, the atrium can offer spaces tailored to respond to this challenge.

Yet, the function of the atrium successfully goes beyond the simple function of furnishing spaces for social and intellectual encounters. It is not about providing a leisure space either. Its flexible design and its open plan enable architects and art students to bump into one another along the corridors and the large staircases, and in the vast cafeteria area. It also helps mix flows of students and teaching staff, and enrols all kinds of material participants in art and design: samples, fabrics, models and working drawings. Architecture, art students and academics working in the building often leave the studio or the lecture room with a paper draft, a quick sketch, an unfinished model, a fabric sample, a portfolio with images. These objects can circulate in diverse orbits in which sporadic interactions among art students and academics may occur and this will make them part of a collective of rather complex nature. And that is why erecting walls between the studios of fashion, art and architectural students and the social spaces of the atrium would contradict the logic of the art world. The atrium design has the means for intensifying the productive encounters of art and architecture academics and students attached to sundry non-human entities (e.g. cardboard and woods, AutoCAD or parametric software, fabrics) and for having the academics and students fertilize one another's research in every possible way. The atrium facilitates and speeds up exchanges, offering numerous spaces to assist them in bouncing ideas off each other and consolidating them; the cafeteria affords lounge spaces for discussion away from the studio and the lecture theatres. These areas inspire informal dialogue over a cup of coffee. The large corridors and open plan staircase improve the likelihood that colleagues will run into each other by chance. Thus the atrium generates cognitive conditions for new ontological mixtures of all the constituents of artistic creativity in an academic context; it becomes a creative space *per see*. These mixtures nurture interdisciplinary dialogues, new forms of research partnerships and art practice.

Extending and challenging the lecture and studio activities in a dynamic way, the atrium is also about 'the capacity to have open, shared display space, which should be a continual reference point for students and staff throughout the year' (Interview with Tom Jarman, 11 November 2015). In other words, it is 'a place where the school could constantly curate both in terms of activity but also in terms of output' (Interview with Tom Jarman, 11 November 2015). Students don't have to come at the beginning of the year and wonder what they will be doing. In the atrium, they can find all the answers all throughout the year: there, they will have the opportunity to share work of all disciplines; there, the work is on display before the end of year show. It is interesting to note that on the degree show days 'the stairs and all of the upper level circulation are really heavily used', notes Tom Jarman, and goes by reiterating that 'one of the roles of the building was to actually be an advertisement for the school. So to be able to take people through the building and show them work was important' (Interview with Tom Jarman, 11 November 2015). This turns the atrium into a gallery that constantly renews and reinvents its content; vertical gallery is the term that comes to replace atrium here.

However, the design philosophy of atrium spaces does not rely simply on maximizing the chance encounters between professionals from different disciplines to spark new directions in research or rethink the formats of creative and curatorial practices that are all constituent of the art education. The underlying assumption is that increased circulation within the spaces will bring people to experience a sense of community within a large building. This feeling is expected to raise the people's incentive to move about in the building along its spatial transitions and various circuits. That is its political dimension: bringing people together, connecting and regrouping them. The Benzie vertical gallery makes different academics and students to congregate despite the segregation of their disciplines. In such a complex building, the atrium gains the status of an important knot of a network of daily research, pedagogical and communicational activities. It becomes a social nexus concentrating and redistributing flows of events, isolating and reconnecting students and professors, campus staff and random visitors, materials and people, making them circulate with greater intensity. The atrium makes a difference in their daily lives: it maps their locations, guides their movements and mediates the transactions among them. It thereby helps the academic building do something more than merely hosting sporadic intersubjective encounters. Through the vertical gallery the building becomes a setting that matters, transforms, engages people and shifts the trajectories of people and things. By prompting interconnections and mixing natural light, air, students, researchers, managers, visitors and the tools, artefacts and the materials from various art practices, the atrium contributes to furthering new creative fusions.

The atrium appears to be a space with internal political programme: it continues the educational programme outside the lecture theatre, it makes staff and students mingle and interact more, it stimulates new dialogues and new groupings. It acts as a connecting mechanism and social centre. As witnessed here, following the stroll in the Benzie building, the vertical gallery becomes an important space for various exchanges. These new connections are vital for the development of innovative research; they condition new links among different people and material entities brought into this space and create new relations and groupings. They are political. The vertical gallery makes us pass through specific places and meet on its generous staircases, an arrangement that invites contacts between floors and causes researchers to cross paths and tell each other of their daily experiences. The visual connections in the space sharpen awareness of fellow artists and designers and encourage continuous exchange of information among students and tutors. Yet, the design cannot determine a particular type of behaviour; it cannot force us all to mingle and interact, to be more interdisciplinary and more social. The academic building invites, facilitates, enables and acts as a mediator that makes particular types of cognitive or communicative activities to take shape, and to diffuse them through networks, to regulate flows, and to actively reshape the relations within the academic world assembled by the building. Yet, in any moment it is not capable of controlling our behaviours, of forcing or steering the same reactions, of shaping the trajectories of people and things in a predetermined way. Space matters, interferes, transforms; design makes a difference: that is its subtle way of being political.

A morning trajectory: Handrails, stairs and elevator buttons

In a hurry for my lectures I enter the Benzie building. As usual, I am immediately confronted with a choice between the staircase and the elevator. Either will guide me to my office. I wonder where to go: the staircase and the elevator offer two ways of reaching the auditorium at two different speeds. The architects confirm this hesitation stood in the heart of the project; the questions of 'how to get people to use the stairs?' and 'how to avoid everyone coming in and using the lift?' were pivotal. The designers aimed to 'make the movement around the building as pleasurable as possible?' (Interview with Tom Jarman, 11 November 2015). At this particular moment, as I rush I do not have the time to enjoy this pleasurable environment. I rush and worry about arriving moments after the lecture theatre is filled with students.

As I decide between stairs and elevator, I do not simply choose between two ways of contemplating the building, between mobility and immobility, activity and laziness, exercised control and self-control; rather, I will be led to share agency with them in a different way.

The staircases stand out aesthetically indeed. They hold a promise for a more pleasurable stroll in the building: reminiscent to beautiful wooden sculptures connected with a set of wooden bridges all forming a geometrical complex, they tempt to sweep us away into a mythical type of Escher-like world. And once I decide for the stairs, the whole Benzie building opens up to me; I remember Tom Jarman saying, 'architecture doesn't stop when you get to the staircase. It's very integral' (Interview with Tom Jarman,11 November 2015). Once I lay my feet on the first step I feel the volume of the stairs ascending dramatically into the air. This is somehow strange. Climbing stairs is usually a very myopic experience: I walk, I pay attention to the slippery surface of the stairs, I try to gain balance over my heels, my eyes hesitantly try aligning the handrail and the stairs beneath my heels, back and forth, back and forth, until I gain stability. I never have the time to pause and contemplate the sculptural splendour of the ascending volume of stairs rising before my eyes. Yet, I do it now. Reminiscent to a clumsy wooden but spectacular ensemble of skyscrapers, the Benzie vertical gallery overwhelms my visual senses, up surging in volume as I climb, balance and hesitantly slow down. Defying laws of gravity, strolling in the stairs makes me feel like dwelling in a mysterious lithograph of Escher: I walk up, and up, and upside down.

The series of staircases and bridges 'make more connectedness and more wholeness between the new part and the existing building' (Interview with Tom Jarman, 2013). The staircase holds a 'vision of the world' inscribed* in its construction, a specific scenario of action, a script*: the width of the stairs, the inclination of the staircase, the materiality of the handrail, all these features of their design are important for me as I climb the staircase. The term script implies that design is *in the world* and helps us escape the modernist division between intrinsic materiality (material, real, objective and factual) or and symbolic aspects (social, symbolic, subjective). Script also hints to the idea that matter is absorbed into meaning (Dubuisson and Hennion 1995; Yaneva 2001), that there is a vision of the world *in* objects, buildings and material arrangements that suggests a specific programme of actions. That is why the materiality of the staircase is not irrelevant to my experience as a dweller in this building. The different qualities of the handrail afford particular actions. In its smoothness and warmth, the rail's wooden surface contributes to the easier gripping actions of my hand as I go up. Its wide and inviting surface makes me lean upon it in conversation with colleagues during the on-stair encounters. The narrow stairs make it impossible to ignore others who I might meet occasionally. The stairs' design facilitates spontaneous face-to-face conversations, making us extend the auditorium or studio discussions. They predispose my body to delegate part of the action to the setting; I feel comfortable when going down the stairs (and not so comfortable when climbing back up them). Not only is the staircase animated by the chaotic intervention of people walking, crossing each other, interacting and sharing the space, but it is also filled with noises and smells coming from the cafeteria. I walk and encounter fellow colleagues and students in the building. Meeting and chatting on the staircases, I find myself involved in interactions mediated by the particular design of the building, the staircase and the numerous artefacts that facilitate my morning trajectory, making my arrival pleasurable.

I questioned Jarman about the specific thinking on the design of the staircase, its dimensions, materiality, width of the handrails and how it works in terms of affordance* and different types of use. He explains modestly,

> I think we got that one wrong, actually. It's interesting because I think the stairs are too narrow, which is probably my fault. It was partly because [this is a boring technical thing], when we went from one model of cladding to another, we lost this much [he makes a gesture opening his hands], 250 millimetres of width, because of the new cladding strategy. And that made the difference between it being comfortable for people to walk past each other up and down and meet, and actually talk, to being a little bit narrower than you'd want. So that was one thing, which we would have learnt and would have done differently (Interview with Tom Jarman, 11 November 2015).

The FCBStudios did not use Space Syntax for calculating and modelling pedestrian flows, as there were too many parameters and the modelling was unpredictable. Jarman elaborates, 'You couldn't say, "Everyone goes to this classroom at this point and everyone discharges from their lecture after one hour." It was much more of a constant flow' (Interview with Tom Jarman, 11 November 2015). And, I can indeed witness this flow as I go up and down, and when I decide to rest on the large parallelogram bridges, providing a long-awaited refuge for my tired high-heeled legs, I witness that flow dissipating in all the directions.

Watching carefully the foyer space I can notice that more people choose to travel vertically using the three elevators. I see large queues of students and staff around the elevators each morning, and due to the open structure, people can be observed disembarking at the first, second and third floors. If I position myself on the second or the third floor, I will notice the crowds going up and down and can distinguish between those who opt for the elevator and those who opt for the stairs. As FCB architects explain, 'it was necessary to cluster the three lifts from a practical point of view, because you just reduce waiting time. (…) So the benefit of the lifts is that they open directly and relate to the long length of the atrium of the front gallery; so even if you nip in and out, you are *forced to interact with the space*' (Interview with Tom Jarman, 11 November 2015). Bodies in the elevator are not passively waiting to be transported. When I push the button, I do not assign the whole action to the elevator, waiting patiently to be transferred from the ground to the second or the third floor, to the auditorium or to an office. I *delegate* part of my action to the floor indicator, and I remain in a state of ambivalent tension, of anxious activity of doing nothing, frightened by the possibility of an accident, or bothered by the presence of other people. Yet, although the elevator cannot compare with the possibilities for social interactions granted by the stairs, in the lift 'you still have some interactions and you still create moments where people *are forced together and have a conversation*' (Interview with Tom Jarman, 11 November 2015). Embraced by the setting, our actions in the lift are finely *mediated* by technical devices: the elevator buttons, the floor indicator and the alarm system all emphasize the social dimension of being together (Hirschauer 2005). If we communicate in a different way in the elevator and on the staircase, it is because they offer two different modes of distributing agency with the environment. Designers have chosen between two ways of *delegating* action to the non-human elements: elevators and staircases, corridors and rooms, handrails and walls.

If the morning trajectory of many university professors like myself is pleasurable, it is because many objects *afford* and *facilitate* our activities, *helping us* to do certain things and forbidding us from doing others. By so doing, they make me reach my students in time, and more often in a good mood. Designers have worked hard to produce a world of objects and environments that aim at assisting and pleasing people inhabiting the building like myself; it is, I will argue here, a specific social contentment that grows bigger when we collectively share the enjoyment of inhabiting built environments together. The pleasure is of a shared taste, a judgement or appreciation that gets stronger when it is being reappraised and *repeated* by many dwellers like myself. Designing is not merely about tracing aesthetic envelopes, embellishing artefacts and environments. Instead, design has social meaning, striving to enrich not to diminish, to fortify not to weaken the public bonds.

Let me pause for a moment and look back at the artefacts that guided me in my morning trajectory. Attempting to describe this routine trajectory, I looked at the university's material environment, describing mundane artefacts in a pragmatist manner. I avoided an analytical frame of mind. This view allowed me to witness what architectural objects do and to understand their practical, everyday meaning. Although in my description I did not refer explicitly to the politics of design, when we come to analyse extensively how different artefacts and designed environments work and how they are capacitated to act, we inevitably touch upon questions of mundane relational politics. Assuming that the structure of the material world pushes back on people, we can argue that buildings, artefacts and material arrangements are designed to shape or even replace human action. They cannot determine but they can suggest, enable and facilitate the decisions we make; they can influence our actions and can change the way we move through the world. By so doing, they play an important role in mediating human relationships, by dividing, regrouping, bringing together and rearticulating connections, thus prescribing political relations.

Doors, locks, key systems and auditoriums

Once on the first floor a swipe card allows me access to studio spaces of the art school. This instant gesture of swiping a card that magically reveals access to the space is very different from the slow entrance through a code-locked door, doors that I am used to open in the Kantorowitch building where my office is located. A code, not a swipe card, is supposed to make me open the resource room (while my key, a key always lost in my bag in the midst of lecture copies and books, helps me access my personal office). And here I am, face to face with the special mechanical code door lock.

One button on the right, then, two subsequent buttons on the left and then ... one more on the right ... two more on the left. I do not remember the code anymore; my hand recalls and hectically reproduces a movement that it has memorized through numerous repetitions, but that my fragile lazy morning brain can hardly recall.... I make my hand repeat it, and here I am in the resource room. This fully mechanical pushbutton operation is quite different than the one my hand has to perform in the morning to set up the house alarm when going out for work. This security method holds several advantages when compared to the standard individual key that opens my personal office: no need to take an extra key with me to open the resource room, no need to lock the door when you go out (it locks by itself when closed); several seconds are enough to change the code where a lost key might force you to remove the lock. This mechanical keyless code door lock system *allows* my colleagues from our research centre to access the resource room, *obliges* us to close the door behind (as the door is too heavy) so as to *impede* random visitors to use university resources and prevents colleagues from other research units to gain access to the room (they cannot dial the same combination of buttons when attempting to access the room).

A simple keyless door lock tells us a lot about the social life of the university and has a political dimension. To understand the lock, we should take Latour's suggestion seriously: 'We should not state that "when faced with an object, ignore its content and look for the social aspects surrounding it." Rather, one should say that "when faced with an object, attend first to the associations out of which it's made and only later look at how it has renewed the repertoire of social ties"' (Latour 2005b: 233). The implications of the particular design of the lock cannot be conferred to the symbolic relationships between departments, disciplines hierarchies, divisions of labour, the university building design, the psychological need of university fellows to double the number of locking mechanisms and key devices that would guide them to their mail boxes and copy machines. We should not try to unveil 'the hidden meaning' of its design; the making of this lock implies a particular way of regulating and maintaining the social relations. Made so as to allow only colleague fellows to access the research group resources and to impede others from using them, this simple mechanical door lock divides and congregates university fellows in a particular way. It empowers colleagues and creates a sense of belonging for those who have it and use it in the university building. It mediates the social relations between researchers, students, random visitors and colleagues from the other departments. Rather than being an intermediary* that would 'express' or 'reflect' university policies, the institutional order and rules (thus serving as a mirror of institutional life), the lock acts as a *mediator* that constitutes, recreates and modifies relations. By *authorizing* only my colleagues to enter the resources room and by *sending away* those that are unable to perform the specific pushbutton operation, the lock regroups university people, and reconnects them differently. That is, *design functions politically*, in the very essential meaning of political as relating to, involving, making sensible, judicious, motivated and interested; by triggering actions that affect many – shaping alliances, constituting groups, reshaping positions and reconnecting entities, design manifests its emergent political dimension. Politics is not *outside* it, at a cosmic distance from its objects. It is *in* the objects' world. Design allows this door lock to take on the conflicting wishes and needs of many university colleagues. 'It *transcribes* and *displaces* the contradictory interests of people and things' (Latour 1992: 153). By using and misusing locks and keys (Latour 1996, 2000), doors and corridors (Evans 1997), we deal with social relations continued by other means such as wood, steel, glass, metal buttons and amplified by their design.

The design of the auditorium where my morning trajectory ends has also an impact on the way I lecture and on the particular forms of social links established with students and colleagues. It creates a cognitive environment adjusted to the task of education. What follows is an analysis of the possible grammar of actions this design can have, rather than of its symbolic language. If I were to teach in a circle-shaped room, the latter would afford an unobstructed view, allowing the students to be seated in a circle at an equal distance from me as a lecturer; this solution also allows all eyes to be fixed on me as a speaker, while also permitting them to see their colleagues. Letting students to see and to be seen by others, it also enables a form of equality. The circular arrangement of space would facilitate a specific type of university communication. It relies on the transparent immediacy of sights, forming a collective mutual gaze. A circular arrangement of the lecture room would mean that students' opinions or questions could appear from all angles. Nevertheless, this type of lecture room has often manifested a persistent problem of diffusion of sounds and speech. Bad acoustics would require the lecturer to raise her voice and to engage in a more 'violent' or authority-based type of communication.

Alternately, a semicircled auditorium would imply a different material arrangement, while also providing a disparate cognitive environment for teaching and learning. Being placed at the centre, the lecturer would draw all eyes towards her, capturing everybody's attention; she can be easily seen and heard. This arrangement of the room offers students, wherever they may sit in the semicircle, a view of the lecturer and the screen next to her. The space in such a room would be focalized by a pole of speech held by the lecturer – the rostrum – and the distance between the speaker on the podium and the listeners will be architecturally regulated. The two types of material arrangements of the auditorium would condition two different types of cognitive design, two distinctive ways of students–lecturer communication and would correspond to two different educational philosophies, two politics of teaching: the circular arrangement would favour mainly visual communication, whereas the semicircled one would rely on speech. The cognitive environment of the auditoriums would also make possible different types of connections between lecturers, students, teaching objects and programme administrators to be created and will facilitate different types of activities.

Yet, I find myself in a rectangular lecture theatre at the Benzie (Figure 3.6). This is indeed a very different shape that is rarely considered in debates on political buildings,

Figure 3.6 Lecture theatre in Benzie building (photo by the author).

and in particular the wide historical discussion of circle versus semicircle shape of assembly rooms. The debate surrounding the choice of the form of the assembly chambers at the time of the French Revolution shows how design facilitated a specific repertoire of actions and had a different impact on the parliamentary behaviour (Heurtin 1999). The rectangular theatre has a more accentuated political texture. It is known that rectangular structures replaced circular ones through time in many archaeological areas around the world. Rectangularity is commonly associated to multi-room buildings and is related to the transition from constructions where the roof is supported on a central pool (squashing together multiple activities under one roof) towards roofless enclosures (Steadman 2006). The rectangular theatre is similar to the semicircular, but it has a better acoustics (Reid 1984). To avoid the sound to be funnelled from the stage to the far corners of the auditorium in an unbalanced way, it has the merit that its sidewalls tend to increase the lateral reflections to the audience, which can be helpful to the appreciation of the lecture. The audience is at a distance, thus reinforcing the formal authority of the speaker. This plan is suitable for lecturing and it provides good sight lines. Speech intensity is fairly directional and the vertical layered rows of the sitting plan keep the audience within a reasonable distance with a forward-facing speaker, reinforcing her authority. Both sound and view can be connected to the power of the lecturer as there are direct sound and sight lines. In addition, there are beneficial reflections of the sound coming from the ceiling and reinforcing the sound, thus facilitating the eventual communication between speaker and audience.

Just as the overall arrangement and the script of the conference room creates a specific environment, impacting the way I lecture and communicate with students the door lock of the resource room alternately creates an environment of privacy and isolation, from one side, and a place for communication with other fellows from the same research group, from the other; this double requirement for isolation and communication better suits the task of research. Design offers us a mechanism for arranging and invigorating the university world, segregating and regrouping, keeping apart and bringing together.

By setting the coded door opening in the same way as our colleagues, we know we share the same research unit and the same little pleasure of making a design artefact work successfully. By communicating in a large lecture theatre, we know we share the same institutional space. This little morning ritual inspires self-confidence – I am here and if the door opens that is because I belong to *this* group, to *this* institution, I share something with *this* community, I take part in *this* institutional rhythm. If you can hear me and if you can see me in the lecture room, this means we share the same social rhythm of teaching and learning mediated by its architecture. The design of door locks and lecture spaces can fill me with a sense of enjoyment. That is another *attachment* to my work that makes my morning trajectories to the auditorium fun and my university work pleasurable. If I feel relieved when the door opens and my hand successfully accomplishes the movement that it learnt years ago, and when the students respond to my talk and energetically engage in discussion. I know that I not only share with the others the same university ID card, but also share a series of worries. Might I forget the code? Or will I make an unfortunate hand move? Will I find the door open and irresponsibly unattended? Was the acoustics of the room good enough? Was everybody able to see my slides? When I open the door and when I get the attention of my students in the lecture theatre, I am pleased, and I know this contentment is shared by other colleagues today; that is, we share something more than the university policy or the institutional rules. We share the possibility of being connected with specially designed doors, locks, lecture theatres and atria. We are connected by design, and that is a social enjoyment. We are put apart, set at a distance, isolated, disempowered; or brought closer, assembled, empowered. There lays the political dimension of design.

Is this political?

If you follow me for a moment, again, in my trajectory, you will witness how the objects and material arrangements from my university mornings (the atrium, my key, the door lock of the resource room, the elevator buttons, the staircase handle, the conference room arrangement) do not stand for social and political structures, nor do they symbolically represent the university's order, hierarchy, divisions of labour or gender inequality; rather, they *perform the social and the political* as we use them, and thus connect us in a new way with fellow colleagues, students and university administrators. We remain linked by using the same architectural objects, by facing the same functional problems, by committing the same ergonomic mistakes. We open ourselves to subjective fragility when the door code is forgotten, just as we enjoy the ways objects function once amplified by a better design. With its networks made of different heterogeneous materials, design guides us in the university spaces, affords our movements, diminishes our insecurities and fears, strengthens our authority in the lecture room and harmonizes our social collaboration with other academic colleagues. Design stands here for what makes the social diversity of a university world hold together.

We cannot understand how a university or an academic community works without appreciating how architectural design helps in shaping, conditioning, facilitating and making possible everyday social links. Imagine how many people like myself are about to perform the same ritual of entering the Benzie building this morning, choosing between staircase and elevator, forgetting their code in front of the resource room and struggling with the door before they finally enter the lecture room. To learn to be a good dweller, I watch the others to see how they use these devices and navigate in these environments, how they share the elevator and struggle with the door code. These are all social acts; without the example of other people inhabiting the building whose mistakes I involuntarily tend to repeat, we would not be able to act socially. Impatient to reach the lecture room I push the button of the elevator, like many colleagues I dial the code in the resource room and follow the gestures of other fellows at the copy machine. That is how design makes it possible for many *imitative* and *repetitive* acts to proliferate and generate new social connections. As Garbriel Tarde put it, *imitative repetition* generates social links (Tarde 1895). All these morning rituals are simultaneously performed by many of my colleagues and my students and that is what makes the use of a university building eminently social. The atrium, the stairs, the lecture theatre, the keys and the elevator's buttons all group and regroup us according to the types of environments we inhabit and enact; they make us feel part of the same institution. Some of these ways of acting acquire, *as a result of repetition*, a sort of consistency and reliability that precipitates them, so to speak, and isolates them from the particular events in which they are embodied.

Design makes us gain access to the social, but it is a microscopic social, discovered in individual objects, dwellers, designers and inventors. If many people like myself do not *repeat* what design has implied, nothing remains of the social. Design ensures that we encounter numerous non-humans (objects and environments) in our routine trajectories, and mediates our communication with other humans. It makes possible the university order, academic collaboration, collegiality and educational philosophy. This order is passed on, not from the social institution (or social group) collectively to the individual, but rather from one individual to another individual, from one colleague to another colleague, from student to lecturer, and that, in the passage of one human into another human, it is refracted. The sum of these associations, from the initial impulse of an inventor, a discoverer, an innovator or modifier, whoever it might be, unknown or illustrious, is the entire reality of the social.

Where is the political then? 'Why does an architecture work take one shape rather than another?' 'How does a building work?' 'How does it bring people together and how does it pull them apart?' 'How do architectural artefacts gain currency?' 'How do they attract contributions from the people needed to support them?' These are all inherently political questions. The problem of acceptance of architecture works and the adequacy of buildings for their dwellers is also political. Thus, in committing ourselves to 'live in' or with specific architectural arrangements and material artefacts, we *ipso facto* take a political decision. Designing in a particular way, following particular arrangements, tectonic patterns and material constraints, we already opt for a specific type of political effects that our design can generate.

Strolling in the Benzie building, an example of mundane politics transpires; an example that stands at cosmic distance from the classic architectural parables of control and social change told around Bentham's *Panopticon* prison or Moses' low bridges. A strong programme, a deterministic one, would assume that bridge-building and prison-shaping is social engineering, because power relations can literally be built into stone and bricks. Alternatively, a soft programme would imply interpretative flexibility so that built environments would be considered as media, which tell something to those capable of reading and listening. Like all texts, everyone may read them differently and will unveil their contingent way of expressing values. Yet, the Benzie strolls demonstrate the irrelevance of both programmes; we can neither say that the Benzie determines a set of actions and human behaviours and always performs them in a particular order; nor can we argue that we interpret its meanings differently according to various subjective idiosyncrasies. And if none of these programmes work, is there a middle road between control and contingency? How is the Benzie example pointing towards these alternatives paths?

The solution we offered in this chapter is rather simple: stroll and discover, let yourself be guided by architectural objects and arrangements, experience them, and you will get access to the ways in which they serve as media of mediation, negotiation and translation between the reciprocal expectations of designers and requirements of people. If we want people to communicate and aggregate or spread and isolate, we endorse the design of buildings and material arrangements accordingly but we cannot determine the nature of effects and patterns of behaviour. Nor is it enough to engage in endless game of interpretative narratives that will retell and reinterpret buildings from various and endlessly changing perspectival angles. The power of buildings does not lie *in themselves*; nor is it invested in the abstract subjectivities imposed on them. Instead, the political agency of architecture depends entirely on how buildings are networked with other things; on how architectural artefacts, skills, builders, materials, settings, designers and affordances are aligned together. Architecture design connects in very specific ways: it divides and reconnects, groups and regroups, aggregates and puts at distance different types of inhabitants.

Buildings do not speak of an asymmetric domination of the world through knowledge; all of them implement instead an openness to what the world has to offer us away from fantasies of domination and control; a bridge cannot exclude minorities, control and filter the access to Jones beach, the MSA building does not determine the patterns of interdisciplinary in the school of arts. They rather facilitate, help. Inhabiting a building implies a symmetric dance of agency: instead of imposing human plans from the outset, designers and dwellers tune their plans in the light of what the building does and makes us do. In strolling, trying out, letting ourselves being guided, we experience a building; we give justice to the many material dimensions of things without limiting them in advance to pure material properties or symbols. This is an example of a non-modern way of organizing our worldly practice. The Benzie building discussed here appears as an ontological theatre, staging dances of agency with inhabitants and designers, resisting to adopt a fixed form.

Strolling in the Benzie building, I have demonstrated that materiality from one side and politics from the other are to coalesce. Buildings are not neutral settings: material arrangement can be political. Yet, they never force us to obey and act always in a predictable way. A good building or material arrangement is one that gives us a chance to deviate the expectations of the makers: designers, planners, builders, renovators. It is through the uncertain variations of the setting, through the oblique mediation of an unstable set up, that the makers can meet a set of surprised wanderers like myself. The political dimension of the atrium will vary according to its light, the type of wood used for the handrail of the staircase will invite us to lean differently; the square of round shapes of auditoria will ask us to talk and think differently. *Here* is the political. The meandering succession of material arrangements and artefacts gives specificity to this form of mundane politics and creates many situations for us to act differently.

4

Experiments in Practice: The Second Way of Becoming Political

To study the practical course of design means to be simultaneously involved in the subject of politics, and in particular, in that type of politics centred on objects. The ontology of design practice, understood as what can be said to exist and how it can be real, is not the ontology of a single practice: there are as many frictions between objects enacted as there are between the practices in which their enactment takes place. That is what turns design practice into a political site. Following how images and models are produced, negotiated and stabilized in the architectural office and how they begin travelling, one would be able to grasp the political. Both images and models emerge as political sites. Unpacking design practice, and how politics is enacted through the work of designers, is the second way to outline the political relevance of architecture.

Following the minute details of architecture in the making, immersing into the world of design practitioners, I will examine here the political dimension of their creative practice. I will follow the composition of entities that assemble in design practice: the objects, the natural entities, the technical practices and the materiality, in addition to the humans. I will trace architects' design moves as they gain knowledge about sunlight, test glare effects, adjust reflection surfaces and rethink the entire cosmology of a building under construction – the New Street train station in Birmingham. The questions that architects increasingly ask in this process are: 'What entities are assembled?' 'Who do we live with?' 'Who is included and who is excluded?' These are questions of cosmopolitics, not simply of big politics; they gradually gain currency at the time of the Anthropocene. Nature appears in this process not as a passive and distant reality; it rather becomes an active element of architectural design that makes us rethink its political relevance and enables us to speak politically.

The natures and cultures of design

Facing the challenge of a geologic epoch of an Earth transformed by human action, the Anthropocene, architecture is confronted more than ever with the need to address the question of coexistence of natural and human entities.

Cosmopolitics designates the search for, as well as the domestication and accommodation of, new entities that try to find their places in the collective in addition to those of humans. The cosmopolitical agenda has inspired work in the field of geography and urban studies (e.g. Whatmore 2002; Hinchliffe et al. 2005; Heise 2008; Morton 2013). Although recent scholarship has focused on architecture at the time of the Anthropocene (Harrison 2013; Tassin 2013), still little is done to explore the cosmopolitics of architectural design, its capacity to contribute to the process of reordering our relationships with nature (Yaneva and Zaera-Polo 2015). The story that I will tell here will illustrate the importance of cosmopolitical thinking in design practice. A number of cosmopolitical thinkers like Isabelle Stengers (2010b), Bruno Latour (2004a,b, 2005a) and Peter Sloterdijk (2005) abandon the modernist idea of nature; nature is not a simple backdrop for human activities, it is not simply 'out there', it cannot be mastered by engineers and scientists from the outside. It is rather to be made, created, instigated; 'it is to be composed' (Latour 2010b). A different, an amodernist attitude to nature will require an active process of manipulating and reworking it 'from within' (Haraway 2003). That is where architectural design could play a vital role: in the light of a cosmopolitical philosophy, it could be seen as the activity of those who cannot any longer count on unified nature and have to redesign every single feature of our common experience. To understand this, we will follow here designers at work as they detect a problem of glare and frantically engage in a process of experimentation and mitigation over which they address, 'talk back to' and put on test a number of natural elements. A different engagement with the political is produced in design practice. By testing, probing and adjusting the parameters of sun, architects can actively transform the coexistence of natural and human entities and can redefine it 'from within'. In this exploration of architectural practice, one will be able to witness the emergence of another kind of political dimension of architectural design – the cosmopolitical.

Design as seen from 'within'

In December 2007, the National Rail and the Royal Institute of British Architects (RIBA) launched an international competition for developing an overarching vision for a redevelopment of the external form of the Birmingham's New Street Station and the atrium roof space (called also the Gateway Project). The RIBA brief for the content shortlist demanded 'a visionary concept designer to create a landmark building and example of cutting edge architecture'. Six architectural practices were shortlisted in February 2008: CRAB Studio, FOA, IDOM UK Ltd, LAB Architecture Studio, UNStudio and Rafael Viñoly. Later this year Alejandro Zaera-Polo was commissioned as concept architect to design the New Street façade and atrium space. In fact, the project started at the Foreign Office Architects (FOA), which later split into two practices, and the project continued with the practice of Alejandro Zaera-Polo – AZPA, later renamed AZPML. The winning scheme of Zaera-Polo was unveiled on 18 September 2008.

Located in the city centre, Birmingham's New Street Station is one of the busiest rail interchanges in Europe. Dating from the 1960s, its age is indicated by poor quality internal spaces and an outdated and unattractive external appearance; the station was considered as 'lacking the requisite capacity to meet the forecast passenger demand'. It was therefore proposed that the station and elements of the shopping centre above are to be remodelled. In addition to these spatio-functional qualms, pedestrian access was judged as poor and not fully compliant with the requirements of the Disability Discrimination Act 1995. Furthermore, the station environment was considered as not only inefficient, but also aesthetically unwelcoming, with dark and cluttered platforms and a congested and haggard concourse area. The resulting space was perceived as an uninviting one for both public and station staff alike.

The Birmingham Gateway is meant to support over 52 million passengers a year, and therefore demands world-class architectural design in order to 'embody the rebirth of New Street station', in the words of Cllr Mike Whitby, chairman of the New Street Gateway Funders' Board (Herbert 2008). The overall Gateway project is a £600 million joint scheme between Birmingham City Council, Network Rail, Advantage West Midlands and Centro. Its aim is to double passenger capacity through constructing a concourse three-and-a-half times its current size. This will be enclosed by a giant, light-filled atrium. Accessible, bright and clear platforms, serviced by forty-two new escalators and fourteen new lifts, will be accompanied by a new station façade. Together, these changes aim to add to Birmingham's growing reputation for good design, whilst dramatically improving pedestrian accessibility (with eight new entrances).

In designing the station façade and atrium, Alejandro Zaera-Polo Architects (AZPA) are conscious of the indispensable position of the station in the City of Birmingham and the large amount of traffic that the station handles (Figure 4.1). Providing expression to the dynamic nature of the railway theme, the proposed design (Figure 4.2) aims at generating a distortion in the viewer's perception of the urban settings of the station. In order to 'ornate the city with the railway animus' (Gateway Project GRIP 4 Report 2009: 9), the undulating, smooth forms of the track field have been transferred and embedded into the geometry of the architectural design. The smooth, curved geometry that results employs bifurcation as a formal system of perceptory distortion, whilst the reflective stainless steel skin will wrap the car park and conceal the roof. The proposed architectural envelope[1] is supposed to create emergent effects irreducible to the underlying context; it deliberately avoids mirroring the surrounding buildings. One can experience the emergent dynamism of the reflective façade, the curvaceous and bifurcating lines underlying the structural or programmatic effects of the envelope. By tilting the upper half of the skin inwards and the lower half of the skin forward at precise angles that depend on the topography and the available distance for pedestrians to move, AZPA architects have set up a field of

---

[1] According to Zaera-Polo, the envelope is the separation between inside and outside, the frontier between public and private realms. It regulates the internal environment, provides security and operates as a representation to the outside world. He also argues that the envelope holds a huge potential for political expression, see Zaera-Polo (2008).

Figure 4.1 Birmingham train station, location. © AZPA (AZPML Principal).

Figure 4.2 The Gateway building, steel façade. © AZPA (AZPML Principal).

reflection that brings together clouds and passengers, nature and railway technology by capturing four types of movements: skies, information, crowds and trains. The façade becomes an active mechanism of reflection: imitating, mirroring and mingling different types of movements and agents simultaneously.

I started following the Gateway Project in 2008 through ethnographic observation in the practice of Zaera-Polo and on the construction site in Birmingham all through 2013. I conducted in-depth interviews with AZPA designers. In this chapter, I will refer in particular to a series of interviews with Alejandro Zaera-Polo, principle of AZPA and Connor Vale, AZPA project architect for the Birmingham train station. They will be complemented by content analysis of related documentation, correspondence between the different stakeholders, official statements and the project website (http://www.newstreetnewstart.co.uk/). One particular moment of the design process fascinated me: in 2010 the engineers from Arup identified 'a risk of glare' and after running further tests both architects and engineers had to tackle the problem as a matter of emergency. I spent months questioning the designers on the glare issue and followed their struggles to resolve the problem and the long series of experimentations that brought up a new cosmological arrangement of technical and sun elements, of nature and culture. As Dana Cuff (1992) noted, the architectural profession tends to favour design as decision-making process while neglecting an understanding of design as making sense of a situation, thus creating an imbalance that could be problematic. To further unpack the nature of design as 'making sense of a situation', I will focus here on how the glare problem was discovered, identified and recognized as a problem, acknowledged, constructed and gradually resolved.

Exploring the nitty-gritty reality of the design process, I will follow how design thinking proceeds in the presence of entities that are commonly disqualified as having nothing to propose: 'natural' entities. I will examine in particular how sunlight becomes a trigger for thinking, generating glare effects and 'talking back' to architects, as well as how its agency is taken into account, who and what is affected by the design, and how. This questions the traditional 'humanist' understanding of the relationship between the nature and the culture of design, and the role designers can play. The story I will tell is not one of architects who become aware of ecological issues and adopt a militant attitude. It is rather a story of how they actively transform the coexistence of natural and cultural elements 'from within'. This will lead us to describe design as a way of dealing with the process of coexistence of different entities and disparate technical practices, thus challenging a modernist view of nature.

Tracing the practices of architects at work, I will tackle how design can be read 'from within': first, as a dynamic way of incorporating as constitutive dimensions the criteria and modes of judgment of a collective practice; second, in the ecology of relationships among other professionals. This implies considering carefully and slowly all the various points of view 'from within', and analysing the emergence of types of knowledge that cannot be disconnected from all the participants in design and from the various entities that share space with humans.

Blinded by the sun

The original concept AZPA developed included a skirt with louvers that would enclose the entire building and would instil connections in massing and in materiality (Figure 4.2). The department store (John Lewis), the shopping mall and the station were meant to be part of one skirt, of one continuing enclosure. Yet, John Lewis as a client wanted transparency and visibility in that part of the building but the entire concrete block structure of the Gateway project was guided by a different principle. To introduce visibility, architects needed the stained steel with multiple reflections. The challenge was therefore to introduce a unit with a transparency in an existing ensemble whose concept was about no transparency and no reflections while keeping the same language across the whole structure. Yet, stainless steel appears as a material that is far from being simple. Endowed with the reflecting properties, steel has a rich and vibrant life of its own; the designed steel façade promised to be far from passive. As early as 2008 Alejandro explained to me that they are aware of the risks that a reflective building might cause:

> These reflective buildings sometimes may reflect the sun on neighbouring buildings. In the case of Frank Gehry, Disney got sued, because apparently some people who live across the street have noticed that in summer the temperature in their living rooms were going up by five degrees as a result of Frank Gehry's building being there. So, they had to solve this locally. We basically learned from this story and we have done some models on how to deal with glare and we also identified the areas where we have potentially to treat the steel. That is what produces this camouflage pattern of different types of sanding so as to avoid the problem of glare of neighbouring buildings. (interview with Alejandro Zaera-Polo, 1 October 2008)

As Alejandro explains, designers have been aware of the risk of glare issues from the very start of the design process and they have done everything to avoid the glare. Learning from the controversial building of Gehry that caused glare problems, they engage in testing and modelling the glare risk. From the beginning there is an awareness of the variability of matter in design; the full deployment of material qualities of steel, including its unexpected and underestimated properties, is part of the architectural thinking about the agency of the envelope. Thus, questions of 'how to deal with glare' and 'how to avoid it' become constituent part of the design enquiry.

> The issue with the glare is that the original building had considered the sun issues, but on a very basic level, just like any typical building where you cut the East and West sections. You do a couple of sections and test different angles to understand the overall sun parameters based on the geometry façade and based on the worst case and the best case scenarios. But because of the curving and non-linear nature of the façade it was more difficult to analyse it. (interview with Connor Vale, 26 July 2012)

Due to the unusual geometry of the stainless steel cladding, it was also hard to predict the agency of the sun and calculate its effects with precision. Architects reduced it to 356 days a year divided by 2 as just half of the year is to be factored for reflections and then they had to consider the range of possibilities of where the light may be coming from throughout the day. That is how 'the sun parameters' entered into the design process of experimentation.

Although architects were aware of the glare problem at the time when the first design was made and the first images released in the public space and they tried to minimize it, the tests of Arup engineers in 2010 demonstrated that there was 'a small risk of some glare'. Further detailed tests were run in 2011 and the glare problem was considered as being of high risk to the train drivers. Then, Arup engineering consultants conducted more detailed tests in May 2011 and produced a movie (WO8b.mov) to demonstrate that the risk of glare was much bigger, identifying one glare spot on the envelope of the building on the west side (Figure 4.3). When I visited the London office of AZPA in November 2011, they already had the results from the glare analysis studies. Arup engineers and AZPA designers work alongside each other to generate the tests: architects provided engineers with a sample of the surface before the engineers calculated the reflectivity; engineers conducted the test by taking an overall plan and all the surfaces, then they ran it through the program of simulation and analysed where the reflection was most likely to happen. When examining all the areas on the train tracks, they realized that when the train is approaching, if the sunlight is coming within a range of 0–30 degrees from your eyesight and it is over the level of 500 lumina, it could reach the level of disability glare. 'It will basically stop the train drivers from seeing the signs: red light, green light', explains Connor, 'and then, of course it is a big problem, because we are bringing 500 people at the train station. The engineers rang the guy who is the chair of Network Rail and the guy who takes care of trains and signalling, and they identified this as a problem' (interview with Connor Vale, 21 November 2011). Rather than discovering a problem 'out there', in a quick and magic wand gesture, 'identifying the glare problem' was a lengthy process of subsequent tests and simulations that took months of involvement for a number of design participants from Arup and AZPA. Addressing the problem was equally a protracted process rather than a quick moment of 'discovering' solutions. As witnessed in design, steel appeared to be significantly more active and vibrant than the symbolic interpretations of architecture would admit.

In their attempts to address the problem of the façade reflection, the architects made numerous tests and developed different scenarios for the façade over five

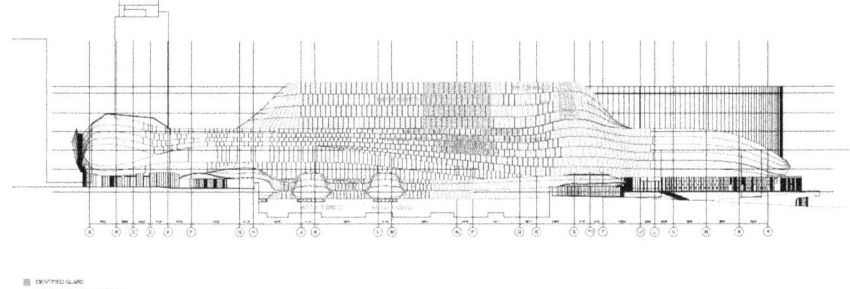

Figure 4.3 Identified glare areas affected by redesign. © (AZPML Principal).

months. This did not affect the entire façade, but a very specific spot on the façade where the reflections are so strong that they can potentially blind the train drivers. During a number of visits in London and in Birmingham, I questioned architects on the nature of the problem, when was it identified, how AZPA architects went about testing and finding solutions and what kind of experiments they ran. Addressing the glare problem could result in changes in geometry and could lead to 'radical reduction of the massing' and the edges of the building as a way of reducing the structure to make it work more efficiently. This could also lead to changes in the reflecting surface of the façade that would echo the sky (blue or grey) and not only the rails, affecting the iconography of the 'image of Birmingham'. Five months after glare was identified as a problem, the images and tests produced at Arup travelled back and forth between the offices of AZPA and Network Rail. Architects and planners had to meet every two weeks to discuss the changes, reviewing the solutions proposed and negotiating the final modification. This process turned out to be lengthier than expected, as while dealing with the sun, many other problems emerged: the car park position, money, mechanicals and changed demands of the client throughout the project.

Testing, testing and testing

Architects from AZPA engaged in tests and experimentation to consider every single possibility of the sun hitting the train drivers. Different ways to moderate and mitigate the glare had to be tested. The first option involved creating shade by blocking the sun with canopies; then architects investigated how they could put the canopies and the secondary structures in place. Yet, this option quickly became very overwhelming and they abandoned it. The second option consisted in changing the surface material. Yet, they presumed this would have a big impact on the concept, and neither the architects nor the clients wished to consider that change. The third option was to alter the geometry and to understand the geometrical constraints of working with glare. And that is the one the architects started exploring. The feedback from Arup helped AZPA architects to modify the geometry, while Arup engineers carried on running their tests simultaneously. To adjust to the sun dynamics, AZPA hired a young architect, Tobias, who had a good experience in software engineering. He started developing computational scenarios by 'playing' with Grasshopper (the Reino software) and he found out different solutions of the reflection problem for a 'quick fix'. He ran a simulation in which he 'bombarded the façade' with sun rays coming from all angles and gave feedback to the other AZPA architects. Thus, they started working in a 3D environment and developed through the means of Grasshopper a tool that proved to be very useful in providing them the calculations to run the software. In this way they developed their own way of using the software and programming so as to be able to run internally quick tests based on geometry, on reflections and on the angles that reflections will hit the train tracks. Such tools are usually developed for engineering companies like Arup and to generate them takes approximately one week, because engineers do a precise calculation of the sun intensity and the sun reflections. For the architects this is a model tool. As Connor clarifies:

> One week does not work for us. We need to be able to make a change quickly – test it, make a change – test it. And since the parameters of the sun and the motion of the sun are so various, there are so many different parameters, it is almost a scientific methodology of trial and error at the beginning. (Interview with Connor Vale, 26 July 2012)

Sun appears to be a complex agent just like steel in the way it manifests itself. Its various parameters cannot be grasped at once. Designers witness the complex agency of sun motion by 'testing, testing and testing what it does' rather than acting to control or manage its manifestations, or else, engage in a quasi-technocratic manner in a process of instrumental domination of nature. Testing, testing and testing is a fundamental epistemological technique in design as architects start to extract knowledge by engaging in trial and error. They begin to detect basic principles and to construct rules such as 'this can't work in these conditions', 'this cannot work in this projection of light' and 'this is an exception of "X"'. Thinking in this way, architects reinvent a language that is truly inspired by experimental reasoning and that will allow for what they term as 'reaction' to work. It is precisely this investigational approach to sun effects and parameters through trial and error that led architects from AZPA to develop the software that will help them reach accurate estimations with quick tests.

Witnessing the cognitive dimension of architectural work, one can follow how design knowledge is acquired in a day-to-day enterprise according to a systematic experimental methodology. The tests aim to probe the parameters and realities of the building within a certain number of limitations. The experimentation happens within a controlled framework and a number of physical constraints were set by the engineers: 'to keep the cladding', 'to sustain the language of the geometry', 'to maintain the material and the gesture that AZPA had with the previous cladding'. It establishes the conditions required for further operations, raises a whole raft of questions concerning the unknown elements of façade and takes into account the ability to cope with the new variables that are added to the existing experimental conditions. Engaging in tests architects try to modify the geometry according to different sun angles, as well as calculating carefully the different reflection angles. They need to adjust the reflections so that the steel façade could reflect the sky and not the car park or the rails. In this process of testing, probing and adjusting, steel becomes an active mediator that regulates the relationship between architects and nature, manifesting itself through sun and glare effects.

To be able to artfully integrate sun (with all its parameters) into the new architectural compositions, AZPA architects engage in an enquiry of gaining knowledge about the sun (light, angles, illumination). In addition, there are a number of agents that happen to speak on behalf of sun: engineers, train drivers, architectural precedents and the various Grasshopper models probing how the surface reacts to reflect the sun. The knowledge obtained helps the architects to integrate sun and glare as active participants in the new compositions. Dealing with glare, architects engage in cosmopolitical design; they attempt at assembling, redefining and modifying the composition when a new non-human (the sun) is brought into connection with humans in an unexpected way. There happens to be more entities to be assembled in this process. If Heidegger considers every object or natural entity to be the assembly of four elements: 'gods and the mortals, heaven and earth', Latour sends the inquiry into the same direction by arguing that 'there are many more than four existing deities, or dimensions, or factors brought simultaneously into play. Any technical or natural imbroglio forces us to count way beyond four' (Latour 2007a: 140). All of them come together and are to be assembled.

At any moment in the experimentation process there was no need to give a new definition of sun or glare. Instead, sun is here what binds together those who refer to it, from designers and engineers, to the blinded eyes of train drivers, the software engineers and the commuters on the station. All those actors have relevant knowledge about it and are to negotiate its meaning. Thus, far from undertaking a unilateral and sometimes aggressive domestication of nature in their attempts to gain control over sun effects, the designers create compositions where a reciprocal transformation of human and non-human entities can occur. They recognize the diversity of the world and engage in testing different ways of assembling it. These new assemblages all emerge not in an attempt to master the forces of sun and mitigate glare, but in a process of integrating, adjusting and skilfully adapting sunlight to the new design conditions 'from within'.

Lost in the sketch folders

Rather than suggesting a 'compromise' or 'a quick fix' to the glare problem, architects from AZPA engage in a long process of testing and experimenting, and thus develop hundreds of variations on the computer. While doing this, they all get 'lost in the sketch folders', explains Connor. Only the final options are presented in the numerous GRIP reports which I have studied carefully while interviewing architects from the practice. When we talk about the glare Connor tells me:

> the glare is something I wish I had two weeks to make a report about. It is really technical. We created a lot of materials. But we never extrapolated that material in a format that we can present with all the options. A lot of the results are really numbers, graphs, and images. Visually they are not necessarily that compelling. We usually work with visuals in architecture. But with the glare story, we had a lot of information that was not visual. (Interview with Connor Vale, 26 July 2012)

Numbers, graphs, tests and visuals are the result of a thorough experimentation process at AZPA, reminiscent of the one described by Bruno Latour and Steve Woolgar (1979) and Michael Lynch (1985) of scientists at work. Inspired by the way ethnographies of science investigated the real-time performance of experiments and the practical discourse of scientists, I have studied elsewhere how architects immerse themselves in experimentation and how at every stage of design enquiry new data about a-building-to-be is gained, and new actors and design requirements are added (Yaneva 2009a). Drawing on the way STS engaged in analysis of science in the making and the scientific practices of visualization (Lynch 1985, 1993; Lynch and Edgerton 1988, Latour 1990; Lynch and Woolgar 1990; Pickering 1992; Galison 1997), the new ethnographies of architecture focused on accounting the hands-on process of experimentation as an art situated within the performance of design practice (Houdart 2008; Yaneva 2009a; Loukissas 2012). These studies contributed to a better understanding of the visualization practices, distributed thinking, instruments, communication, material culture and design environment.

Coming back to the glare case, one can witness that using a quasi-scientific methodology architects analysed the sun angles and reflections and worked closely with Arup engineering while they ran control tests to analyse the amount of sun hitting the tracks and the kind of luminosity this created. While all these tests were run, architects stayed in line with the same 'architectural language'.

Parameters pile up

To address the problem of glare architects engaged in a long and painstaking 'geometry exercise' playing with the reflection, calculating the sun angles and gradually proposing to modify the façade geometry so as to be able to mitigate the glare effects on the train tracks. 'At the beginning we wanted a quick fix', explains Connor, 'we thought we could modify things slightly from here and there and try to make things work. But then when we started this design, we saw that there were actually other design parameters that came into play at the West façade' (interview with Connor Vale, 21 November 2011). The experiment started from the question 'what are the parameters?' Yet, modifying the sun parameters will lead to a number of changes in other parameters of the West façade. These parameters were there before, but they became an element of consideration after architects began the study on glare. One element that came into play is the service platform with a bunch of mechanical equipment placed on the West façade, adjacent to the car park. The initial plan was to use the façade of the car park to hide the equipment; a loose skirt was hiding everything. Architects had to deal with this and respond with a number of options.

> One solution was to entrust folds, and the other solution was, that on the East side of the car park we had these large louvers and we direct all the reflections towards the ground at that point, towards the tracks. Essentially what we did is cutting down all the façade that was reflecting back and that was inclined towards the sky; and this was all on the Southern part; the Northern side we could keep because it was not causing any glare. (Interview with Connor Vale, 21 November 2011)

This solution of introducing louvers changed the cladding and meant that (Figure 4.4) all the reflections are supposed to focus down. To be able to stop the sun reflection, the elevation is cut into pieces in a way that instead of reflecting the skies like the envelope

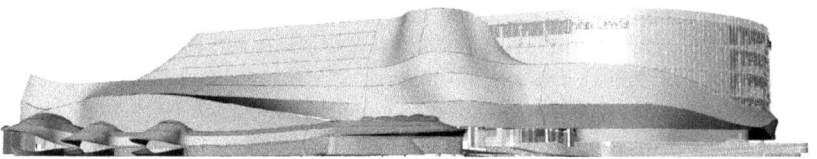

Original Concept

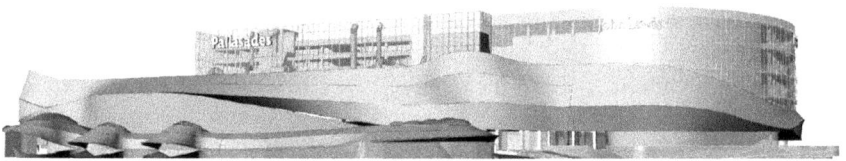

Option 1: Metal Mesh

Figure 4.4 West façade of the Gateway building. © AZPA (AZPML Principal).

did before (a large surface reflecting everywhere), it has now a more acute angle and it is reflecting back down the movements on the ground, other tracks, the John Lewis store and so on. As a result, the envelope would become very heavy, chunky and in this way would lose its continuity and flow. The clients were not very happy with this proposal and after a good discussion architects had to 'start from scratch again'.

Thus, while dealing with the glare issue, some of the parameters have changed. As the mechanical equipment was removed, the space was not needed any more. Since the car park was associated with the John Lewis store, an overflow was not needed to create a bulky mass. Architects started from scratch and tried the possibility of putting a simple cladding on the car park, wrapping it around tight and then, creating connection from the cladding of the car park to the rest of the façade so as to ensure continuity. It was very important that the car park did not become an independent object so as to add a third agent to the envelope. This added an additional parameter to design experimentation. The idea was to keep the attention only on two elements wrapped into one continuous envelope; to maintain this uninterrupted geometry designers had to avoid the introduction of a third building type.

Then, the architects engaged in an exercise led by the experimental question: 'how can we treat the massing?' – with the strategies they developed being: with small louvers, with two or four creases, or with inverted louvers. Designers did numerous tests that showed what was going to be reflected in the façade. The idea was not to reflect the car park below, nor was the intention to reflect the back of the structure. The concept consists in reflecting the train tracks surrounding the building areas. The solutions they explored with smaller louvers were based on Brigitte Reedley geometrical patterns of openings and nodes for a design developed for a Chicago building.

Connor talks me through the different options and concludes: 'Using what we learnt in the past and identifying the advantages in terms of reflection and in terms of glare, another idea that came in was the idea of having better natural ventilation and having openings in the façade for day lighting like in the car park' (interview with Connor Vale, 21 November 2011). In the new massing plan, a collection area for the John Lewis customers that used to be covered now became exposed to the rain. For John Lewis as a client, this was a problem, stating: 'we want our customers to be protected'. This aspect of the design came as an additional factor to consider in the process of glare mitigation. Another one emerged soon after: the maintenance issue. The clients wanted to get rid of an existing maintenance truck to service and architects were asked to provide access either by walkways or other means. Another factor was the condensation of heat, which appears to be a problem with concave surfaces and reflecting surfaces. The latest issue that emerged was the new design restraint for the panel sizes that can be used for the cladding. The architects had incredibly long panels, sometimes 1.5–8 meters long, and the contractors said that it was impossible to work with them as it was limiting the panel sizes. Architects therefore had to go through an exercise of changes, with some significant alterations emanating from that exercise. As a consequence, there were now new technical aspects to resolve while considering what the cladding was going to be. Thus, in the process of dealing with the parameters of sun and glare mitigation, architects had to consider a number of different problems as the envelope was supposed to work as one structure. Parameters piled up and modified the envelope.

The glare testing changed a number of other aspects of the design starting from the stainless steel cladding. It also made architects rethink the initial concept. It affected a number of aspects of the design, which were not considered previously: the car park position, John Lewis' branding, customers' platform, ventilation, massing, maintenance issues and heat condensation. The changes in the project reflected on changes to the image and the clients required updating it. The glare experiments led to small adjustments in the geometry, they enticed new discussion with a broad and diverse public of representatives of the retail industry and the planners; they also triggered software innovations, and brought new actors on the site. All these actions were aimed at 'slowing down' reasoning and activating thinking about the impact of design. Resisting the consensual way of dealing with glare, architects 'slowed down' and created through testing, probing and option making a space for hesitation where different concerns were voiced and the glare issues were addressed. They resulted in further fuelling the discussion around the different options, eventually leading to a solution with enduring transformative effect.

Exploring options, crafting cosmologies

While exploring various options and engaging in a tedious process of technical and geometrical testing, architects attempt to 'stay within the same language'. The façade iconography is connected with the geometry, which is related to the construction process. Since the construction had already started, the geometry is supposed to follow its technical constraints. They are all naturally linked with the meaning of the image. Experimentation, geometry and image narrative all intertwine. As witnessed in the observation of the glare testing, the recurrent concern in this process was to ensure that the image would reflect the skies, the movements of the clouds and the trains, the crowds and the publicity. Yet, the glare experimentation proved the need for the image to capture a much larger cosmology of elements of which sun was an important part. Architects wanted to either reflect the skies, or the train tracks below, but 'if there is sun in the sky you can't reflect the sky!' – that is what they are reminded of while experimenting with glare. The envelope opens up to accommodate the sun in the new composition of elements where it will appear as a dynamic element with varying parameters. As a result, one can witness the making of a complex façade with three distinct levels, of surfaces reflecting the sky and surfaces reflecting the tracks, and in between those there are many surfaces that when reflecting the surface below also reflected themselves in the sky. This caused double and triple reflections, which architects had to take into consideration. Breaking up the massing also created a much more complex façade with many more elements. By following the architects engaging in glare testing and exploring the various geometry options, one can also witness the crafting of the meaning of the envelope. The different options for the glare mitigation opened up new meanings and interpretations. The architectural meaning, and the narratives that will accompany this iconic-to-be image, is not to be attached after-the-fact to a solid technological system; instead it is crafted and reinvented, thought and refined in the process of glare testing.

As witnessed in the glare-driven design process followed here, architects participate in the work of 'diplomacy' as they provide a voice for those whose practice, mode of existence and identity are threatened by the quick political decisions of planners and politicians: sun and glare, retail industry, commuters at the Birmingham train station and train drivers. Designers' knowledge is not accepted as relevant; their roles differ from the one of the experts (engineers, scientists, construction experts). That is the reason why designers engage in consultations, convoke natural entities with differing ontologies and explore the ways that those entities interact with humans. They test new conditions, make explicit the connection of humans to those entities and create new spaces for their cohabitation. By so doing, they actively contribute to the formation of new compositions that turn the problem related to glare into a cause for thinking and suggest that non-human entities such as sun, water, heat, light, condensation and pollution are to be part of the collective thinking of design.

The cosmopolitical ecology

In the analysis of the design experiments with glare presented here, one can witness how sun is no longer a natural element 'out there' waiting to be discovered by architects; it is not a simple and obvious assemblage. Instead, it has been entirely rethought and its parameters redesigned many times in the glare experiments all the way to the degrees of lights, the angles and the facets of steel reflections. This example illustrates that even the natural world of sunlight is not passive distant nature, but rather an assembly that is to be redesigned by all those who have relevant knowledge about it. 'Dasein is design', as Sloterdijk famously put it (2009), meaning to define the activity of those who cannot any longer count on any natural untouched entity and have to redesign every single feature of our common existence, including in this case, the cosmology of sunlight and glare reflections. The glare experiments are not simply 'about nature' or about human conflicting interests, but about humans, sun, the risk of blinding the train drivers, retail economy and train station design. As it unfolds, an assembly is slowly being built around this heterogeneous assemblage of cultures and natures, and the reintroduction of the sun agency into design experimentation creates a complex political imbroglio.

The glare story also illustrates the distinction between political and cosmopolitical ecology. Political ecology affirms that all knowledge is objectively produced and verified by experts; only engineers from Arup can produce objective knowledge about glare. In political ecology, politics is commonly reduced to an empty game, leaving astray all the entities that are producing or destroying our worlds: non-humans, such as sunlight, glare. However, when there is 'an issue that not only does not allow itself to be dissociated in fact-value terms, but also needs to be given the power to activate thinking among those who have relevant knowledge about it' (Stengers 2005: 1002), one can witness the regime of cosmopolitical ecology. A cosmopolitical perspective would acknowledge that there is no 'objective definition' of a glare that everyone will share. A detached definition of sun and other natural entities accepted by all would not produce a better understanding of the glare impact on design. Instead, one needs to account for the active participation of all those whose practice effectively engages in multiple modes 'with' the sun or 'with' the glare: designers, software engineers, train drivers, commuters and John Lewis customers. That is what will give us access to the 'cosmos' constituted by 'multiple divergent worlds' (Stengers 2005: 995). Cosmopolitical ecology will therefore handle all the objects of human and non-human collective life bearing on complicated forms of associations between beings: regulations, equipment, consumers, institutions, habits, retail industry, solar energy and sun angles.

> There are so many little idiosyncrasies that are developing with the façade itself. Whereas the façade before the glare was some kind of uniform system that we apply everywhere, now we see 'oh, on this side we need to do something special, and we have to tweak it'. And on the South it has to perform very differently because we are very close to the property line so we cannot use the same angle. So tweaked it in another area. On the East we also need to tweak for some of the glare. On the North, there is a tramway going around the North, and the clearances, the permissions, were too tight, so we had to curve into the façade. So, there were all these types of idiosyncrasies that appeared and we incorporated them into the language. From design intent to parameters, from the contractor to construction, to now the small idiosyncrasies to adjust for specific on-site local parameters. And we are all trying to keep it work, to keep it homogeneous. (Interview with Connor Vale, 26 July 2012)

What architects describe as 'a tweak here' and 'a tweak there', that is a process of adjustments according to local idiosyncrasies, is a very cosmopolitical process. Rather than 'liberating' architecture from the undue weight of political influence or natural forces, cosmopolitics accounts for the sort of politics that follows the path of design. Addressing the glare problem becomes a political question, not in the sense that everyone should agree about it, but politics in the sense of the progressive composition of the common world that we share (Latour 2004b). Glare experiments place design at the trading zone between the natural and social sciences and bring together the two of them by reinventing them. The solution to the glare problem could not be imposed by politics performed by power actors such as the Birmingham city council, Network Rail, John Lewis or others; it should be 'cosmopolitically correct' (Latour 2007b).

As the glare issues appeared to be too intractable and too enmeshed in contradictory interests, architects had to become scientists and artists at the same time. They did not engage in representation of natural elements. Instead, they engaged in an active enquiry of gaining knowledge (not discovering) about the phenomena under scrutiny: AZPA architects studied the glare effects and gained knowledge about reflections, they reinvented and adapted the software, got lost in the sketchbook of options. In other words, they introduced a form of architecture making that went far beyond an understanding of design as 'expressing' what was hitherto hidden. Learning from scientists and nature the experimental method, allowing them to organize the contest of their proposals, to challenge them collectively and to revise their preset views of the world, designers activated thinking about the sun. In the process of design, they asked 'What world do we assemble?' 'With whom do we align?' 'What entities do we propose to live with?' 'Who do we integrate, and, who do we exclude?' Tackling these questions, designers literally tried rearranging the world. Not symbolically.

The glare story illustrates how design turns nature into food for thinking and mobilizes a variety of entities in new compositions. Immersed in cosmopolitical experimentation, architectural designers question and refresh these compositions. They contribute to redesigning the relations with nature. In the process of experimentation, designers 'slow down' the quick narratives of ecology and sustainability and invite us to rethink the microelements of an architecture threaded by climatic issues. Addressing the primordial question of coexistence of humans and non-humans at the time of the Anthropocene, architecture requires skilful reinvention of the specific techniques for capturing the coexistence of natural and material entities with humans through generation of habitable spherical units and design envelopes where they can all leave together and survive. This compels us also to rethink the role of architectural practice as important cognitive and political *loci* for crafting cosmopolitically correct answers.

5

The Multiple Natures of a City: The Third Way of Becoming Political

I will continue to follow architects as they engage in design and planning of the Gateway project in Birmingham. In this chapter, I will explore in particular the politics of architectural imaging and I will trace the production of visuals related to this new development. I will analyse their scalar and ontological specificity, their composite nature and versatility. The analysis is based on extensive study of the Birmingham New Street project in the UK through design and construction (2008–2014). Tracing design and planning moves, following the paths and flows of the images as they circulate in design, construction, city councils and planning sites, I will show how the Gateway images succeed in capturing, assembling, recomposing and re-enacting the city of Birmingham; how they synthesize all its relevant emergent features, talk about its multiple identities and perform the city dynamics. As Birmingham cannot be removed from the practices that sustain it, its reality is multiple. Through image making, the city becomes a reality that is manipulated in practice. The images trigger various enactments of the city. Different enactments entail different ontologies. They come with a different way of 'doing' the city. These realities are not random; they are ontologically political. The image holds them all. That is a third way for architecture to become political: by grasping the multiple realities of a city.

Assembling a city

The growing influence of the pragmatist philosophy has gradually changed the way we think of our cities and urban realities and has shifted the focus from architecture as meaning to architecture as process and becoming, from the lives of those who inhabit the cities (de Certeau 1984) to the life of buildings, streets and other material entities, including images and scale model as actors in urban design. Paradoxically, the divide between subjective interpretations of the city (through the perspective of the *flâneur* experiencing, walking in and perceiving it) and objective interpretations (the city as an objective frame, a map, a set of artefacts, a city guide) is still so much alive in contemporary urban theory. Recently, architectural studies questioned the boundaries between these two types of interpretations and attempted to circumvent this divide by tracing cities *in concreto* (Zitouni 2010; Doucet 2015).

Cultural geographers (Lees 2001; Graham and Thrift 2007; Jacobs et al. 2007; Jacobs and Merriman 2011; Strebel 2011), archaeologists (Buchli and Lucas 2001; Buchli 2013), sociologists and science studies scholars (Houdart and Minato 2009; Yaneva 2009a; Loukissas 2012) shared a renewed attention to architecture as an ongoing process rather than accomplishment (or artefact) of human doing, and engaged in path-breaking research that aimed at deciphering the making of buildings, cities and urban phenomena (see Chapter 2). They advocated an approach to the urban that consists in tracing the urban: suspend the zoom, multiply the adjunctions between the different views, relocalize the sites where one talks about a city, and you will see a city that is invisible (rather than visible, perceivable entity), that is to be composed, to be recollected, to be aggregated (Latour and Hermant 1996). By unpacking the different material registers of architecture and tracing the paths and flows of a variety of non-humans that circulate within cities, we are able to gain a better understanding of cities.

Drawing on the recently developed pragmatist approach to architecture, I will question here the specific relationship between city and the various images of buildings and urban realms that talk on its behalf (or *represent* it, in philosophical parlance). I will unpack how architects reconnect through the process of image making the various rhythms of urban life scattered across distant and disconnected sites. That is, I will argue here, an inherently political process. My ambition is to account and better capture the practical relation between the large-scale and the modification of the human and non-human associations. Instead of maintaining the traditional preconception that politics is always bigger and more complex than the mundane practice of design, which are small, minute and insignificant, and could only end up projecting the complexity of big politics, I will rather advocate a different approach. In the spirit of reversed reductionism, one can argue that 'the small is always more complex than the big' (Tarde 1999: 39). Yet, my argument here is different: a better understanding of cities could be gained by literally keeping our compass sights on the paths of image making in design process, following the routes that link the humans with the material world, the subjective with the objective, the built with the inbuilt, the small with the big. To miss to follow these traces and account for these paths is to miss what a city is; and how it can be reassembled in design.

In other words, I aim to further here specific questions: 'How can architectural images assemble the variable qualities of urban life and recollect the city features?' 'How is a city grasped, made present and enacted *in concreto* through the quotidian process of image making in design?' The city that inspired these questions is one that I happened upon whilst conversing with the architect Alejandro Zaera-Polo in 2008: Birmingham. We have already witnessed AZPA architects working on the specific problem of glare and engaging in cosmopolitics (Chapter 4). Here, I will explore further the political dimension of design process, and in particular the daily routines of image making, through attending to the phases of design and construction of the Birmingham New Street Station. Engaging with my desire to understand the specificity of the city and how it connects to the images that talk on its behalf, I asked architects 'What kind of city is Birmingham?' in addressing how the city could itself be grasped. This question was followed by a more repetitive and persistent one: 'How do you generate an image that will become a spokesperson, a spokes-image for Birmingham?' Curious to understand how the modalities of its urban life could be unpacked, I persisted with such questions. These came to form my research agenda.

The chapter offers a practice-driven perspective to the composite nature of the Gateway images, attending to their scalar and ontological specificity, and accounting for the particular way they capture and assemble the city of Birmingham. I trace their making at the architectural practice of Alejandro Zaera-Polo (AZPA), and how they become *real*. I explore their modalities of action and account for the nature of the entities that make the images real, as well as for what can be said to exist *through* them. To do this, I use a variety of sources ranging from participant observation in the office of Alejandro Zaera-Polo in the period of 2008–2013, to in-depth interviews with AZPA designers working on the project, content analysis of project-related documentation, correspondence between the different stakeholders, official statements and also studies of the Gateway website (http://www.newstreetnewstart. co.uk/). I have also been able to compile and carefully assess an image archive on the project in order to get a rounded understanding of the image ontology, its transformations, travels, compositions and recompositions. Engaging in the complex process of capturing, assembling and recomposing the urban, architectural images attend to the manifold reality of a city. A city that is multiple but at the same time one.

Politics of architectural imaging

The Birmingham I found as my study progressed was not that recollected in history. Rather, it was recollected and re-enacted in design. The first image I found to adequately capture the city in its current state of flux was itself mid-production in the office of Zaera-Polo, before being submitted to further transformations, decompositions and synthesis through design and construction processes (Figure 5.1). Generated on the computers of AZPA designers, morphed and inspected, retouched and enhanced many times, small and large-scale images of the Gateway flooded the screens. Architects spent long days and endless nights zooming in and out these images, morphing their sequences, adjusting parameters, retouching their contours with Photoshop, rendering colours, choosing textures or 'populating' them with human and non-human entities. The production and use of design images always happened to be a collective venture distributed between designers, software engineers, planners, citizens and politicians. Reproduced and rendered in different versions and according to different types of anticipated viewers, these images left the small office at Curtain Road in London and travelled the world. Touring back and forth between London and Birmingham, they talked on behalf of planners and architects, and enrolled different publics of supporters and critics.

A closer look at these images tells us that architectural visuals are pixelated, rendered and reproduced, yet also animated, enlivened and versioned. They

Figure 5.1 Image of the Birmingham New Street Station, concept design of the station envelope. © AZPA (AZPML Principal).

are far from being black-boxed pictures, witnessing for iconic design or certain urban knowledge, highly anesthetized static illustrations of urban visions or mere documentations of different stages of design. They capture knowledge about the city of Birmingham and as such they are dynamic cognitive objects, tentative and open, vigorously impacting the city reality. They are versatile as they constantly change to accommodate the new knowledge about the city. Dynamic also because of their numerous travels and flexible trajectories, that all constitute the course of design. Underpinning other forms of visualization (models, animations, simulations), architectural images define the working visions of architects and at the same time cultivate the expectations of many different participants in design who view the images and act according to them.

The reason for choosing to focus on the Gateway images is twofold. First, following the making of these images will allow illustrating how the city qualities of Birmingham permeate design practice: how they are grasped, translated and synthesized. Second, the images are central to city-making practice across the fields of architecture and urban planning and they are crucial for how city phenomena are to be seen by all participants in urban design. Thus, architectural imaging is unravelled here as a set of everyday techniques for attending to the specificity of the city of Birmingham. Although the grain of analyses will not be as fine-grained and meticulous as an ethnographic account of these practices will imply (Yaneva

2005, 2009a,b; Houdart 2008), as long as the practicalities of image making is part of our story, it is a story about design practices. The Gateway visuals form a tentative collection of working images that help grasping the complexity of the city of Birmingham, its multiple facets, rhythms and diversity. They encapsulate the 'working object' of designers and planners: the city-to-be. The visuals enact four aspects of the city in a hologram way: the industrial, the multicultural, the informational and the infrastructural. Clouds, information flows, crowds and trains move together at once, mediated and enhanced by the steel reflections (as seen in Chapter 4), thus shaping four versions of Birmingham, four distinct realities, four facets of it that make it one.

The Gateway: 'New Street, New Start'

The RIBA brief for the concept design encompasses the primary aim of 'ensuring that the architecture of the new station building *meshes* with the different urban qualities of the surrounding area – both in terms of the existing fabric and that of proposed new developments' (RIBA Brief 2008: 4, author's emphasis). The design is also expected to 'reflect the aspirations of modern day Birmingham'. These ambitions are encapsulated as follows: 'Birmingham is the UK's second largest city. The significant investments and regeneration activities that Birmingham has attracted in recent years have transformed the City' (2008: 5). A long list of such investments follows, before adding that 'the redevelopment of New Street Station lies at the core of the City Centre Master plan that aims to further Birmingham's position on the world stage' (2008: 6). Commenting on the design after the design review panel, chaired by commissioner MJ Long, on 29 April 2009, the Commission for Architecture and the Built Environment (CABE) concluded that the design of the wrapping façade is a 'striking and imaginative response to the brief' (CABE letter to the Birmingham City Council, 15 May 2009).

The AZPA design aims at 'providing the station with an adequate envelope, which will give a long-lasting impression to those visiting the city, and the appetite to discover Birmingham' (Gateway Project GRIP 4 Report, 2009: 8). Beyond initial impressions, the proposal's explicit objective is to produce an iconic architecture, one that will be able to communicate the function of the building to the public via railway-specific iconography and other related and recognizable content.

In designing the station façade and atrium, AZPA architects were conscious of the vital position of the station in the City of Birmingham and the large amount of traffic that the station handles. Birmingham, as the most important regional centre for the Midlands, receives a large influx of visitors, and many of them access the city through New Street Station. It is effectively the first point of contact for many visitors to the city, hence has the potential to form dramatic Gateway. The latter therefore heavily influences the first impressions of the large, 'floating' population that enters the city on a daily basis. This is judged to be of critical importance by the station's architects, who argue that its current design (and the quality of the surrounding public realm) is inconsistent with the ambitions and calibre of the city. In addition to their ambition 'to correct' the situation, AZPA's explicit objective is to produce an architecture that will be able to communicate the function of the building to the public via railway-specific iconography and other related and recognizable content. Architects elaborate this as an attempt to 'capture the animus of the railway'. By this they mean the potential energy or power contained in certain objects within, and the holistic orientation and arrangement of the train station itself. Taking inspiration from the bifurcating patterns of the rails, or the distortion of perception produced by movement, the undulating, smooth forms of the track field have been transferred and embedded into the geometry of the architectural design; the resulting smooth and curved geometry will employ bifurcation as a formal system of perceptory distortion, whilst the reflective stainless steel skin will wrap the car park and conceal the roof.

How do architects know and research the specificities of Birmingham's 'situation' so as to learn what this icon-to-be should encompass? How do they extract knowledge of the local, cultural and environmental circumstances of the city, before urban theorists package them as 'context'? As I follow the making of the aforementioned envelope images, I witness that such understanding must come from a mixture of both material sources and also practices. These are found not only within the textual sources of the brief, drawn from written and verbal feedback from the planner, but also through the practice of actual engagement with the client and the many other participants in the project. This multiplicity of contextualizing sources is crucial to acknowledge, yet 'context' remains the wrong word. It is not a stable framework standing 'out there'. While it is important to consider the relationship of design to the characteristics of its locality, this does not imply a one-way projection of the city as an embracing framework onto the works of design.

The movability of context lies at the core of AZPA's conceptual design. The proposed architecture is supposed to transform: to create emergent effects irreducible to the underlying context. It is this transformative and thus political power, I will argue, that is being communicated by the images such that the envelope actually triggers contextual mutations; it produces versions of Birminghamness. What one can see in it is not the bright future of Birmingham, traced in a manifesto style, but mundane crowds, flows of information, trains and the variegated shades of Birmingham's sky. One can rather experience the emergent dynamics of the reflective façade, the curvaceous and bifurcating lines underlying the structural or programmatic effects of the envelope. Architects hope the building will gain autonomy (an *animus*) while maintaining a pragmatic effort 'to find formal efficiencies that exist beyond expression, in order to avoid becoming a caricature' (Gateway Project GRIP 4 Report, 2009: 9). Notably, the station's envelope deliberately avoids mirroring the surrounding buildings. By tilting the upper half of the skin inwards and the lower half of the skin forward at precise angles that depend on the topography and the available distance for pedestrians to move, AZPA architects have set up a field of reflection that brings clouds and passengers, nature and technology together. The façade becomes an active mechanism of reflection: imitating, mirroring and mingling different types of movements and agents simultaneously.

A history of past attempts to refurbish Birmingham train station precedes this brief. Some proposals, notably that of John Mcaslan, were denied planning permission and so the required redevelopment was delayed for quite some time. There have also been efforts to build a new station at the outskirts of the city as it proved difficult to design an upgrade of the existing structure. Despite such challenges, the final decision of planners was to maintain the central location and to embrace this aspect of its regeneration. The current city planners were cautious in broadcasting the envelope images, given the failures of their previous attempts to refurbish the station.

Alejandro explains the tension this decision lies upon, 'they were very nervous that if you put an image in the public realm, the people are going to make you accountable for it'. The images produced during the competition did not pretend to illustrate a 'promise' as such. From an architectural point of view, 'everybody knows that the building will never look exactly the same. Everybody understands that things will change, and [this] will be a process in which technically a lot of problems will be solved'. Alejandro also highlighted Network Rail's fear of accountability to a strict reproduction of the image, were it to be broadcast. All parties involved in the decision-making process (mainly Network Rail and Birmingham City Council) ensured a restraint on the announcement of preliminary images and their dissemination in the public realm. 'There were a lot of questions to be answered before the architect came with a final image and they didn't want to publish anything', reiterates Alejandro in an interview in September 2008. On the 18th day of that month in 2008, following a lot of discussions and negotiations, Network Rail sealed the deal with the city. The people of Birmingham and the West Midlands were presented with visionary new designs for the station (Figure 5.1). Released in the press, presented and discussed by the designers in public presentations and widely distributed on the web, these images also 'landed' as large panels on the old station and decorated its premises during the construction process. In this way, the old station served at the same time as a site and as a material support of the visionary new design; it mediated this exchange through its very contrast to the proposed new development, prepared the public opinion and helped shaping the right expectations. For politicians and city authorities, this image did much more than bringing skies and passengers together. The image, indeed, held an important promise, which returns us to the difficulties noted as inherent to its public release.

Despite this, the first public reactions were very positive, explaining that 'the striking concept designs, clad in shimmering, reflective metal, will create a bold, modern gateway to the city for the millions of people using the station each year'. AZPA's design is defined as 'world looking' and 'breath-taking': a design that 'places Birmingham on the international map for very high quality, daring design' (Herbert 2008). The critics argued that 'Alejandro Zaera-Polo's bold architecture symbolizes Birmingham's arrival over the last few years as a globally relevant city looking to its future, as a connected international hub, to the advantage of citizen and investors alike' (Herbert 2008).

What makes this image an intriguing object of study is the fact that the architect's role in this project is a very specific one. The engineering company Atkinson is hired to do the design. However, no matter how efficient their design and engineering work is, they are not expected 'to give image to this new development'. As such, Alejandro Zaera-Polo is given this role serving as the crux of the project: 'to give image' to a city. This is a city that he barely knows. Commenting later on the design of the John Lewis store, AZPA was commissioned to do as a part of the station concept, Alejandro reiterated that their work consisted in 'wrapping' the station, that the remit of the architect is reduced here to 'dressing' the building. Yet, the images of this 'wrapping' have important scalar and ontological, composite and rhythmic dimensions.

Adopting a 'slow' mode of enquiry (as explained in Chapter 2) as opposed to a 'quick' understanding of urban reality that relies on stable definitions, the analysis presented here will step aside from a simplistic characterization of Birmingham. To understand this city, one must attempt to account for what is specific to it as revealed in architectural design and by reclaiming the art of dealing with and learning from what some may consider messy and contingent design process.

The making of the Gateway images

It is October 2008. I am at the office of Zaera-Polo in London and I follow the operations of image making: generating, morphing, inspecting, retouching and enhancing small and large-scale images of Gateway. I watch architects at work and account for the alternating rhythms of scaling the images as they zoom in and out on the computer screen as they morph sequences of images, adjust parameters, retouch the contours of Photoshop images and allow themselves to be surprised by the results displayed on the screen. Gathering my ethnographic data as such, I trace the making of these images, unravelling the complexity embedded into the micro-operations of rendering a colour, choosing a texture, parametricizing, morphing sequences and populating an image with both human and non-human entities.

In order to produce these images, architects use a computational engine based on quasi-dense three-view algorithms. In this quasi-dense image reconstruction from un-calibrated sequences of images, all geometry is computed based on resampled quasi-dense correspondences, rather than the standard sparse points of interest. This not only produces a more accurate and robust reconstruction due to the highly redundant and well-spread input data, but also provides sparse reconstruction for visualization application (Lhuillier and Quan 2002). Alejandro explains, 'my generation is blessed. For us computers became tools for design. I think that you can work on the computer and still remain a designer. In a way we witnessed the first integration of technology into the practice' (interview with Alejandro Zaera-Polo, 10 October 2008). For him, an engagement with these tools is crucial in gaining knowledge about the computer rotation and the dimensions that would allow for the production of different designs. Once familiarity with the digital tool is gained, a concomitant improvement in one's knowledge of the design options is made available and the designer can intuit immediately what the geometrical determinations of that form are and define that intimate relationship between quantifiable data and design.

The superior accuracy and robustness of quasi-dense sparse reconstruction is important in accommodating non-human actors into the image: this includes trains, crowds, clouds and digital information. Thus, the making of such images involves a multitude of operations ranging from matching the colours, to defining the sky bluish and reddish nuances, morphing sequences of images, defining the number of parameters, setting up an algorithm, testing the geometry of reflection, measuring the angles of the skin, tilting the surfaces upwards and downwards to make them reflect trains, crowds and clouds, testing how to control the image reflections, adjusting the variable geometry of tracks and bifurcations, modifying colours depending on the sky and the height of the sun at different times of the day, and changing the relationship between quantifiable data and design shapes. Transformation, morphogenesis, combination or superimposition, alteration and also simulation, reproduction, enhancement and augmentation are but a few of the techniques architects employ in the execution of these often-complex design procedures.

As I follow Alejandro and his colleagues' computer-based 'craft' in defining the intimate relationship between data and design, adjusting parameters, rotating and rendering images, I witness the reproduction of details and their parametricizing, in defining the façade performance, putting people inside, adding trees, trains and clouds, turning the black of the sky into blue and enhancing the effects of the image, I am in the world of computational design. Through witnessing first hand the making of the computer image, one can find that it consists of an immense array of entities: humans, colour shades, parameters, sequences, settings, rotating and pasting devices, amongst others. For any so-called 'small' rendering to be produced, the designers must collect and consider millions of colours, hundreds of material samples and millions of repetitive moves in retouching the image. Far from being reduced reflections of the complex realities of the city of Birmingham, the images of Gateway reveal themselves as being more complex, multifaceted and composite. Their making is slow, complex and gradual, requiring painstaking operations of adjustment, fine-tuning of colours, transformation, combination or superimposition, simulation, reproduction, enhancement and augmentation.

The multiple natures of the city

What is the ontological specificity of the images described thus far? How do they encapsulate Birmingham and aid at the same time our understanding of the city? Following architects at work, I witness that drawing and retouching the numerous images of the Gateway allow architects pragmatically to approach the city of Birmingham as knowable. By so doing they do not simply rearrange its different facets, but also gain in this process new knowledge about it; knowledge about its sound reality, knowledge that is not graspable otherwise.

The stories of the architects about how they get to the city specificity do not expel the reality of the city of Birmingham. They talk about it for it is everywhere: in the materiality of infrastructures, in the industrial history, in the movements of crowds and trains. It denotes a suffocating reality, it has noises; it is dense. Hundreds of images witnessing for historical and current developments are collected; pieces of evidence are brought after every design meeting. Letters fly between CABE and AZPA, AZPA and Network Rail, Birmingham City Council and CABE. Moments of disappointment. Waves of excitement. More calculations pile up in the GRIP reports. Experiments with software. Long hours spent on the computer generating millions of versions of the same image. Long evenings in the office at Curtain road. Long afternoons in the construction office at New Street in Birmingham before rushing back to London. Events are made to happen by several types of actors. Words and drawing software participate too. Paperwork, building and construction documents. The local news from Birmingham city council circulates on a daily basis. Words exchanged in planning meetings. Glamorous images shown at public presentation. A model touring the city of Birmingham to meet the citizen. The images of the station are spread all over the sites of design and construction. Buildings. Words. Visuals. Archival images. Publicity snapshots. Flows of information. Crowds. Ticking clocks. Movements of trains and clouds. Design happens among all these things and people.

To witness how the city is enacted in design, I remain interested in the techniques that the designers use to capture its dynamics. Architects tell me that knowledge about Birmingham is gained via the processes of design, as well as through a number of subsequent meetings on the construction site (Figure 5.2). Alejandro relates this to the specificity of the city as a crux of mobility,

> at a certain point I was going there very often. That is where my image of the city comes from. It is a large city with a large immigrant population ... It is a city that gathers people. People go through Birmingham. The city "processes" them and then they go back to Pakistan, Canada or Germany, etc. For me, the centre of Birmingham has more this kind of transient character. This was something that we had detected already through the competition stage. You talk to people who

Figure 5.2 The Birmingham New Street, the construction site (photo by the author).

work on the project and nobody lives in Birmingham. They commute. The city itself is almost hollow. (Interview with Alejandro Zaera-Polo, 20 July 2012)

Acting as a nexus, as passage point for different groups, this city of Birmingham welcomes people from all over the places, integrates them into the economy. Grasping the character of the city is essential to the design process, yet that of Birmingham I have found to be multiple and composite. It is difficult simply to isolate one central characteristic. During the research phase, architects 'select a number of elements that belong to Birmingham' and assemble them together to 'synthesize an image of the city' (interview with Alejandro Zaera-Polo, 20 July 2012). In identifying and distilling these elements, the architects traced the city's history back to the time of the Second World War, during which the city had been completely destroyed. From this they aimed to understand its current condition and geographical location.

Endeavouring to understand how Birmingham was transformed into a hub for transit, AZPA's design opts for a train station envelope that is suited to the task of reflecting this evolutionary history. In this sense the challenge, explains Connor, was

> to understand on a macro scale the immediate neighbourhood and the reconstruction that is going on, in and around Birmingham, and also the impact that the development of the public realm around the station will have on the pedestrian flow; thus recreating a city centre which does not exist now, but which I have seen taking shape in the process of construction. (Interview with Connor Vale, 26 July 2012)

The accumulated reflections of designers emphasize the point that there is no one particular identity of Birmingham, one city nature – stable, given, acknowledged by everyone – that would be captured by one image in the process of design and construction and would inspire a specific architectural form of expression. Rather, a number of features emerge and are synthesized as architects engage in learning about a city that reveals itself through multiple realities.

The image of the station comes as a result of recombining manifold elements in a new composition: the famously black sky of Birmingham turned into blue blended together with the spaghetti junction experiments in the 1970s, along with the experiments of transport and infrastructure, the pollution and the frantic circulation of people and trains. As the architects put it, 'we collected a number of qualities or things we can build the image from' in forming a computer image that would communicate this 'vortex' character of the façade. This will be made by agglomerating the swarms of people at the train station, coming and going, and the train tracks going under the station, to visualize the city going through the station. As such, the image is made, and in its making Birmingham is enacted rather than observed and represented. It is at the same time composite as it puts together different entities in a new relational arrangement, and dynamic as it sets all these entities in motion. By fusing and recombining elements of the city that will be reassembled in the shared pixelated space of the image, architects do not engage in a work of representation. They do not strive to grasp a certain essence of a city by reflecting its unique nature, generating new urban symbols and icons. They rather engage in the much more complex series of operations of composing, recollecting and reassembling. This generates a versatile image that will resist all further interpretations of its iconic-to-be nature.

The envelope is made to reflect all these qualities recollected in design research, to gather a number of entities and grasp their movements.

> We were wondering how to use the fact that the tracks are going here, and to play with the reflection of the façade, so that when you look at it you will see the tracks reflected on it. So, basically we are reflecting the tracks, the trains, and the crowds of commuters. We are reflecting the station, and we are inserting content from the public information system. These are four layers of movements: clouds, information, crowds and trains. All this is captured by the skin. (Interview with Alejandro Zaera-Polo, 27 October 2008)

These four layers correspond, I will argue, to four versions of Birmingham that are 'extracted' through the process of design. These together give us four different ontological layers of the city; four distinct realities of Birmingham emerge and are being enacted in the image-making process.

The first reality is the industrial one; the black and grey skies of the city are immediately associated with its pollution and the related steel industry (Figure 5.3).

Figure 5.3 Layers of Movement, public presentation, Redevelopment of New Street Station, Birmingham, April 2008. © AZPA (AZPML Principal).

As Alejandro puts it, 'Birmingham has a famously black sky. It was a very industrial city. The black sky was very famous because it was overcast [laughing], like most of the UK, but apparently more. It also used to have a lot of heavy industry – steel, coal, etc. and therefore high-level pollution' (interview with Alejandro Zaera-Polo, 27 October 2008). The industrial history of the city is emergent in the processual reflection of Birmingham's sky in the steel surface, as it clears: not grey, but blue. The blue hints at the death of the economy and the birth of a city with an altogether different form of pollution. It speaks of the developers transforming it into a city with offices and shopping centres, rather than factories and production lines. Clouds appear and disappear from the envelope as it reflects the various shades of sky above it. Birmingham emerges in the image as a city in flux.

Another feature of Birmingham that is considered in the process of composite image making is its sociocultural diversity. The image should reflect the ethnic composition of 'the first majority/minority city in the UK, with the youngest population in the UK; the most "multicultural" city'. This is quite literally illustrated as one can see different crowds of people with various compositions reflected by the steel envelope (Figure 5.3). A sense of the ethnic mixture responsible for the city's vibrancy is gained as I follow different groups of people in transit: going in and out, mingling and flocking into both crowded and emptying spaces. The moving crowds animating the envelope emphasize this quality of the city: to collect, often temporarily, people from many different cultures.

The infrastructural variation is also very present as the station 'was also the place where in the 1970s the experiments with "spaghetti junctions" took place. The highways around Birmingham are incredibly sophisticated and the most extravagant loops were built there at that time almost like experiments of transport and infrastructure' (interview with Alejandro Zaera-Polo, 10 October 2008). 'Spaghetti junctions' is a nickname given to describe the massively intertwined road traffic interchange that resembles a plate of spaghetti; it refers to specific urban developments in Birmingham in the 1960s. The term was originally used to refer to the Gravelly Hill Interchange on the M6 motorway in Birmingham, UK. In an article published in the *Birmingham Evening Mail* on 1 June 1965, the journalist Roy Smith described plans for the junction as 'a cross between a plate of spaghetti and an unsuccessful attempt at a Staffordshire knot'. Since then many complex interchanges around the world have acquired the nickname of 'spaghetti junctions'. One can get a sense of the existing infrastructure as one follows the train tracks and junctions projected on the envelope (Figure 5.3). The visual reference to the tracks plays a crucial role in successfully conveying the local infrastructural specificity. The station was built over pre-existing tracks, with the city standing a further level above; the trains running below the station thus outline a plurality of holes hidden in the middle of the city. This gives the façade a unique ability to capture the movements of trains, whilst itself producing an unfolding loop of the dynamic processes at the train station, rather than an opaque flat surface of symbolic projections.

The fourth level is informational. The envelope will contain information drawn from the public information system, and a number of screens will be inserted in the building skin on the top of the main gate (Figure 5.3). They will broadcast information about the operation of the building or the content. Thus, the reflective wrapping will adapt and convert its own content to enliven the surrounding city. The station will continue the city effort of public space development across Birmingham as a number of similar screens have been placed in front of the city hall and at various other locations. The result will be numerous flows of public information circulating through the reflecting envelope, joining the circuits of movements of clouds, trains and passengers' crowds.

The four layers of the Gateway image discussed here do not provide different individual perspectives on a single reality of the city of Birmingham seen from the point of view of different participants in design – spanning the industrial, the infrastructural, the sociocultural, the informational. These are not four essences of the city, neither are they alternative constructions emerging from the past. Instead, they are different versions, different realities of the city that coexist in the present and help enact it. Different, and yet, related. The image holds them all.

However, the image is also false, unfaithful. Yet that is precisely why the rendering is capable of bringing the viewers into a different dynamics of the city. The image, instead of faithfully reflecting one urban essence, is 'populated' in the process of design with people and objects of all kinds: from trains, tracks and 'spaghetti junctions' to shops, cars, screens and benches, and of course skies. Every relevant element from the digital catalogue of things, be it a human, a tree or a track, is submitted to the same process of encoding, importing, cutting-pasting and correcting, regardless of their ontological differences. Since the very first renderings appeared on the designers' screens, a specific thinking about how to bring together trains and clouds, different ethnic groups and information flows, retailers and developers, jobs seekers and commuters, blue and grey skies, new and existing buildings was brought to the fore. Akin to the hybrid space described in Sophie Houdart's ethnography of the rendering process in the office of Kengo Kuma (Houdart 2008) where people and forest, animals, fairies and muses would create a new cosmology of harmonious cohabitation of humans and non-humans, the Gateway image presents a novel cosmopolitical assemblage (like the glare assemblage described in Chapter 4). The envelope creates an impression of three-dimensionality, populated by differentially sized entities with varied ontologies arranged within several non-overlapping steel surfaces. The resulting image effectively exemplifies the cosmopolitical question of co-habitation of different entities and brings together within a single, visually coherent space all of the entities necessary for the Birmingham station redevelopment.

The result is a dramatic envelope with immanent tensions of surface reflections, irregularities and curvatures, with visual interrelationships between the different parts. The image is as dramatic as it is full of action. Action, furthermore, implies relationships and interactions between reflected entities found in the same visual space. Nothing stays constant on the reflective façade: the clouds alter their shades, the information changes, the crowds come and go and the trains move. The resultant image thus can vividly demonstrate how it is that a number of previously disconnected entities may coalesce in a single continuous rhythmical movement. Each movement of one entity garners meaning through a series of related movements of the other. The envelope 'moves' and regroups the accommodated entities according to their different inherent regimes of enactment.

The image captures the station dynamics. Architects themselves fully traversed the station studying the geometry of reflection and testing the tilted surfaces to ensure their ability to capture and reflect decisive moments of what happens around the station, not the surrounding buildings. The designers explain, 'We are capturing from a number of positions the distance from which you look at the building, and depending on that distance, [depending] on the relationship between the public and the building, the angles of the skin have to change in order to show something' (interview with Alejandro Zaera-Polo, 10 October 2008). There is an intrinsic dynamic component of this image: it contains and enacts the life unfolding around the station, the variegated dimensions of Birmingham, in such a way that they become its own image; it is not the image that becomes Birmingham. Each reflection reacts to and acts upon others, on its facets. Each type of entity reflected on the façade merges with the actions and reactions of the multiple actors whose movements are captured. The moving image introduces us into a world of universal variations, universal undulations; a world that has no axes, no centre; one that has neither left nor right, no politics.

As the envelope never maintains a single shape or colour, but constantly changes in capturing the different movements, its image will never embrace one specific iconography either. Alejandro explains, 'When the reflective skin is tilted backwards, thanks to the ambers, it reflects the sky and clouds, and when it is tilted downwards it reflects the crowd or the tracks' (interview with Alejandro Zaera-Polo, 27 October 2008). Constantly seeking 'a certain effect of reflections', its dynamic nature is expressed in two ways: through the changing arrangement and composition of entities, and through alterations in colour. Once it is wrapped with the reflecting envelope, the building will change colour depending on the sky and on the height of the sun at different times of the day: at 12 am it may have bluish colour, in the afternoon – a more reddish hue. Its image therefore should also capture this constant lack of aesthetic stasis and it will be impossible for it to reflect big politics. The planners' demand to fix the representation arguably goes against the image's inherent propensity to vary as it grasps, in a dynamic and rhythmic way, the multiple realities of a city.

The city 'reassembled'

'Now, I understand what kind of city Birmingham is', says Connor, as we walk around the construction site of the Birmingham train station in 2012 (Figure 5.4). Following architects at work through the processes of design and construction of the New Street Station, Birmingham appears as far removed from a vision of the city as merely an objective frame, or context, wherein one may place a building. It escapes the simplistic, yet widespread, divide of urban theory between subjective and objective perceptions.

Speaking of Birmingham *tout court* without mentioning the design images of its new developments, the imaging techniques, the disputes in design meetings, the

Figure 5.4 Construction site, July 2012 (photo by the author).

changes of the façade geometry on the building site or any other modality of enacting the city will require bracketing all practicalities. Birmingham would appear in isolation, ready to reflect big politics. Yet, if one follows the practices of image making, the city of Birmingham would appear as a flux of information, as a flow of moving clouds changing their hues according to the reflecting steel surface of the façade, or as an important vortex of movements of crowds and trains, connecting the small to the big, the big to the small. That is a city that has many variations, but at the end is one.

This chapter illustrated the meticulous design work needed for the production of the images of this new development. Exploring design process ethnographically, I followed the making of these images as they emerged in the office of the concept architect and how they became political, I analysed their scalar and ontological specificity, their composite and versatile nature. Tracing the making of the Gateway images one can see that at any moment in the study of AZPA one does not witness a radical shift from face-to-face interactions to bigger social structures, from the pixels on the designers' computers to the genuine context of Birmingham, and to big politics. A sense of Birminghamness is gained in the process of design, in the recollection of the multiple realities of the city; Birmingham is rendered and reassembled. Thus, tracing the actions of architects allows us to witness a city that is very different from the one that appears through the many subjective experiences of the Birmingham *flâneurs*, the station commuters or the building experts. I remained sceptical to the appeal of urban theory that 'people, not spaces and structures, animate the city' (Beaumont and Dart 2010). Rather, I illustrated the potential of images to connect the different scales and to 'capture', 'animate', 'assemble' and 're-enact' a city.

The story I tell here is very English. If I slightly altered the lenses of my study, if I were to travel to Birmingham and London every day, if I were given access to every single design meeting, if I were able to witness every move of the designers' hands and software, attend and record every public presentation of Alejandro and follow every model and image of this new development, I would tell different stories. The specificness would differ. However, what would not alter is the coexistence of different ways to enact Birmingham. There is a multiplicity that stays the same. As long as the practicalities of enacting the city are kept unbracketed, the varieties of Birmingham multiply. In the process of design, the city appears to be more than one – without being fragmented into many.

All these images of the Gateway do not represent Birmingham; they rather attend to the multiple reality of the city. As the city cannot be removed from the practices that sustain it, its reality is multiple. Through image making, the city becomes a reality that is manipulated in practice. The city that one is able to attend to by following the practices of architects is never alone. It does not stand by itself. It depends on everything and everyone that is being active while it is being practised. The city is not 'out there' ready to mirror and represent political power. The city is being done in design. Big politics is not 'out there' either, ready to give shape to this new development. The images carry new realities with them. They trigger various enactments of the city of Birmingham. Different enactments entail different ontologies. They come with a different way of doing the city. Yet, the realities produced by AZPA architects are not random. They are ontologically political (Mol 1999). Ontology defines what belongs to the real, the conditions of possibility we live with. If the term 'ontology' is defined with that of 'politics', then this suggests that the conditions of possibility are not given. That reality does not precede the mundane practices in which we interact with it, but is rather shaped within these practices. So the term 'politics' in this context works to underline 'this active mode, this process of shaping, and the fact that its character is both open and contested' (Mol 1999: 74–75). Other variations of Birmingham than the one presented here possibly exist and may be enacted in other architectural practices. Enactments of realities are not a matter of free creative choice; they are always socio-material workings.

The Gateway images are far from being passive and illustrative, their role is rather performative: images serve as astute devices used to train the eyes of those who make the city – to teach designers and viewers how to see and how to think architecturally, but also to educate planners and builders how to read the images of this new development. In other words, the images perform the political. They also invoke a number of workaday choices: which software to use, whether to retouch renderings, how many copies to render, how to teach planners to read them. Through their reiterative performance, new knowledge about the city is gained and new urban knowledge is communicated.

Redescribing the operations of image making illustrates that a building is not simply inserted into a context that exists 'out there' and prior to any process of design. It is rather an object that will redefine the city, will reshuffle it and set it into motion. The station becomes an extension of Birmingham, 'a variation' of it; its images act as sophisticated reflecting machineries that drive the city to 'go through the station' and trigger contextual mutations. Relying on recomposition, not representation, the images also convey an idea of architecture that is very different from the traditional understanding of buildings as static structures placed into space. Flipping through changing arrangements of entities, the moving envelope image makes it impossible to perceive a building as an aesthetic object, as a flat projection of politics or as an embodiment of symbols. No matter how overwhelming and complex the Gateway building is meant to be, it is impossible to grasp it in one instantaneous moment; its perception has temporal and rhythmic qualities.

Political interpretations of architecture commonly consist in critically addressing the role of architecture in tackling social issues, in solving the political problems of the day. In the Gateway case, this line of interpretations would imply connecting to the diversity and ethnic composition of the city, to political conflict and change of power in the Birmingham City Council, to politicized controversies surrounding the preceding proposals for developing the station. To raise a political question often means to reveal behind a given state of affairs of architecture (project, vision or building) the presences of forces *hithero* hidden (as discussed in Chapter 1). If we were to reveal the hidden political forces or intrigues behind the Gateway project, we would have fallen in the trap of 'political explanation' and we would have spoken *about* big politics. Yet, I have chosen an alternative path: to *speak politically* following the composition of the city images, to re-emphasize the political relevance of architecture. There are more entities to be included in the mix in addition to architects, engineers, mayors and developers: renderings pixels, shades of colours, steel and glass, clouds and sun. Planning decisions, ethnic diversity and conflicts – all these features of big politics that impacted on the design project are also there – not as causal elements bringing explanation, but as part of the whole mix. As argued in Chapter 1, both the understanding of architecture and politics can fail if they do not measure up the number of entities that assemble at the first place: the objects, the natural entities, the technical practices, the materiality, in addition to the humans. As witnessed in this chapter, the meandering succession of images of the Gateway, followed here, gives specificity to the political. The shifts and differences in making, rescaling, retouching, staging, synthesizing, publishing, presenting and circulating different images of Birmingham create many situations for the humans to react differently, to disagree, to differ. No one knows if a shift in the image making setting will make the image a good site of the political; every variation of the images can give birth to a new design scenario or a new feature of Birmingham that is to be added to the ensemble. Adding new image versions to assemble different features of the city becomes a political process.

Following the production of the Gateway images, I travelled through hybrid spaces and was able to witness a city that is not made by powerful men, politicians, planners, decision makers and visionary architects. I rather witnessed a city that emerges as its images trace many intricate relationships, involving a variety of material and natural entities. Follow the Gateway images and you see Birmingham, not on the images, but *through* them. Watch their variations, and you will be able witness its multiple natures. When designers and planners meet in design meetings, when viewers inspect a huge scale model of Gateway, when builders and citizens of Birmingham cross paths on the construction site, they all together jointly give shape to the reality of the new train station; they make Birmingham reassemble.

6

Sites of Politics: The Fourth Way of Becoming Political

There are many sites where political action is being performed. We have already visited three of them and we have witnessed together three ways of activating the political in dwelling (Chapter 3), in design experimentation (Chapter 4) and in the practices of image making (Chapter 5). We followed how these sites become political as different views are being expressed, fought for, shared and negotiated. We witnessed how politics is enacted at the level of the building-in-use (Chapter 3), in the process of designing a building-to-be (Chapter 4), in the practice of capturing and assembling the city (Chapter 5) and through the work of designers, builders, planners, their repertoire of actions, drawing practices, consultations with stakeholders, risk-taking and negotiations. In this chapter, we will analyse another political site – building renovation. Following the difficulties, unpredictable turns, surprises and drifts in the process of renovating and transforming old buildings, I will visit one site in Vienna and one in Moscow. The chapter aims at shedding light at the social and cognitive complexity of 'renovation in the making'. It argues for the important *mediating role* that an old building can play to guide, afford, redirect and facilitate the political dimension of architecture. Instead of being passively submitted to interventions, buildings-in-renovation become active participants in design. Shifting the source of variability to the building itself rather than to the multitude of subjective interpretations or opinions about renovation, the building as object of manipulation differs from one practice to another, its reality multiplies. The architects, the planners, the renovators, the visuals, the technologies of preservation, all of them are more than one, more than singular, more than unique. This triggers the question of how they are related and that is what makes renovation a political site. The forth way for architecture to become political is by tracing the sites of building transformations.

Renovation in the making

Conservation studies have taught us for decades that buildings are valuable for their historical substance and symbolic significance gradually acquired with time and that is why they should be protected. Old buildings should be preserved because they are valuable for their architectural quality, 'patina of age' (Ruskin 1989), building substance (*Bausubstanz*), symbolic significance, 'age-value' (*Alterswert*). They implied that the 'traces of age' and the signs of premature ageing (Dehio and Riegl 1988) are the qualities considered as being the most important features of historical buildings that guarantee 'originality' or 'authenticity'. Structural integrity and spatial stability are considered as distinctive qualities of buildings, as compared to other cultural objects (art works and valuable objects) and are conditions *sine qua non* for buildings to acquire significance and meaning. On the other hand, buildings are regarded as important 'documents', evidences of social history and 'monuments' of collective memory transmitted over the centuries and this gives preservationists another reason for protecting old buildings. Conservators often face the dilemma of 'preserving the building fabric' and the architectural quality as defined by the original architects and builders or 'preserving the readability of history' so as to retain all the conservation interventions and traces of history on the building surface. Focusing their efforts on identifying the symbolic value, original substance and historical layers of old buildings, conservation studies interpret them only on the basis of what they are and what they mean. They often ignore to account their potential to change and manifest their agency in situations of interventions on their fabric. Buildings were for a long time excluded as actors in conservation and preservation studies.

The reason why buildings were given no chance to play any role in renovation theories is also due to the very definitions of actors and agency. Action is interpreted as what 'intentional', 'meaningful' humans (conservators, renovators, preservationists) do on the passive tissue of a building, and their actions are called 'interventions' (as acts of intervening in a situation and becoming intentionally involved in it, trying to change it). That is why it is hard to see through the lens of these theories how a building, a fresco, an arch or a columns' grid, could be active. However, intervention holds also a different meaning, of *interaction* with an existing building, granting a certain degree of agency to the object whose process of transformation architects, renovators and builders are intervening in, thus conveying an implication of subversion.

Questioning the politics of preservation studies and their understanding of buildings and agency, in this chapter I will explore the process of renovation of the seventeenth-century *Alte Aula* in Vienna (2004–2006) and the nineteenth-century Bolshoi theatre in Moscow (2005–2011) by tracing their unpredictable dynamics. I begin with the questions: 'Is it possible to restrain from understanding the renovation of the *Alte Aula* in Vienna, and the Bolshoi theatre in Moscow as predominantly political, symbolic or cultural?' 'Is it possible instead to understand buildings-in-renovation as *things* manipulated in practice?' 'Or, else, can we escape perspective?' There are different interpretations of the Bolshoi theatre or the *Alte Aula* buildings that would connect the buildings to the specific local histories, and scandals during and after the renovation. In an understanding inspired by 'perspectival flexibility', one can witness how the different interpretations of the buildings will vary while the buildings will recede behind these interpretations. Stepping away from the dominant perspectivalism in architectural theory, here I will rather foreground the practicalities, materialities and events of building renovation that appear to be so visible in the process of renovation, in the disagreements of the renovation actors, in the controversies surrounding renovation that have far-reaching effects. I will trace the practices of designers, planners, renovators and constructors in these processes. By so doing buildings will cease to be treated as passive objects that can be perceived from different perspectives. The analysis would escape perspective. If we take this step, Bolshoi theatre would not be any loner a political or cultural symbol, the *Alte Aula* would not be any longer a precious Jesuit relics, but they will rather become a part of what is done in design and renovation practice. Thus, what follows is not two studies of the opinions of the Russians or Austrians about key buildings in their capital cities, but rather two accounts that tell us what buildings in renovation *do* in practice to all those who relate to them. Tracing renovation in the making will reveal the 'aperspectival objectivity' that shifts the source of variability from the multiple variable subjectivities towards the reality of the built object.

The driving question here is no longer how to find the truth about the renovation of Bolshoi theatre or about the *Alte Aula*. It is rather about 'how the building as an object of manipulation is handled'. This shift in philosophy of knowledge draws the attention towards ethnographic interest in knowledge practices. Thus, I will direct the ethnographic attention to the vibrant matter of a fresco theatre in Vienna and its surprises, and the meticulous gilding techniques of the restorers of Bolshoi's imperial glory tracing their practices as they discuss architectural plans, materials and clients' demands, as they gather on the building site or on online fora debating renovation.

Renovating the *Alte Aula*

In 2000, the Viennese architect Rudolf Prohazka was commissioned to renovate the seventeenth-century building of the Old University of Vienna, known as the *Alte Aula*. This building is a part of the university quarter built in 1623 when the Emperor Ferdinand IV entrusted the theological and philosophical faculty of the University of Vienna to the Jesuit Order. The building at *Backerstrasse* 20 was used at the time as a college building that also served to host university festivities and theatre performances, and accommodated different programmes throughout the centuries.

In the summer of 2004, shortly after I began to work for the Austrian Academy of Sciences, which currently manages the *Alte Aula*, I decided to follow its renovation process and its architect on his way to redesign and restore one of the oldest buildings in the centre of Vienna. The building was supposed to accommodate a science museum of new type – The Gallery of Research. The process enrolled a number of institutions such as the Federal Office for the Protection of Monuments (*Bundesdenkmalamt*); the Ministry of Economy and Labour (*Bundesministerium für Wirtschaft und Arbeit*); the *Bundes Immobilien Gesellschaft (BIG),* the largest property owner in the Federal Republic of Austria; the *Burghauptmannschaft,* a subenterprise of the Ministry of Economy and Labour responsible for the management of public buildings in Vienna; and the building company *Swietelsky*. Individual actors such as the architects, the preservationists, the clients, the engineers also joined along with non-human actors such as the building façade, the natural stone used for the floor, the columns' grid, the fresco and the layers of paints. I followed these actors at numerous places of planning, discussion and negotiations throughout the whole process until the final completion of the building in 2006 and witnessed how they engaged in the long-lasting venture of reshaping the building and redefining it time and again, how they expressed their concerns, modified the criteria, communicated their expectations and engaged in negotiations. Following these actors, I was able to account renovation not as a series of personal 'heroic' battles of an architect with the unchangeable 'historical substance' of an old building, but rather as a collective venture – tentative, difficult and controversial – to reshape and redefine, rearticulate and re-establish the building of the *Alte Aula*. I used a variety of other sources as well: interviews with the architect, with the representatives of the building company, the client and representatives of the Federal Office for the Protection of Monuments, content analysis of archives of the Jesuit University and the Jesuit Theatre, of regulation and preservation documents of the Austrian Chamber of Architects and Engineers (*Bundeskammer der Architekten und Ingenieurkonsulenten*), of documentation on the competition and the planning process, as well as photo documentation. For the purposes of the actual study, I have consulted the following archives: *Staatsarchiv* (the State Archive) – *Allgemeines Verwaltungsarchiv* (General Administration Archive) and *Haus-, Hof- und Staatarchiv* (Imperial Archive); *Wiener Stadt- und Landesarchiv* (Archive of the City of Vienna); *Universitätsarchiv* (The University Archive).

I will first examine the renovation process dynamics and will then focus on the specific mode of action of the old building undergoing renovation, accounting for the process in which action is shared and actively distributed between transforming agents and a building that *resists* transformations. This offers a possibility to witness the variability situated within the *Alte Aula* building.

Dynamics of renovation

Rudolf Prohazka's first encounter with the building of the *Alte Aula* was in 2000 when he was invited by the Academy of Sciences to participate in the international competition for its renovation along with nine other participants. Although the winning project of Prohazka set clear objectives and means for its realization, the process of renovation I happened to witness in the period 2004–2006 appeared to be unpredictable and non-linear, guided by 'drifts' and 'surprises', driven by 'ruptures' and 'modifications of details'.

The architect denotes the impossibility to plan the different steps of renovation with exact precision and the need to constantly correct and adjust the outcomes of the activities that were initially planned:

> I had never had any project in my carrier that had no restrictions at all. There are lots of fixed restrictions such as norms, laws that exist anyway. It is simple for instance *to plan* to use blue materials, but it will make the additional expenditures much bigger when they are afterwards corrected and adjusted. (Interview with the architect Rudolf Prohazka, 3 May 2006)

A number of renovation issues provoked disputes and disagreements among the participants in the renovation, and made it impossible for the architect's original plan to be realized with precision and exact anticipation of the outcomes. These issues were usually debated during the meetings in the building company over which both technical execution and costs were discussed by architects, builders and representatives of the *Burghauptmannschaft* and the client. Discussions over financial issues were time-consuming and more difficult as compared to the disagreements over technical issues and execution. The building company *Swietelsky* answered both technical and budget concerns by providing exact calculations and technical solutions. Every deviation from the initial project was negotiated and justified. While debating additional costs or technical execution, the renovation actors constantly referred to the specifications in the call for bids and the offers.

The actors in renovation process engaged on numerous occasions in negotiations that changed its course and reformulated its objectives, modified the nature of the actors and the compromises reached by architects, planners, clients, preservationists and ministries. One can witness that renovation did not begin with a well-informed and predictable historical enquiry that served as an inspiration of clever design solutions and was incorporated in design plans, realized according to the expectations of all participants in this venture. Instead, the modified building appeared as being the unexpected and improbable result of a tentative process of disagreements, of daring and sometimes arbitrary design experimentations, of trials that modified the architect's initial choices and subjected them to alternations due to unknown or neglected factors. That is how renovation could attain, sometimes, accidental results.

Renovation progresses in an unpredictable way also because a building that undergoes renovation is not a fully masterable object: it often resists to interventions and shows itself as a disobedient object. Clients, builders and architects witness their incapacity to anticipate and fully control its modifications, as the building has prepared them a lot of 'surprises'.

'Surprises' in renovation

As a Viennese, the architect Rudolf Prohazka was previously intrigued by 'the strange urban situation of this building'. Renovating this building meant for him first and foremost a strong challenge of urban intervention, as thorny and challenging as every intervention in the city centre's fabric of one of the oldest European cities might be. Commenting on the nature and the ambitions of the project, Prohazka stated in one of the longest interviews: 'The task of transforming and giving an entire new life to this building fascinated me' (interview with Rudolf Prohazka, 3 May 2006). To renovate meant for Prohazka 'to clean' and 'liberate' the building from all the remaining traces of previous uses, of recent constructions and interventions, so as to re-establish as much as possible the initial building fabric. Instead of engaging in attempts to learn about the intentions of the 'original planner' so as to discern the building 'original substance' (*Originalsubstanz*) from other additional layers that were accumulated in time, the architect had to find other ways of detecting the old building and make it reveal itself to architects, planners and builders. Besides using literary sources about the building history like the book of Mühlberger (1993), considered as a main reference in the research stage, the architect argues that:

> *the real information source was the building itself.* And there were so many things that were not documented, or unknown, like the parts of frescos, some differences were found out, the techniques... all the time there were *surprises* in a negative sense: Why did they build it so bad? Why did they need these wooden parts? Lots of things should be corrected that would be normal for a new construction. I would not say that it's unusual for a building at this age to have foundations that are not perfectly laid like the foundations of a recent building would be. And if we were to build it today we would find it difficult to think about the stability of the building in 400 years. If you leave it open and unfinished it will simply gain quality. (Interview with Rudolf Prohazka, 10 December 2005; author's emphasis)

The question of learning *about* the building – something that every renovation or design project begins with – becomes rather a question of getting to witness those specific techniques through which a building-in-renovation makes itself knowable and lets itself being known. Old buildings accommodate new activities, but also guide visitors through spaces, 'house different types of programmes', provoke debates and disagreements. At the same time, the building's materiality and history neither fully determine the actions of all the 'interventionalists' (architects, builders, conservators, preservationists) nor is the building under renovation a simple backdrop for human action. The renovation process situates us between the full causality of the old building and its sheer inexistence. To understand *what happens* in renovation, we are led to describe the multiple modes of action of the building: how it affords, surprises, renders possible, suggests, facilitates and influences other actors and possible doings.

A surprise can derive from the discrepancy between the received knowledge on the building (preceding the renovation process) and the knowledge that was gradually acquired *in the process* of renovating it. The architect would stop and wonder, questioning retrospectively the building's fabric: 'Why was it built so? Why were these wooden parts used? Why were not the foundations of the building laid in the way architects would lay them now?' These questions will then trigger a process of corrections and adjustments of the building using the available contemporary techniques.

Yet, more often the surprises in renovation come from the building itself. Prohazka explains that the work is progressing according to plan, and that it should be finished in time: 'However, "unforeseen things", like discoveries of all sorts might always happen' (meeting with architect Prohazka, architect Mandler and representatives of the client, 3 May 2005). I have chosen to account such an 'unforeseen' event triggered by some fresco parts that let themselves accidentally visible in the process of renovating the sidewalls on the second floor. This manifestation of recalcitrance of the *Alte Aula* had also a strong impact on me and the network of participants enrolled by the 'surprise'. That is the reason why I will slow down the analysis here, and I will engage in a more fine-grained description of how exactly this surprise occurred, reconfigured traditional definitions of building and agency and reinstated the variability of the building.

Everything changed for me that morning of May 2005, when after unlocking the old squeaking entrance door on the side of *Wollzeile* Street, I entered the empty building site, as usual, in search of a new excitement to begin the day with. Having the key from the aged Jesuit building was as exciting and as sinister as it might be to have access to an inhabited site richly loaded with history. And, as usual, my morning walk began with a quick stroll among the columns in the arcaded space on the ground floor, followed by a longer moment of contemplation of the view to *Riemergasse*. Then, I climbed the new staircase near the glass elevator designed by Prohazka, and skipping as usual the first floor, my morning visit guided me impatiently to the fresco room on the second floor (Figure 6.1).

This amazing space concealed a variety of dwellers through the time. Having studied these spaces and the archives on the university quarter in Vienna, I often imagined the anatomy and the pathology lecture halls, situated on that floor according to an inventory of 1821 for the New University Building (now the Academy of Sciences) [University Archive, CA 1.3.376]. Another updated inventory from 1865 pointed also that the lecture room for physics and the room for machines, as well

Figure 6.1 The fresco room, the old Jesuit theatre of the *Alte Aula* in Vienna (photo by the author).

as the observatory and the natural history cabinet with its adjoining rooms and a laboratory were all located on that floor. However, what always incited my fascination and made me spend hours in the empty 800 m² hall was the ceiling with one of the largest hanging frescos in Vienna, painted by Anton Herzog, and the remaining of the stage of the Jesuit theatre. At the time of the Jesuits, this *theatrum* was not only used for performances but also for promotions and university festivities. The *calendarium academicum* of 1693 shows an image of one of these events. Built around 1654 with the financial support of Emperor Ferdinand IV, the *theatrum* on the second floor was used both as an auditorium for festivities and as a place for presenting scientific experiments. The stage was constructed at the time in Regensburg and shipped to Vienna via the Danube. Designed as a *solemne theatrum* with all its mechanical appliances, decorations and scenic changes, the stage and all the baroque scenic techniques were meant to impress the spectator by all means.

> [...] that day of May was richer in surprises: I was strolling in the empty fresco room, engaged as usual in a childish 'find the differences' game. Striving to find out the minute changes made on the building the day before, my eyes paused for a moment on the sidewalls of the former Jesuit theatre stage. There, I saw yellowish parts of paints, regularly spread in different layers; no instruments, architectural plans and visuals were left from the day before. This was surprising, I thought, to leave the sidewalls in such a devastating state, only months before the building was supposed to be completed. These yellowish minuscule strata worried me, and this escalating feeling of worry partly spoiled my morning excitement, that usually used to charge me with energy for the whole day. [...] It was strange that no architectural traces were left behind...
>
> [...] a few moments later, architect Prohazka greeted me with a dry but polite '*Gruss Got*', and staring at the sidewalls he sighed: 'this building *surprises* us every day.' (AY: Fieldwork diary)

In that morning of May 2005, the parts of fresco on the sidewalls had on me an effect of surprise and amazement reminiscent to the one that this stage with all its spectacular machineries and scenic settings used to have at the time of the Jesuit plays. So was its impact on the architect, surprised as I was, to find himself being surprised *again* by the building. Prohazka followed the building closer than myself and knew all its details and corners and had already acknowledged on different occasions its disobedient nature. Yet, his surprise was bigger than mine and so was his knowledge about the building. That situation of 'surprise' lingered for months and provoked debates among all participants in renovation who brought various instruments and equipment in the fresco room to investigate it and make it talk, and by so doing enrolled more materials, tools and techniques in the process (Figure 6.2).

A couple of days after that May morning visit, new parts of fresco also showed up on the ceiling of the first floor, a space dedicated to temporary exhibitions. This new 'objection' of the building enrolled new actors in the discussions – representatives of the Academy as a client, curators, artists and conservators. During a meeting in the building company on 16 June 2005, we vividly discussed the material that should

Sites of Politics: The Fourth Way of Becoming Political 117

Figure 6.2 The 'surprises' of the fresco, the *Alte Aula* in Vienna (photo by the author).

be used for repainting these various fragments of fresco on the basis of the expertise provided by the conservators. A solution discussed at these meetings was to cover the fragments with 'Reversill', and then repaint them with the same paints as the rooms so as to erase the traces of the building indocility. The client was concerned with the way the exhibition halls will look and wanted homogeneous neutral spaces that would not compete with the pieces on display, and also a predictable space that will no longer 'disobey' and astonish.

The renovation and preservation documents show that it is anticipated that the old building will remain a stable object, a black-boxed entity that could be rather predictable. The documentation gives privileged status to the systematic and stable knowledge about the old building, knowledge that is accumulated through centuries and laboriously documented in archives. However, in the course of renovation interventions, the *Alte Aula* expected to be a coherent entity, suddenly multiples. Not one fresco but many fresco fragments; not a single renovation practice, but many diverse practices of intervening and transforming. The participants in renovation face new uncertainties and engage in new networks of materials-shapes-architects-historical layers-and-conservators. That is the regime of intense and enduring 'surprise'. The fresco 'surprise' shows that once reopened, the building starts to act as an agent that enrols further more materials, renovation techniques, clients and preservationists. We witness how renovation attends to the multiplicity of the building that cannot be removed from the practices that sustain it.

'Surprise' points also to a different epistemology of the practice of building renovation – one that requires all the participants to redefine and mobilize their knowledge, competences and artistry in the moment when the routines of the renovation are 'breached' (Garfinkel 1985). Acting as a 'breaching experiment' of the renovation, the fresco 'surprise' implies an empirical inquiry in which normal interaction is interrupted and the constitutive expectancies are infringed radically causing the participants in it to become confused. Seeking to re-establish balance and attempting to normalize the renovation activities, constrained by deadlines and tight budgets, the participants in renovation engaged in reconstructions of the building history. As the debates around the fresco layers unfolded, they were led to go back to the building archives and recall its different uses; from its Jesuit foundation, through to the nineteenth century when it served modern institutions such as the journal *Wiener Zeitung* (from the 1890s until 1938), the Imperial and Government Printing Office (*Österreichische Staatsdruckerei*) that moved in the building in 1866, and after the Second World War, the Central Statistical Office (*Statistisches Zentralamt*), up to the recent decision to renovate the building and prepare it for contemporary uses of the Austrian Academy of Sciences. In this historical discussion triggered by the 'rebellious' fresco wall, we were all led to believe that most probably the yellowish strata were leftovers from the scenic paintings that used to frame the experimental theatre during the seventeenth century. Throughout the eighteenth century, the sidewall paintings and sculptures in the window bays were hidden behind curtains to make sure that the attention of the audience is focused on the theatre plays. Between 1756 and 1773, the theatre on the second floor was used for public demonstrations and experiments, while the adjacent room housed since 1715 a physico-mathematical museum as well as a natural history collection brought together by the Jesuits in their travels (Hamann et al. 1986). Recalling this history in more details allowed us to find certain aesthetics in the yellowish and pinkish spherical wall spots.

'Surprise', in the words of Prohazka, of that morning in May 2005 referred also to a tentative notion of building agency rather than to the stable knowledge about the building. The source of agency was questioned, and it provoked disputes and new negotiations among clients, preservationists and sponsors and thus modified the state of affairs in which the building emerged gradually as an actor. To test the building agency, we should ask the question: 'Does the seventeenth-century building, its fresco layers, its paints and its columns' grid make a difference in the course of some other agent's action or not?' Yes. The fresco manifestations of resilience changed the course of renovation and reshuffled the definitions of all participants of what a good renovation is, of what to exhibit in a seventeenth-century space means, of what preserving a building loaded with history implies. It is that specific experimental trail allowing all the actors to detect the difference that we term here 'renovation'. Far from being a passive surface of interventions, the building emerges as an active *participant* in the course of renovation.

In the interviews, too, many participants in the renovation venture defined the *Alte Aula* as a building that reacts to them and responds to their attempts of smoothly transform, alter and manipulate its fabric and agency. Although the term of 'intervention' remains in the technical professional jargon of conservationists from the Federal Office for the Protection of Monuments and the Ministry of Economy and Labour, and is equally present in the relevant documentation and minutes, their actions could be treated as 'responses' to the building. One can witness a different meaning of renovation, not as an intentional intrusion into a passive object, but as a complex *trans*action based on the interactions of a building that gradually lets itself being known by architects, clients and builders learning about it *in the process* of renovation.

'Surprise' describes also the intense mode of being in a situation that we seek to understand and that can be accounted as transactional, a situation in which the building manifests itself as a design agent that talks back to architects, preservationists and clients, causing them to apprehend unexpected situations, *making them do more*, engage with and reassess the building history, materiality and technicality. Revealing some methods of reality construction, the fresco 'surprise' entailed such an accountability of the renovation actions that redefined the connections among the participants in the renovation and created new relations and groupings. It acted politically.

Political valence of building recalcitrance

Far from being mere ostensive objects, buildings-in-renovation are more reminiscent to recalcitrant microbes or chemical elements (Stengers and Prygogine 1988; Rheinberger 1997). They come to light as *performative agents* that can hardly be mastered by architects, preservationists and planners; they stubbornly resist their interventions, hinder or facilitate specific ways of accommodating the programmatic requirements. In many cases, the *Alte Aula* had no scruples in objecting to the architects' and builders' actions by 'behaving' in undisciplined ways, blocking the renovating operations, obstructing the plans, suspending the builders' deadlines, disappearing from view, disclosing unknown layers of its history and showing a selective 'attitude' to different materials. Like a concert that was being performed in a complex setting, it vanished from the viewers' eyes when it was no longer performed.

Yet, to argue that a seventeenth-century building is an actor does not mean to claim that it operates as a strange quasi-theatrical machinery from the Jesuit time or that it literally talked to us in that early morning of May 2005. For a building to act, it is to be a part of a network, in which each element 'relays', 'prolongs' and 'overtakes' the action of the building and the whole collective without either of them ever constituting a source of action in itself. The fresco 'objection' that led to surprises was prolonged by many sets of agencies of all the participants in renovation. As a result, its capacity to act is the effect of the associations of a heterogeneous network composed of architect-fresco layers-conservators-visitors-visuals, instead of being assigned to a powerful master architect or to a single architectural object that could determine the course of action.

The way architects, builders and clients responded to the 'objections' of the building showed their constant uncertainty over the nature of this entity. No matter how thorough the research on the building history was, the building often happened to reveal a hidden layer of it; no matter how systematic the knowledge on its materials and construction was, they often happened to manifest new properties. The *Alte Aula* acted (and transformed action) in unexpected ways not merely repeating and relaying it. Distorting and modifying the meaning attributed to it instead of faithfully transporting it through the centuries it manifested its political valence. Both its history and modalities of action were probed and redefined through the moments of 'surprises' and led us to question traditional definitions of buildings as static backdrops of activities, as subservient to the laws of technical causality.

Renovating Bolshoi theatre

The recent boom of urban developments in Russia left conservation studies confronted with a challenging dilemma: preservation of the architectural quality or conservation interventions. A topical example witnessed for this dilemma – the renovation of Bolshoi theatre in Moscow. In this case, legally only renovation was possible, but in fact reconstruction happened. Moreover, this process happened to be extremely controversial. The length and the scandalous fame of the building during the reconstruction initially intrigued me. Then I found myself teaching at Strelka in Moscow and got fascinated by the renovation process of the theatre. Sitting sumptuously in the heart of Moscow, at walking distance from the Red Square and right next to the Malei theatre, Russia's famed Bolshoi theatre (Figure 6.3) has been covered by spiky scaffoldings and its rose-and-white-columned façade stood shrouded in construction curtains for six years and three months – from July 2005

Figure 6.3 Bolshoi theatre in Moscow (photo by the author).

until 28 October 2011; the new Bolshoi opened doors again with an inauguration concert on 2 November 2011. This first spectacle triggered questions about the whole 'spectacle of the theatre's renovation'.

For decades Russian politics was enacted on the stage of Bolshoi theatre: the SSSR was founded on its stage, its walls, heavy curtains and golden ornaments witnessed numerous important gatherings and ceremonies of the communist party. As a major cultural but also political scene of Russia, Bolshoi theatre was in the last seventy years a scene where communist ideology was staged and important rituals were performed. The signs and symbols of their domination were there for all to see. In 2004, the theatre still had the Hammer and the Sickle on the façade and thus represented the last bastion of Soviet culture. Therefore, it is very tempting to produce a narrative of the political importance of this building in the Soviet Period, and to explain Bolshoi theatre's architecture with big politics, with political change and shifts in ideology. The literature along these lines is ample (Barnett and Skelton 2008). A number of interpretations written in the spirit of mainstream social sciences can be found and they all refer to social, political and cultural factors; they all elude the building specificity. They underline the symbolic power of the nation's most popular theatre; its meaning is either treated as a reflection of Imperial glory or the symbolic system of the Soviet Union; ballet is seen as nostalgia for power (Sporton 2006). The 'social explanation of' of Bolshoi's architecture is largely explored. Yet, to say that this building simply embodies Russian politics would be to indulge in facile politization; to accept that its difficult building renovation can be explained as projecting the facets of new political climate is a form of anachronism. A causal explanation between political changes in Russian society and its cultural institutions will not explain Bolshoi's specificity.

The theatre building has its own life and strengths and its trajectory is very revealing of the 'turbulent' life it has had in periods of wars, revolutions and political turmoil. The building was erected between 1821 and 1825 following a project of Ossip Bove. In 1853, it was severely damaged in a fire; the renovation of the building was completed by Albert Kavas in 1856. The second reconstruction took place in 1921–1923 and that is the moment when the concrete foundations were laid down. The building was damaged again during the wars and restored in 1942–1943; another major restoration took place in 1958. Between 1998 and 2003, different projects for the reconstruction of the theatre were developed but none of them took shape. A crucial moment was reached in 2005: it was announced that the dilapidation of the building has reached a critical 70 per cent and on 2 July 2005 the building was closed for renovation.

What was about this building that it 'died' so many times and 'resurrected' subsequently? What kind of actors responded to the theatre actions and claimed to speak on its behalf? To understand Bolshoi, we need to recollect its history in periods of war and peace. The recent renovation debate brought back this history and made us rethink the social life of the building and in numerous analyses of the renovation we witnessed discussions about the history of the Bolshoi, its amazing social biography: a building that burnt in fire so many times and nevertheless 'survived'.

Yet, Bolshoi did not cease to surprise during its recent six-year renovation and provoked many reactions and disagreements. The renovation developed according to its own logic to the extent that it is impossible to explain its dynamics or the most salient arguments with current Russian Politics, with mafia scandals, or the inherent rivalry in the artistic world. Big (Bolshoi) theatre cannot be explained with big politics. Tracing the controversies surrounding the renovation of the theatre rather raises the questions of the inherent political dimensions of the renovation process: 'how many actors are involved in a process of renovation?'; 'how different are their voices, disagreements and transformative actions?' If we follow the actors in the process of renovation – architects, renovators, building companies, politicians, artists, citizen groups – we would be able to witness how they mediate between different understandings of the cultural heritage of Bolshoi. All these stakeholders have different interests, different visions *about* Bolshoi; this would allow us to produce an interpretation that would embrace its 'perspectivile flexibility'. Yet, all these actors have a different grasp on the process of renovation and handle it from their own material perspective; if we follow the building variability and the 'surprises' of the nineteenth-century building of Bolshoi, we can witness how these actors all meet on the site of the theatre, how they disagree and how they handle the building-in-renovation. Witnessing what this building *does* to those who interact with it on a daily basis, in a multiplicity of events, will allow us to escape perspective and to trace again building renovation as a political site.

The Bolshoi building appears as much more complex than this symbolizing regime implies. Rather than staging big politics (hence the name 'Bolshoi', meaning 'Big', in Russian), Bolshoi is made up of the little dramas of design and construction, of forces and events; of the discordant voices of its makers just like contested 'architecture is made up of intensive forces: actors' disagreements, concerns and the extensive maps of their displacements. A building is not a static entity composed of symbols, but a flow of trajectories' (Yaneva 2012: 20). Following the flow of trajectories and transformations triggered by the Bolshoi renovation, one can witness that the renovation of a building with such a historical and cultural importance for Russia provoked a great amount of reactions within the architectural community and the journalist community, artists and public administration. A lot of groups felt concerned by the Bolshoi renovation in these six years and expressed reactions of agreement or disagreement on internet blogs and in the press, various newspapers and specialist journals, such as *Archproek,* the Russian journal 'Theatre'. The renovation process made all the actors to revisit the history of the theatre and its re-constructions; it made them to evaluate its major importance for Moscow and made them appreciate how many actors, other than artists and politicians, make it work today.

Tracing the Bolshoi controversy

The protagonists in the controversy came from different sides: cultural institutions, political, construction, media, renovation and restoration. The theatre's $760 million renovation was considered to have many flaws. A number of aspects of the renovation were discussed as problematic and were criticized openly: the stage was uneven, so uneven that dancers were said to look at the floor all the time to avoid being injured; the use of papier-mâché and other materials spoiled the aesthetic appearance of Bolshoi's imperial glory. The theatre was supposed to be completed in 2008, but it was found that the entire foundation has to be replaced, carefully setting the giant structure on thousands of metal supports and pouring new concrete footings underneath. This delay triggered more discussions about budgets and the quality of the renovation.

The artists as a group were very vocal in this controversy. They complained saying they have been treated as 'guests' as they were never consulted about the renovation. Nikolay Tiskaridze, a premier dancer of the Bolshoi Ballet who joined in 1992, spoke very critically about the reconstruction project from the outset, calling the result 'vandalism' (Osborn 2016). He commented on the renovation decisions on a number of occasions discussing both the functionality and style of the new building. In his criticism he went as far as comparing it to a Turkish hotel: 'it's impossible to lift a ballerina ... she's going to hit her head on the ceiling'.[1] He was concerned that the dancers were constantly falling on the tile and some serious injuries have already happened; also, the floor of the new building was very cold and this was too dangerous for the artists who act almost barefoot; the new rehearsal rooms were also judged as 'catastrophic'. In 2013, a senior violinist and veteran of the Bolshoi theatre for four decades Viktor Sedov died of his injuries after falling into the orchestra pit.[2] The artists remembered the old building and spoke with nostalgia about its features, Tiskaridze recalled, 'I know exactly where the gold was, which handle was where, where the stucco was' and as a 'wild amount of money was spent on gold, I just want to see the gold'.[3] Judging mainly the aesthetics of the new theatre other artists joined too: the soprano Anastasia Meskova complained: 'They knocked down a cathedral and put up cardboard'.[4] The conductor Vladimir Jurowski, who conducted the first public performance of the reopened theatre, also commented on the quality of the theatre stating that the sound was 'terrible'. The artists blamed the administration for the many flaws in the renovation and for ignoring the artists' opinion. The main disagreement seemed to be between artists and administrators. The ballet community largely discussed Russian corruption that can be witnessed everywhere; they said that 'corruption had come to the Bolshoi in the past few years'. One of the prima ballerinas, Anastasia Volochkova, summed up the artists' position stating: 'today Bolshoi's artists represent Russians who lost their belief in their state management and in law enforcement agencies'.[5] She argued that 'The leadership is not paying enough attention to the creative process, but rather to business, commerce, and money'.[6]

[1] http://www.nytimes.com/2011/10/29/world/europe/joy-and-nostalgia-in-moscow-as-bolshoi-theater-reopens.html, downloaded on 3 September 2013.
[2] http://www.independent.co.uk/arts-entertainment/classical/news/bolshoi-violinist-viktor-sedov-dies-after-fall-from-stage-8720494.html, downloaded on 10 September 2013.
[3] http://www.bloomberg.com/news/2013-03-19/bolshoi-head-dismisses-ex-ballerina-s-pimping-claims.html, downloaded on 10 September 2013.
[4] http://www.spearswms.com/good-life/travel/43457/inside-the-controversial-renovation-of-moscows-bolshoi-theatre.thtml, downloaded on 10 September 2013.
[5] http://www.theguardian.com/stage/2011/mar/22/bolshoi-rocked-by-scandal.
[6] http://www.theguardian.com/stage/2011/mar/22/bolshoi-rocked-by-scandal, downloaded on 3 September 2013.

The second very vocal group of actors in the controversy was the group of the theatre directors. The theatre director Anatoly Iksanov was dismissed after the artistic director of the Bolshoi, Sergei Filin, was attacked with acid in February 2013 and nearly made blind. Commenting on this criminal attack, Filin said that this vicious infighting is related to the 'government investments, which have increased the yearly budget to $120 million'.[7] The leading dance scholar Vadim Galevsjky stated, 'The theatre acquired the spirit of freedom, but it ended in scandal.'[8] Iksanov had nothing to say, but to reiterate that when there is a conflict between artists and administrators, it is natural to expect that the public opinion will be on the artists' side. Vladimir Urin, newly appointed director of the Bolshoi theatre, joined the controversy. According to Dmitry Bertman, head of popular Moscow musical theatre Helikon, Urin was supposed to be the 'first aid' for Bolshoi theatre. He explained: 'Vladimir Urin is a true "knight" of the theatre. He is a man who loves artists and always invites interesting directors.'[9] Described as a particularly non-controversial figure by the journalist and highly credited for rebuilding Moscow's second-tier theatre, the Stanislavsky and Nemirovich-Danchenko Music Theatre, Urin spoke openly about the problems at Bolshoi: 'It is true that there have been problems at the Bolshoi, but these are often artificially created problems.'[10] He admitted he needed time to find out what the problems are and to prepare for the role of Bolshoi's director: 'I am no revolutionary, I am a man who solves problems one by one.'[11] 'I perfectly understand that one person cannot do anything in the theatre or in any other field on his or her own. I do hope that the majority of talented and wonderful people working here will be my allies. Only together we can solve problems that exist today at the Bolshoi theatre.'[12] Another theatre director joined the controversy, Aleksandr Titel, artistic director of the Stanislavsky and Nemirovich-Danchenko Theatre. Commenting on the dismissal of Iksanov, he stated: 'A number of squabbles and scandals exceeded an acceptable limit, even taking into consideration that backstage intrigues are common in theatrical companies.'[13] He argued that Iskanov has been prematurely dismissed. Yet, he praised the professionalism of Urin, stating that it is a fact that the new director is an experienced manager. He was the only one to mention the quality of the renovation: 'During the long-lasting renovation of the theatre, Mr Urin succeeded in creating technically equipped theatre space and an interior which Moscow residents consider as one of the cosiest in the capital.'[14] The quality of the renovated building is seen in two radically different spectra: for the artists it is a dysfunctional, even dangerous space that can hardly compare with the imperial glory of Bolshoi; for

---

[7] *Moscownews*, June 2013.
[8] *NYTimes* (July 2013).
[9] http://voiceofrussia.com/2013_07_09/Bolshois-new-chief-highly-professional-will-hold-on-to-the-talented-expert-1488/
[10] *BBC* website and video recordings (July 2013).
[11] Ibid.
[12] http://voiceofrussia.com/2013_07_09/Bolshois-new-chief-highly-professional-will-hold-on-to-the-talented-expert-1488/
[13] http://voiceofrussia.com/2013_07_09/Bolshois-new-chief-highly-professional-will-hold-on-to-the-talented-expert-1488/
[14] Ibid.

Moscow residents, it is a modern and technically advanced space, hosting a warm and pleasing interior. The debate is driven by 'perspectival flexibility': the opinions of different groups about the quality of the renovation and the speculations about the attack on Filin pile up at the same time; the interpretations vary; the perspectives of artists, theatre administrators and Moscow residents change, and their viewpoints swing every time we hear a new voice on the BBC, on the pages of *New York Times* or *Guardian* or on the *Voice of Russia, Moscownews* or *Izvestia*; their individual difference can be hardly reconciled.

As expected, politicians played an important role in the renovation controversy. A key figure was Yuri Luzhkov, former mayor of Moscow, who for a long time personally supervised the progress of the work and participated in meetings of the Board of Trustees. He resigned as co-chairman of the Board of Trustees in February 2006 when early scandals in the reconstruction of the theatre broke out. The budget issues were critical and Luzhkov was a witness in a criminal case of theft of funds from the bank of Moscow. While Luzhkov reiterated many times in political statements that 'it is very important to open the theatre in 2011', says music director Alexander Vedernikov in 2009, 'I always think that it is not so important *when* the theatre opens because the reconstruction is very difficult and complex. Instead, in this situation, the quality of what is going to be done is far more important... I have nothing to expect but a disastrous result.'[15] Vedernikov argued that the theatre was putting bureaucratic interests before artistic ones. This statement resonated with the overall concerns of the artist expressed above. He went as far as to claim that 'it's become clear that the Bolshoi theatre does not possess the slightest traits of an artistic organization.'[16]

The role of Mikhail Shvydkoy, special Envoy, International cultural cooperation, was very crucial. In 2000, he came to the Bolshoi as a Minister of Culture and he realized that the theatre building is in a state of disaster. Only cosmetic repairs were performed since the 1980s when it was deserted. He explains, 'When I was the head of Roskultur, we reported to the President on the need of reconstruction of the Bolshoi theatre. The budget estimate for the reconstruction was 25 billion rubbles in 2011, and further increased to 30 billion.' Because of the high budget, the project was revised several times and it took some time before the renovation started. Commenting on the difficulties of the renovation, Shvydkoy stated, 'The building was exhausting: the walls had vertical cracks. The entire theatre was actually held on this plaster. There was a high probability that the building will simply collapse in the process of reconstruction. I had to spend the extra money to put special temporary pilings that supported the theatre.'[17] It was also found out that under the parquet the wood panel was replaced by a concrete slab, perhaps during previous processes of renovation. Speaking on behalf of the building, as he did Shvydkoy offered a number of adjustments, such as the use of papier-mâché. All the boxes were made of papier-mâché. Papier-mâché was there originally for the project because 'it is sonically better than wood'.[18] Instead of

---

[15] http://content.time.com/time/arts/article/0,8599,1910930,00.html#ixzz2dSdiQOVn
[16] *Guardian* (March 2011).
[17] http://www.apbspeakersinternational.com/speaker/mikhail-shvydkoy downloaded 10 September 2013.
[18] http://teamuz.ru/publication/mixail-shvydkoj-vosem-istorij-o-bolshom-teatre/

preventing all renovation activities, an attempt was made to regulate them by way of these local adjustments. By introducing different materials, Shvydkoy was able to make the crowds aware of the impact of some big interventions on the building fabric, without resorting to political speeches. Because this solution was not generated by big politics it met little resistance and, in the attempt to devise a better use of the building, an agreement was reached. This example illustrates that renovation cannot be reduced to simple interventions. As the process of renovation unfolded, all these actors interacted with the building and weaved a web of connections that might hurt or repair its balance. Thus they craft different renovation adjustments. Instead of acting 'against' or for a bigger budget; against and for the original fabric of the building, against radical interventions and for preservation of the nineteenth-century glory of the theatre in a blatantly political militant way, Shvydkoy acted 'from within', raising awareness of the disastrous state of the building, and offering new local adjustments that would craft the building more adequately.

The press actively followed the debate too. Katerina Novikova, Bolshoi theatre spokeswoman and press secretary, was a key voice in the controversy. The Bolshoi theatre's management has distanced itself from the allegation by stating that 'the money set aside for reconstruction did not go through the Bolshoi theatre.'[19] Novikova also confirmed on behalf of Bolshoi's management that all financial issues were handled by the agency, which was created by the Culture Ministry. Yet, she did not comment on the quality of the building renovation. Another important media figure was Nikolai Uskov, Editor of Snob. Commenting on the attack on Mr Filin, he stated in *New York Times* that 'what once seemed like rumours and intrigue, now, after the tragedy with Filin, has moved into the territory of a moral imperative.'[20] The renovation was qualified as an experiment and the danger for Uskov was that 'the Bolshoi is turning away from our traditions. In our mentality, turning away from the Bolshoi's tradition is like betraying your homeland: it is a synonym of betrayal.'[21] Another Moscow-based journalist, Tina Kandelaki, voiced her concerns about the quality of the renovation, and in particular the cracks in the walls. In November 2012, she posted photos taken in the theatre by her business partner, who went to a show. The photographs exposed cracks in the walls and crooked painted with gold paint plastic instead of gold leaf. If some politicians like Shvydkoy spoke from 'within' building renovation, attempting to grasp the specific rhythm of the building variability, the media moved the balance back towards 'perspectival objectivity'.

Who spoke on behalf of the building?

Many actors talked *about* the building and expressed views *about* the renovation commenting on the different aspects of the scandal: corruption, chaos, artists' rivalry, struggle for the leadership and mistrust of authority. Only the renovators,

---

[19] http://www.nydailynews.com/news/world/suspect-detained-acid-attack-bolshoi-director-article-1.1279585
[20] http://www.nytimes.com/2013/02/07/arts/dance/bolshoi-ballet-figures-swap-accusations-in-interviews.html?_r=0
[21] Ibid.

some architectural historians and museum professionals praised the renovation and continued to speak, as Shvydkoy did, on behalf of the building. Olga Sviblova, director of Moscow's multimedia art museum commended the renovation of the new theatre by saying, 'I think there is a delight in the details here that is an indicator of culture. This is what was lost in the Soviet time,' and she went, 'You cannot understand how happy it makes me unless you saw how it was before.'[22] At times more than 1000 restorers were working at Bolshoi; they continued work until 2011 right until the opening of the theatre. They were the ones who talked on behalf of the building and the challenges of renovation from 'within'; they situated themselves in the variability of the object. The objects that populated the interior happened to have many complex layers inherent to the architecture of the Renaissance, Baroque and Rococo.

Vera Babich, expert in polimont gilding, and her practice were commissioned for the job. The time constraints were enormous: they had to start the interior renovation whilst major building work was still underway. A lot of time was spent on cleaning up and removing dust. Little tents were used to stabilize the temperature and protect the objects that were undergoing gilding and other transformations. At the end of 2009, restorers from Buro Vera Babich began work on the decor of the auditorium of Bolshoi theatre. They were expected to recreate the acoustics of the original main scene, so they began to restore the decoration of papier-mâché.[23] The legendary acoustics of Bolshoi theatre, they argued, would depend on this tiny detail: the quality of the papier-mâché. Like a tree, papier-mâché, has a cellulose base and does not burst of small deformations, which are inevitable in the theatre (for instance due to sound vibrations of some musical instruments). The restoration of details of papier-mâché in the theatre was a very difficult job as it implied clearing and restoration of lost parts of the décor following a technology that is eighteen to nineteen centuries old. It was necessary to remove the six layers of paint to get to the very first original layer. The restoration finishing touch was applied cautiously so as to avoid distorting the original appearance of the mouldings. Some lost items during previous restorations were replaced with inserts made of gypsum.

The gold surfaces and interiors in Bolshoi were also carefully restored. Let us depict a typical scene of renovation: On a four-foot scaffolding, a gilder sits on the side of her hip, her knees and feet tucked in at her side. She uses her finger to spread petroleum jelly on the back of her hand. She picks up a fanned brush made of squirrel tail hair and brushes it over the thin layer of petroleum before touching the top of the brush to a thin leaf of gold resting on a suede pillow. When she picks up the gold leaf, it shivers. The tiny, lustrous square is hand-hammered so thin that light shines through it. It is a tenth of the thickness of a spider's silk. It will cling to every crease of a fingerprint on an oily finger. 'Rub it between your fingers and it disappears. But place it on moulding that has been prepped with clay and egg and a swipe of distilled alcohol like vodka, and the frail leaf bonds to it, creating the illusion of solid gold', explained Vera Babich,

[22] http://www.nytimes.com/2011/10/29/world/europe/joy-and-nostalgia-in-moscow-as-bolshoi-theater-reopens.html
[23] http://www.vera-babich.ru/news/zolochenie-bolshogo-teatra.html

'No golden paint will have such a noble effect, such a bright colour. Over time, gold paint darkens and never achieves the same look.'

Referring to traditional gilding techniques little used during Soviet era, reintroduced by her father, Babich explained further the secret of the glowing gold surfaces and interiors of Bolshoi. Few people have mastered this technique: it consists in moistening the surface with vodka after applying primer, then applying the gold leaf. It takes a lot of work and delicate touch, but once it's completed the ornaments will gleam for two to three centuries. 'The technique is time-consuming', Babich elaborated, 'You have to do it all by hand. Gold leaf has to be rolled till it is very, very thin. It's a bit wrinkly but that doesn't matter. When it is applied it will be completely smooth. And then we polish it till it shines like a mirror.'[24] Commenting on the techniques and the intensity of the process, Babich stated: 'Restoring the Bolshoi, I feel I have reconnected with the art form'; 'you only get a job like this once in thirty or forty years. Basically once in a lifetime.'[25] Discussing the repair of the chandelier, the restorer Yevgeni Vassilev, argued, 'this chandelier has been hanging here for centuries. It is a symbol of Bolshoi theatre, just like the sculpture on the front'. On the website of Buro Vera Babich, we can see videos of training sessions in Russian, where we witness her teaching this ancient technique to more restorers. Babich personally trained sixty of the workers who were involved in the Bolshoi theatre restoration, including her two daughters. She recalled how difficult it was to learn to master the technique: 'my father was a gilder and took me to his projects. I didn't have to study – he taught me to gild and polish on every job. Not everyone catches on so easily. Sometimes it takes two years just to learn how to prep the moulding'.[26]

Commenting on the technical aspects of the building, art historian Grigory Revzin stated, 'It turns out, that a square meter in the Bolshoi theatre costs almost ten times more than its European analogues...Yet it still can't be named the most high-tech, cutting-edge or the biggest in the world'.[27] The building agencies and contractors formed another powerful group of actors commenting on the renovation. PO Teplotekhnik were hired in 2005 by federal reconstruction agency and funded by the culture ministry; they worked on the project for six years. The involvement of company ZAO Kurortproekt turned out to be very controversial. It was argued that 'ZAO Kurortproekt was paid three times for the same work at a time when the Kremlin was trying to crack down on corruption.' The construction firm Summa Group, best known for building oil pipelines and cargo ports, was another actor in the controversy. As representative contractor of Bolshoi's reconstruction, they endorsed the renovation quality. Their spokesman Mikhail Sidorov stated, 'Now we've returned to the theatre's original 19th-century acoustics.' The theatre has gained a second stage with a sound-reflecting floor coating, specifically designed for opera, and a ballet stage returned to its once-famous four-degree angle that is able to absorb impact, making jumping safer for dancers. 'This was developed to extend dancers' lives, to

---

[24] http://www.youtube.com/watch?v=05qSN5uX69M
[25] Ibid.
[26] http://www.hemispheresmagazine.com/2011/09/01/dance-revolution/
[27] BFM.ru.

prevent their legs from breaking into pieces.'[28] In their evaluations of the renovation, the construction companies responded to the artists' concerns: the safety of the new stage and the quality of the acoustics, arguing that 'Bolshoi has now been returned to its former glory'.[29]

The political effects of buildings' vibrancy

Both conservatives and modernists pretend to speak on behalf of old buildings in disputes over building conservation and renovation (Strike 1994). Yet, in many cases they ignore the agency of buildings and fail to consider the variety of other entities that are being propelled on the scenes of renovation and preservation. At the same time, our way to tackle buildings' agency differed from the interpretation of constructivist studies, which consider agency as 'what returns to people when the building is narrated and reinterpreted – discursively made anew' (Gieryn 2002) and by so doing constructs identities and structures political relationships. Accounting the multiplicity of human and non-human actors that partake in renovation, I tackled the dynamics of the renovation process of the *Alte Aula* in Vienna and I traced the networks of renovation surrounding Bolshoi theatre in Moscow that revealed the repertoire of actions of buildings-in-renovation: their docility, obedience, but also counter-actions and recalcitrance. This vibrancy of buildings made impossible for them to engage in the simple register of the reflectionist regime (to embody and reflect big politics) or the social constructivist regime (to shape identities and construct political relationships). Challenging the process of renovation and the building's capacity to act led us to redefine the political valence of architecture.

The study of the two buildings in process of renovation challenges the traditional substantialistic understanding of buildings as permanent and timeless entities. Exploring the political relevance of renovation, I illustrated here that renovating is not about transforming a passive and subservient object; it rather offers an experimental situation in which one can witness the building capacity to manifest itself as disobedient as possible to the protocol of renovation, to resist the attempts of control and to 'surprise' its makers; that is, to protest and enact disagreement, to become political. In situations of renovation, buildings manifest themselves as complex agents that skilfully redistribute the agency among human and non-human participants in renovation, provoke contextual mutations, transform social meanings and by reshaping the alliances modify the political valence of architecture. Instead of manifesting themselves as entities that stand and endure with time, Bolshoi theatre and the *Alte Aula* buildings appeared as buildings-in-becoming.

Speaking of these buildings *tout court* without inspecting the images of their renovation, the engineers' and gilders' techniques, the online traces of controversies,

---

[28] http://online.wsj.com/article/SB10001424053111903392904576512761179504804.html#ixzz2dqakI9yf
[29] http://news.sky.com/story/894705/curtain-comes-back-up-on-world-famous-bolshoi

the disputes in design meetings, the surprises of frescos or gold leafs, will require bracketing all practicalities. This will make the buildings appear in isolation from the practices in which they are enacted, and will place them within the larger frameworks of Soviet, Russian or Viennese politics. Instead, if we focus on the practicalities of enacting a building, it becomes clear that it is no longer possible to embrace a critical or iconic discourse; it is not possible to bring big politics as an explanation of fresco restoration or gilding techniques. Tracing renovation we witness that the variability is located in the object itself: *in* the process of renovating the Bolshoi theatre or the *Alte Aula* architects and renovators engage in adjusting and renegotiating the relations between historical fabric, modern technologies, Austrian or Soviet Politics, briefs, regulations, the city fabric, and the protests of various civic groups.

Following renovation in the making reveals that the chief source of variability shifts from the multiple viewpoints and variable subjectivities towards the reality of the built object, and that is an 'aperspectival objectivity'. In renovation, the building itself comes into being with the practices in which it is manipulated. And since the object of manipulating tends to differ from one practice to another, reality multiplies. The architects, the planners, the renovators, the crowds, the technologies of preservation: all of them are more than one. More than singular. More than unique. This triggers the question of how they are related. That is a question of politics.

As an experimental situation, renovation allows witnessing the objectivity of an old building that does not refer to any specific quality of its building fabric, to any *Originalsubstanz,* as stated by traditional conservation studies. Instead, it relies on the participation of an actor, which has been rendered 'able' to object to what is told about it in the history archives, and counter-reacts to what is done on its fabric in a series of interventions. Renovation provides a unique situation in which buildings can flip-flop their agency, thus making shambles of architects' and clients' attempts to fully control and modify them according to their scenario. This allows us to reassess the political dimension of the sites of renovation.

Circumventing the dualism that opposes the active and the passive will imply taking seriously the vitality of buildings-in-renovation, and the flexibility of spatial forms while accounting for the political. Buildings-in-renovation appear here as active form. Considering the variability of buildings leads us also to take into account the vibrancy of matter (Bennett 2010) and the political production of vibrancy (Bartolini 2015). Analysing renovation processes implies an understanding of buildings as entities whose inherent materiality does not do anything in its solid state. Buildings are rather lively in a number of ways and it is essential to understand the political effects of their vibrancy; to question how materials and people passing through a building and taking part in renovation get transformed and how their interactions mediated by the building create vibrancy.

Although the two cases are very different and the dynamics of renovation has been traced with different methods and in different time spans, what remains the same is the fact that there is a multiplicity that stays the same. Renovation attends to the multiplicity of a building. No planner, no renovator is singular; no fresco and no building foundation react in the same way; all their actions vary according to the steps in renovation. As long as the practicalities of enacting the building are kept unbracketed, the varieties of Bolshoi theatre or the *Alte Aula* multiply. They cannot be removed from the practices that sustain them; their reality is multiple; and if it's multiple, it is also political. As we know, 'ontologies are brought into being, sustained, or allowed to wither away in common, day-to-day, socio-material practices' (Mol 2002: 6). The renovation ontologies inform and are informed by the bodies of renovators, planners, architects, designers and builders, their visualization and scaling devices, the frescos and the golden leafs. All of these; all at once; all in tension. Following renovation, the buildings of Bolshoi theatre and the *Alte Aula* appear to be more than one – without being fragmented into many, or else, pluralist. They are not the outcome of different individual subjective perspectives and interpretations. Both Bolshoi theatre and the *Alte Aula* can be described as a part of the renovation practices and the debates surrounding the renovation in which they are enacted. Bolshoi revealed various aspects in renovation, but at the end it was one. Its reality was varied. And so was the *Alte Aula* in Vienna.

7

Urban Publics: The Fifth Way of Becoming Political

After we followed how images and models are produced in the architectural office (Chapter 4) and how they travel outside the architectural practice and get modified, juggled, revised, retouched and negotiated on construction sites and building renovation locales (Chapters 5 and 6), the next step will take us to trace how they start affecting different interested parties, prompting reactions and activating groupings; how people gradually enrol in larger groups that eventually become design 'publics' (Iveson 2007). If we have witnessed earlier how visuals become political sites, here we will see how they get displayed, staged and arranged in different presentational set-ups to be able to generate political effects. Architectural presentations provide another site where to explore the political dimension of design and the process of formation of urban publics. They encapsulate an experimental form of public action in contemporary societies.

I will follow here three different formats of architectural presentations and will account for the specific techniques used by architects to re-enact buildings and urban concepts in public and make arguments of civic importance. I will explore the technical and rhetorical modalities, the economy of persuasion, the cognitive and visual languages of these presentations and their material dimensions. This will allow me to analyse the new forms of experimenting and creating public 'arenas' with architectural means as spaces specifically designed to showcase design related events; spaces where architects use persuasive techniques to make participants in presentations witness a building, share reactions, but also challenge design knowledge and subvert architectural practices. The analysis is based on the study of three architects: Andrés Perea in Madrid, Rem Koolhaas in Rotterdam and Moshe Safdie in Singapore. The chapter also questions the role of architects as political actors in contemporary technological societies and reflects on the boundaries between the expertise of architects and non-architects. Fostering participation and engaging participants in design to gradually form publics is the fifth way for architecture to become political.

The capture of publics

Ensnared in complex networks, architects appear as public figures on various experimental 'arenas' of design – architectural presentations, exhibitions, competitions, press conferences, blogs and internet forums – to present a building and demonstrate it *to* a public. There, buildings, city plans, urban issues and design concepts are being explained with, and redefined according to a number of concerns of clients, neighbours, urban activists and communities affected by design.

It is commonly considered that architectural presentations are demonstrations, which similar to demos in technology, consist of exhibiting an object (building, master plan) in front of a chosen audience, following a carefully elaborated scenario. But unlike technology demos used to show the feasibility of a technological approach or the running of a prototype or product (Rosental 2003), architectural demos tackle uncertain objects and knowledge that often deviate from set plans and scenarios. Architectural presentations rely on explicitation and are related to the cognitive potential of the presentational setting. Like other forms of demonstration, presentations in architecture mix technologies of proof and exhibition of practices, and include also experiment and 'display of virtuosity' (Collins 1988). By engaging different types of participants and larger groupings, they bring architecture into democracy (Callon et al. 2001; Latour 2004a); they reaffirm the importance of architects as crucial political agents in contemporary societies.

Previous studies focused on the grammar and the cognitive style of the PowerPoint presentations of architects. Stark and Paravel, for instance, analysed the seven architectural finalists in the Innovative Design Study for the World Trade Centre and explored the technical and rhetorical modalities of digital demonstrations as well as the cognitive styles of computer-assisted argumentation of architects in search of successful persuasive techniques to convince a variety of publics (Stark and Paravel 2008). Yet, the economy of persuasion of the architectural presentation does not rely simply on the digital morphology of PowerPoint (Tufte 2006). The architectural presentation in its typical forms seldom limits its repertoire to digital demonstration or computer-assisted presentation, especially in case of presenting a project-in-progress or an architectural concept that is not public yet. Its cognitive repertoire includes a variety of media, objects and spatial techniques, as well as timing and spacing devices. Such a heterogeneous setting yields investigation for two reasons.

First, by designing a presentation architects create a specific space that is meant to facilitate reflection on space and displays techniques for addressing a number of architectural issues. That is, a setting that should be cognitively adjusted to the particular task of questioning architecture. If in their routine practices designers often conceive program-driven spaces, only in the process of designing presentations they deal with the difficult cognitive and political task of envisaging an issue-oriented space, in which the building is not reduced anymore to program, but is instead explained with, and redefined according to, a number of issues and concerns (of potential users, of environmental groups, of clients with changings demands, of communities of neighbours). Investigating the techniques for designing an issue-constituted space will also shed light on the practical tools architects mobilize to organize its publics.

Second, an architectural demonstration/presentation does not simply imply a way of enrolling people in a project or addressing a previously shaped entity (audience or group). Instead, presenting in architecture implies a focus on the potential of objects or materials to actively contribute to mediating publics in practice. In presentations, the properties of a building-to-be are shown as emanating from, but also detachable from the materiality and the spatial topography of the settings, from their distinctive cognitive and visual repertoire, technical and rhetorical modalities. Design practitioners rely on different techniques to affect and sensibilize their publics by the specific material arrangements of the objects they display, their modes of selection, modalities of action and performances; the concrete spatial topography of the presentational setting – dimensions, spatial dispositions, distances and proximities among speakers, objects and material arrangements – is vital for the success of the presentation. In situations of demonstrating the ability of an architectural project to address issues of public importance, architects rely on the capacities of things to facilitate, inform and organize engagement.

The notion of 'public presentation/demonstration' refers to the process of formation of a particular type of public. If the empirical interest in the materials, technologies and settings of public engagement is closely linked to the wider 'object turn' in social, cultural and political theory (Knorr-Cetina 1997; Latour 2005b; Lash and Lury 2007), architectural theory still deals with an old-fashioned Aristotelian notion of public as marked by inaction, as a 'passive mass'. The classic idea, again Aristotelian, that participation in public affairs requires social actors to disengage themselves from their everyday material concerns and take part in public debate cannot be sustained any longer. Yet, if we follow how architects plan, organize and stage presentations, as a part of their daily design work, we can begin to witness the mechanics of formation of publics, and account for the material dimension of political participation. In architecture, we deal with publics that organize by material means, with 'material publics' (Marres 2012). Following architectural presentations we will stand away from a notion of 'public demonstration' as a device for the enrolment of otherwise disengaged publics, towards an analysis of the difference that particular architectural objects (models, drawings, PowerPoints and videos) and specific set-ups make to the constitution of urban publics. Thus, challenging the traditional preconceptions of publics in architecture as pre-established, well-structured and predictable groupings of users and communities, this chapter will further the understanding of how a public can be made with architectural means.

The ethnographic study of three presentational set-ups will guide us to explore here the mechanisms of public-making unfolded in presentations. Through careful comparison of different settings, I will analyse the distinctive techniques developed by architects to bring democracy into the realm of embodied experience. In presentations, the architectural object is not simply taken from within the architectural practice and abruptly displaced into a distant public realm, 'unveiled' to a previously disengaged and ignorant public 'out there' who is meant to react to or engage with it. Instead, public engagement has a socio-material situatedness that begins at the very level of design practice and gradually enrols more participants. My aim here is to trace how design practitioners assisted by different material and spatial machineries make people engage with or feel concerned by numerous thorny issues of design. I ask: 'What capacities to act are performed in presentational settings?'

'How do design presentations "engage" people?' 'How do different presentational repertoires and practices transform experiences and affect human trajectories?' 'How do the various experiences and performances coexist?' Investigating the techniques of staging the design presentations as sites of political action and the events they enact will shed light on the practical tools mobilized by practitioners to affect people in a transformative way and to redefine the modalities of experimental forms of public action.

Presentational displays and the grasp of reality

In situations of presentations, the architect can be compared to a warrior; the presentational 'arena' would become a battlefield. The skilful architect just like the skilful warrior invests his strategic thinking towards minimizing 'armed engagement'; he makes sure that everything is played out at early stage in the determination of events when dispositions and manoeuvres can be adjusted, and special tactics devised. Skill in warfare depends on the 'potential born of disposition', or *shi*, an important concept used to explain a different strategic thinking in warfare. As disposition *shi* 'consists in organizing circumstances in such a way as to derive profit from them' (Jullien 1999: 32). Decisive and direct confrontation in battle is central to modern European concept of war; there are means for achieving predetermined end. If the Greeks gave priority to the immediate use of forces, to confrontation and heavily armed infantry, the Chinese mastered the art of manoeuvres and tactics, harassment and evasion and their strategy aimed at using every possible means to influence the potential inherent in the forces at play even before the actual engagement, so that the engagement would never constitute the decisive moment, which always involves risk. War was conceived for the Chinese from the perspective of propensity and a shaping of effect; the notions of means and end were replaced by the notions of a set-up and its efficacy. Through *shi*, whatever stems from the circumstances and seems to elude one's initial calculations naturally finds itself again contained by them. The disposition that generates the potential in a battle includes the configuration of the lay of the land, the terrain, the character of the land, the elevation, the climate, the number of troops and their dispersion in space. The entire situation can play a negative or positive role on the troops.

A good general, like a good architect, manages with the help of *shi* to achieve maximum effect with minimum effort. Disposition includes the particular arrangement of objects as well as the situation at hand. It is effective and renewable; it is flexible. Through *shi* one can get a grip on the process of realty. Thus, the term *shi* will designate here the configuration of power relations in the same way as it denotes the strategic set-up of objects, distances and viewing positions in a presentational setting. Reminiscent to the disposition that generates the potential in a battle, the material arrangement of architectural presentations, the dimensions and the character of the room, the display of objects and the positions of the viewers according to these objects, in brief, the whole situation can exert a positive or negative impact on the efficacy of the presentation. The question of the architectural display is how to exploit strategically the potential born of disposition so as to be able to win a battle before it had even started? According to the variability of the display, the architectural presentations will have different efficacies and architects, just like warriors, will manage getting a grip on the reality in different ways.

Scenes of action: architectural mechanics of the political

Three settings will be analysed to witness how architects present buildings and architectural concepts and to retrace the formation of architectural publics. Using an ANT-inspired approach to the architectural presentation to shed light on the processes of gaining-and-presenting knowledge in architecture, I will depict three situations following both the human actors and the variety of non-humans that gather around the architectural objects in situations of presentations, accounting their reactions, their ways of engaging with the objects, the techniques for collecting reactions and integrating them into design.

The first presentation is staged in the Office for Metropolitan Architecture of Rem Koolhaas in Rotterdam in 2001. We witness an office presentation of the proposal for the extension of the Whitney Museum of American Art in New York (the NEWhitney). The building concept is work-in-progress and as such is a non-stabilized entity; architects are struggling to accommodate and reconcile numerous contradictory demands. The presentation happens in-house and is afforded, mediated and facilitated by the ample and versatile materiality of the office foam environment; a number of people who might be potentially interested in the building are invited; we witness the formation of a proto-public. The building in this presentation is captured in the process of becoming public.

The second presentation takes place in Madrid in 2005. It is a public presentation of the Spanish architect Andrés Perea of his proposal for the *Palacio de Congresos, Ciudad de Leon*. Perea is one of the finalists in an international competition won by Daniel Perraut. The building is a quasi-stabilized entity as the potential questions and concerns of the audience cannot influence back the design. Yet, the architect and the audience can communicate. The presentation is staged in a neutral space, a lecture room, and no connections with the practice and the design approach of the architect are established. I analyse the presentation and I study additionally the practice of Perea. The proposal is presented to an already structured audience with specific expectations and knowledge about it.

The third presentation is drawn from a presentational video of the Marian Bay Integrated Resort project of Moshe Safdie in Singapore from 2006. It presents its conceptual design, but also situates the project within the larger context of Singapore and Asian green architecture. The concept is clear and stabilized; it is not open for discussion to a public. Safdie talks and draws; but we also see the investors and developers presenting the ambitions of the project. The concept is stable; there are no 'unknowns'. The audience is 'out there', anonymous, invisible.

If the three settings are different it is not because the first one is staged in Rotterdam, the second one in Madrid and the third one in Boston and Singapore; nor is it because we deal with three different architectural styles and refer to dissimilar moments in the trajectory of a design project. Instead, these settings display differently what it means to present in architecture for they embrace a different rhetoric, imply individual cognitive repertoires that are inseparable from their material dimensions; as socio-material arrangements these presentations engage humans (architects, developers, investors, potential users) and non-humans (models, visuals, books, materials) in a distinctive spatial topography that makes possible to enact an architectural event with a variable intensity. To redescribe these three settings, I draw on a variety of sources: conversations among architects at work in the process of planning and preparing a presentation; in-depth interviews with architects and participants in the presentations, video footage and images; presentational materials: books, diagrams, photo documents, models and material samples. In the three scenes, I will trace three distinctive ontological dynamics of the formation of publics and how they are shaped according to the problematic mode of a specific design issue.

Scene one: In the midst of models

In a cold and hazy February afternoon in Rotterdam architects from the Whitney team get together on the ground floor and frantically start moving models and images to the mezzanine. Rem has invited a number of people in the office for a presentation of the NEWhitney project. I studied OMA ethnographically for two years and I have published on a number of their projects (Yaneva 2009a,b). I had access to the OMA and AMO archives, and I had the chance to conduct numerous interviews with architects from the practice and to follow and document visually different types of presentations in the office. And here I am again going back to this material, and that very first presentation of an OMA project witnessed in the misty February of 2002. The presentation begins with a visit of the office; the master architect 'walks and talks' and invites the guests to follow him. The invited participants are given the opportunity to see other projects OMA is currently developing; they witness the office energetic process of making and can situate the specific project they are invited to review within the larger net of ongoing office activities. They are also offered the possibility to see tables of models that display the painstaking process of experimentation and showcase the office creativity. There is not just an expectation to theatrically impress and affect a previously constituted group – a public. The presentational walks in the office have a different strategy for making the participants form an opinion, take a stance and make them constitute as a group. The walk is supposed to introduce and familiarize the guests with the type of material practices developed at OMA. As they stroll, handle models on various tables, inspect drawings and chat to architects from the different project teams, their actions are finely mediated by all these objects and tools of architecture making; they find themselves organized by materials and physical arrangements, that is, they form a proto-public of design.

Before we witness the presentation and the reactions of the guests, let us rewind the film: a few days earlier, I followed the architects who prepared the presentation. When planning the office presentation, architects from OMA pay equal attention to its format, timing, location, physical décor, spatial setting and even the architecture of the room where the presentation will take place. In other words, the disposition, the *shi* plays an important role in the planning of presentations. I follow the architects when preparing a panel for the Landmarks Commission in New York; they need to know ahead of time what the size of the room is, how many people will be viewing the projects, what will be the spatial configuration of the setting. They also consider very precisely the design of the presentational space: whether it is going to be a round-table presentation, which will allow them to show models of a particular size, or a podium presentation where the panels will be more visible.

The number of people attending the presentation, the scale of it, the time needed to set up and to clear up, the disposition of the actors and the entire physical spatial setting in which the building is presented – all these make a difference to the understanding of the architectural project. In the preparation meetings, the materials are discussed along with the presentation scenario, the elements of the building and its various meanings. Thinking about the building and how to present it – with what kind of materials and what strategy – are inseparable parts of a rhetorical scenario intended to draw the attention of a client or a public. Yet the preparations do not involve the shaping up of a repertoire of arguments and counterarguments. Instead, designers are concerned with the specific architecture of the space where a discussion about architecture will take place; they carefully rethink the details of the space in which space is conceptualized and made emergent for others. The reason for this is that, 'most of the viewers are not even able to appreciate an architectural project', explains Erez Ella, an experienced architect from the Whitney team. And he goes, 'they are just not able *to see it*'.

> I am sure they are not going to appreciate it. Even judging by the time that is given to us for the meeting – 30 min, this means, they will not be able to understand the project. Even if I am an architect and I am looking at that building and somebody tries to explain it to me in 30 min, it would be hard for me to understand the project. (Interview with Erez Ella, 5 September 2002)

Architects do not rely on educating the public, on making them understand or see the building; information plays a minor role in the political space of presenting. They rather think about the appropriate disposition, the 'format', the timing, the spatial arrangements, as well as a multitude of other contextual details; all of them, all together will make the building manifest *in situ*.

The visitors of OMA witness first the display of the CCTV project in Beijing – a headquarter of the TV station in China, still work in progress at the time of that visit (Figure 7.1) and stop for a while on the seventh floor to contemplate it. Let us pause for a moment too and inspect this display together with them.

Figure 7.1 Vertical display of models of the CCTV tower, OMA, Rotterdam (photo by the author).

A multiverse on a table

Commonly such huge model displays are witnessed in architectural exhibitions. Yet, they are typically composed by closed, stabilized models that tend to evacuate the work of artistry, as well as the whole polemics among actors: clients, technical consultants, future users, community, city councils, media and large public. They provide anaesthetized versions of what is an inherently sculptural process. In contrast, an 'open' model shows the variety of, sometimes fuzzy or controversial, concerns, demands, attitudes and expectations implied in the construction of buildings; it acquires more details, more layers, more fields of action. Presented as such to various people – clients and users, connoisseurs and investors – models trigger reactions. The display of CCTV models drifts away from the tendency of installing increasingly collectable and exhibitable models as stabilized architectural objects (Clarisse 1993; Frampton and Kolbowski 1981; Millon and Lampugnani 1994; Schwanzer 1994). Instead, it shows open controversial, unfinished, models-in-progress, models that 'talk' about their 'tribulations' and address specific design issues. Model making is not a simple venture of narrating the reality, be it the sophisticated highly expressive architecture or the banal architectural environments. It is instead a conduit for actively transforming reality by reconciling different aspects of a building-to-be.

In spite of the contemporary architects' fascination with the potential of digitally conceived work, architects from OMA choose to experiment with what could be perceived as an anachronistic form – physical models (Yaneva 2005; Yaneva 2009a). A simple visit in the office shows the omnipresence of scale models in space. Scattered and recollected many times during design process, models always travel together to present the building. Arranged next to each other on the office shelves, staged on the tables of models, distributed in the client's quarters, they all talk about the same building. The presentation we witness (Figure 7.1) puts on display not just *a* model of the CCTV building, but a fanciful variety of models. It is not their singularity, but their multiplicity in connection with many requirements that the OMA guests will witness.

At the very beginning of design process, architects enlist a variety of aspects that have to be 'accommodated' by a model: site location, program, volume, urban fabric, district fragmentation, circulation, mechanicals, zoning envelope, city politics, users' expectations, historical landmarks, building philosophy and community concerns. Some of them are requirements of the client considered as 'givens' for the architects, others are parameters established by architects themselves. What makes model-making a complex process is not simply its painstaking and time-consuming process (Busch 1990; Bonfilio 2000), but the fact that so many constraints and controversial demands are to be taken into account, so many actors are to be assembled and reconciled in a whole. Hence, model making is about bringing all these aspects in a whole new ensemble. As Erez explains, the model should '*show how well it is able to accommodate an almost random number of things;* and that is even more important to show the ability of the scheme to develop a multiplicity of qualities' (interview with Erez Ella, 5 September, 2002). Moreover, the model houses not only different elements, but also discussions and research needed for their definition. It also denotes a particular moment in design process when all these disparate elements are *assembled* together in a new entity. To accommodate them means to take them into account, to house them, to put them and to provide room for them to stay, to embrace them all together. 'Accommodate' points also that the model has enough space for all these elements to reside in it. To define the model as an accommodation, as an assemblage, is also to consider it as a specific agreement among the various actors, which enables them to live together and to compose a common world. That is, models and model-making are inherently political. Modelling is not about imposing a shape over a matter according to certain political, scientific or juridical conventions; imprinting big politics on passive substance. It is about assembling a collection that gradually gets richer, more consistent and consolidated.

Scale models show the composite character of buildings and are intrinsically political entities in which a variety of concerns and requirements are fitted together, and surprisingly disparate, local and conjectural connections, expectations and needs are made visible. A model shows that it is impossible to imagine a new building without taking into account the adjacent buildings, the adoration of their worshippers, the disagreements of their reformers, the busy traffic of the city, the dense network of the districts, the zoning fragmentation, the marks of history, the majesty of the government, the controversies of city politics, the sweet pieties of neighbours' relationships. A model becomes possible only because it can bring together a distinct assembly of parties and weld them all into a new working entity. That is how various types of models take shape: structural, program, circulation models.

A *structural model* of the CCTV building in Beijing talks about a particular method of avoiding the isolation of the traditional high rise by turning four segments into a loop, coupling them in regular intervals to establish a composite stability. It also breaks the pattern of the traditional tower that merely goes up and down at four points, and replaces it by a loop that unites and confronts various elements. It illustrates an agglomeration of concerns of stiffness, redundancy, robustness and torsion capacity.

In the *circulation model* of the Beijing television tower, an additional variety of elements is mobilized to present the same building: the circulation between the two towers braced against each other at a height of 160 m, the distribution of the floor space in the two portions of the building, the mechanical power, the escalators, the view on the city. The model points to that mobilization of elements that are meant to present the circulation logic for flows of visitors, which will trace many circulation paths to and through the space. It shows another aspect of the building by telling us 'look at the circulation model and just imagine you are the tiny red figure on the ground floor; many other visitors like you can be seen within the transparent tissue of the circulation model'. Only visitors and circulation paths through the building are being visualized in red (escalators, elevators and staircases). So, if you are staying down there, how would you go to the top? Many up- and down-movements are rendered visible through the circulation model, pointing 'where' the visitors are allowed to move and how exactly they are meant to traverse the building. 'Where' refers here to the vertical and horizontal relations the travelling trajectory of a visitor is composed of.

Nothing suggests a certain relation between the structural model and the circulation model of the CCTV building, and the many other models on the plinth. How do they relate to the same building? What exactly do they refer to? Aren't they sketching just two distant, lonely and discrepant images of the same? Aren't they related just because the same architectural firm scrawled a signature on them? They are always staged together and travel together to represent the building, but what is it that holds these assemblages together as features of one? What kinds of relations embrace them mutually into a whole?

Looking at the structural model, then at the circulation model, then back at the structural one, nothing suggests a certain relation between them. Something moves from one model to the other and forms a relation of adjacency, and that is what architects rely on in design process and presentation; adjacency is also a way to call their togetherness. Resting as 'neighbours' on the shelves in the office or on plinths and table of models, they remain related in a way that they do not possess common sources and origins; they are not deductible from each other. If an element from the structural assemblage is changed, it will not recall immediately some consequences for the circulation assemblage. Set next to each other *by chance*, having external and accidental connections only, none of them refers to the other for a logical reason, reaching a cause for its existence in it. This points to such a relation between the models that the zoning model cannot be anticipated and conceived out of the circulation model; thus, they remain logically ignorant – they stand for themselves.

There is no way to get out of the structural model without getting into the site model or the circulation model; the structural model prolongs and completes the site model, the circulation model extends the programmatic one. That is why all models sharing the official solemnity of the tables of models and plinths are continuous. One leads to the other, borders it, prolongs it and passes to it without requiring necessary interrelations. The fabrication of the circulation model is independent from the site model production; the generation of the structural model has no necessary causal relationship with the conception of the programmatic model. However, once installed next to each other they tangle together to shape the building. Being mutually adjacent, or contiguous, these models find themselves associated with each other. Every new model comes to the 'table of models' as a graft of a tree, to form a branch of it to redefine the whole tree; that is how the apparent disorder on the table of models of the NEWhitney or the plinth with models of the CCTV can be considered as a particular order holding the simultaneously generated versions of the building.

It is the absence of dependences and causal relationships among the elements of the collection of models that makes them contiguous, adjacent. Since no model is the first 'original' prototype of the building, they find themselves not in a relationship of time succession, but rather in a relationship of nextness. On the tables of models, we see no predecessors and successors, but neighbours. Not mutually dependent on each other, but *associated* in order to happen or exist, they meet and touch each other; there is nothing behind their here-and-now presence. They all form an additive entity, that is, a plurality. Nothing suggests that they are meant to present the same building. Nothing suggests how many models will come to be *added*, and how they all together will shape a building. The circulation model will not tend to replace or repeat the structural one; so it comes to be added externally to it, then to the other models – programmatic, site, conceptual models – thus, sharing a quiet and uncontroversial nextness. At the same time, it might vanish from the table or plinth of models without the rest of them having to change. Future models are just attached to the models presented there without depending or demanding a strict generic relationship with them.

Following the different setting of models and their *mise en scène* for clients and visitors, we can argue that there is no strict direction towards a terminus or completion of this particular process of assembling the building; instead, there is a cumulative move of adjoining, setting and readjusting, staging and restaging, displacing, bringing together and accumulating models in a way that a building comes through. When the circulation model is added to the structural model sitting on the table along with many other models, samples and options, it means that it is brought in adjacency with other entities to increase, complete or improve the assembly in a way that the building refers to all of them; it is composed by a 'range of starting points'. Each of these models says more, different things add up – programme relationships, entrance conditions, circulation trajectories, shading requirements; various aspects come to be collected in a way that it becomes difficult to count, and encounter through the process, the number of things in connection that have to be physically organized as a building, the actors whose opinions and disagreements have been reconciled. A small model of the Chinese television has to 'accommodate' 500 m² foot gravity-defying trapezoidal loop, ambitions to build a headquarter of the Chinese flagship, state-controlled television network, fibre optics, structural redundancy, architects aspiration to redefine the skyscraper, new patents for broadcasting media, Chinese urban explosion and the shift that the country is undergoing by its entry in the World Trade Organization. All issues and scenarios are installed on the table of models, standing together to sum up the range of potentials and possibilities for the building to happen. By gathering all these models together architects also assemble requirements of new wireless technologies, and digital compression coalesce, stiffness and torsion capacity, resistance to windstorms and earthquakes, Chinese modernization patents, globalization and communist politics. That is why to show the building again, we need to recollect it – to displace many models from the working table to the presentation table, from Beijing to Rotterdam, and back to Beijing. The building appears in the movement of displaying, reassembling and adjusting many adjacent models again and afresh; it emerges in an effort of collecting various concerns and disagreements into a whole.

One bunch of CCTV models remains for a long time displayed on the working tables and the wooden plinth in the OMA, and that is what our guests have seen in that cold misty Rotterdam February of 2002. Another bunch of models is travelling around the world and are being designed in a tiny workshop in Beijing, preparing a presentation for China's political leaders to convince them that the building would actually stand up. Thus, the fact that two different collections of models present the building in two opposite parts of the world shows that neither logical dependences nor internal and deliberate connections are maintained within the assembly of models. They are not parts of a whole, related in a system, a system that would make them interdependent and affecting each other; a system, in which the whole determines the parts and the parts explain the whole. Nor are they particles of a mere aggregate shaped by mathematical nextness only, in which the adjacent models each contain their boundary and stand peacefully next to each other. Every gathering of models can travel to present the building, assembling and accumulating different figures of it. No logical identity, inner fitness or coercive sequence can link the models from the Rotterdam assortment of the building or the ones from its Beijing setting. Their relations are conjunctive rather than connective, their tie is that of sharing a common time and space, their form – a collection rather than a system.

That is why all models travel together and share on the table of models a quiet and well-meaning neighbourness. The building never derives from one definite and huge realistic model of the whole, from *a* universe. Instead, a building comes from *many* requirements, issues, claims, considerations and potentials; that is, a dissipative entropic entity. It derives from a multiplicity of models that are all *additive*: their adventurous relations obtain the building. The CCTV tower now, as seen in this office presentation four years before it was built as a skyscraper in Beijing, is a stabilized gathering of few models, tentatively adjusted together and arranged in a whole setting; each of them presents it, each of them contains it, and only through their collection the building exists. The CCTV building only has a being as it enters in some way into

Urban Publics: The Fifth Way of Becoming Political   145

the being of its various scale models as different assemblages of concerns. It is not outside its models, a reality to come through anticipation or mirror projection; it is rather coalescent and conterminous with them. A building, as witnessed in office presentations, is an assembly of assemblages, pluralistically constituted, genuinely additive, marked by manyness. A building is a 'multiverse'.

After contemplating the CCTV model display, the small group of visitors heads up to the mezzanine, where as usual designers from OMA have put on display a fanciful variety of models in the middle of the office, all staged on a huge table, and surrounded by large printouts. Here one can witness a typical office presentation (Figure 7.2). The people around Koolhaas are curators and artists, invited to evaluate the proposal for the NEWhitney. He starts by discussing museum extensions at large: 'I am very curious to see what you think about the notion of museum, and museum extension. We are going to work on it now.' Then he expands and talks at large about big politics, Colin Powell, 11th September and how this had an impact on museum projects. He notes, 'Even columns are seen as threat now' (...) 'They [Americans] don't want to build in an American way any longer.' Elaborating more on a number of current projects of OMA in the United States – the LACMA in Los Angeles, the NEWhitney

Figure 7.2 Rem Koolhaas presents a project in OMA, Rotterdam (photo by the author).

in New York, the Guggenheim museum in Las Vegas, the gallery in Lehmann Maupin Gallery in New York – he goes 'these projects are important because we have to witness what is going to happen to American artists now'. Then, the guests stop in front of the LACMA table of models and Rem tells them how 11th September has had an impact on this project as well. The artists get fascinated by the transparent roof; they discuss at large the possibility to make clouds and different lights so as to create special effects and suitable interiors for the specific exhibition projects. One of the artists takes the roof of the large-scale LACMA model and starts discussing the flexibility of lighting and special effects. They finally move to the NEWhitney table and gather all around it; the discussion on the NEWhitney internal display and lighting begins. Rem goes back to a number of other projects of recent extensions: 'Nothing is like what it is used to be in the Tate' he says.

> The question is what is the space and how the space is done. There is something about the circulation, some mixture of modernist labyrinth and classic display. I cannot define it, but there is something wrong with the space (…) The same thing happened to the Centre Georges Pompidou. I remember at the beginning the display in Pompidou was so beautiful, and then something happened when it got reopened. (Field notes from the architectural presentation, 22 February 2002)

The guests listen to Rem's concerns about big politics, they get increasingly intrigued by that 'something' that happened both in the Tate and Pompidou cases; soon they understand that is the real concern of Rem; that is precisely what he wants to avoid in the NEWhitney case. And, that is why they are here, in the OMA. A successful extension, we read between the lines, is one that does not leave us with the feeling that there is 'something wrong' in the museum space; and by extrapolation, one that makes us to wish to persevere the way the space worked prior to any extensions. Curators (among them, a former curator of Dokumenta), artists and museum professionals all listen to Rem, they stand at distance from models and other visuals, but are allowed to approach, touch and change the small collection of models and visuals that the designers have carefully selected so as to expose the building's multiple facets. They are all staged as a coherent composition on the table. There is no public previously formed in an abstract space ready to view the models and evaluate the project. The master architect stands in the middle, close to the table of models, with the presentational book in hands, surrounded by the guests. The visitors all turn around the table of models, touch different parts of the models, ask questions to Rem, Erez or other architects from the Whitney team, look into the presentational books, go back to the models and suggest alternations. There is no particular scrip for Rem; no scenario is followed. It is by going back and forth between models and presentational materials, in a space discursively and materially mediated by the presentational settings, that the visitors start sharing a space and begin voicing concerns that make them gather as a more coherent and constitutive entity, a 'proto-public' (Yaneva 2009a). By 'proto-public' I mean the group that witnesses the coming into being of a new non-stabilized design object, in a tentative and object-centred setting of demonstration/presentation, and actively participates in retouching, adjusting and reshaping the models, thus expressing their concerns about the museum lighting, display and interior design. They do not talk or argue; they just move around, touch and adjust, move and manipulate objects, and this quasi mute but skilful tactile dance of rearranging dispositions is reminiscent to the material dance of agency witnessed in design (Yaneva 2009a). They do not say 'yes' or 'no', argue or agree, vote or protest, they simply stroll around, handle objects and material samples, drawings or printouts; they choose viewing angles; they test lighting conditions, they bend themselves to view the models. And so does Rem and the other architects in their attempts to 'provide answers': they move back and forth between panels and scale models, go back to the presentational books or lean on the table to spend more time adjusting a foam model. To show concern the guests get closer, to express a view they move a model from one spot to another, to make a suggestion they adjust a piece of foam. As their reactions in the form of tactile moves and skilful manipulations of objects on the presentational table are often integrated into the project, they see themselves becoming participants in the making of the building-to-come. We witness the emergence of an object-centred grouping. The participants in the February presentation do not find themselves at the OMA to solve the problems of design in the spirit of a technocratic politics of problem-solving. They are called into being by a specific issue – the lighting and display in the new extension of Whitney museum – and therefore they differ morphologically from the communities of stakeholders to whom the project will be presented commonly constituted out of experts such as Board of Trusties, members of commissions. The tentatively formed proto-public is shaping materially around the issue of lighting, and that is why it is a 'material public' (Marres 2012). 'The material public does not just face an epistemic problem of representation, in which the question is how, *given* a political ontology of "issue affectedness", actors and issues can be adequately represented in the public institutions and language of issue formation. In the pragmatists' account, material publics are faced with an ontological problem: they are problematically entangled in issues' (Marres 2012: 56). Thus, the public shaped materially by the concerns of better lighting display in the new Whitney extension is not just another larger community of stakeholders whose concerns and wishes are to be taken into account. Rather, it is marked by a distinctive problem of relevance – how to achieve a better lighting for the art works in the new extension; how to avoid 'that something' happens to the NEWhitney just as it did in the Tate or Pompidou. This proto-public consists of a few artists and museum professionals, prone to be affected by the lighting display, and they show that they are intimately concerned by these issues; yet they are far from being formal participants in the larger networks and platforms of issue articulation: official presentations to the Mayor of NYC, to the Landmark commission in NYC, to the Board of the Trusties of the Whitney museum.

Scene two: Between panels and screen

The second case provides us with a completely different spatial setting of presenting an architectural project: a public presentation of an entry for the international competition for the *Palacio de Congresos, Ciudad de Leon*, which took place in Madrid in 2005. I conducted a series of in-depth interviews in the practice of Andrés Perea in Madrid in 2010. I also had access to the archives of the *Palacio de Congresos* project, the drawings and the project documentations, as well as the video presentations and the architect's slides. The public presentation in Madrid is very different from the one witnessed in Rotterdam; we do not anymore see an architect and a number of visitors in his office gathering around a table of models and visuals. We rather see an architect in a public presentation in a conference room, seated between two types of visuals – wall panels and a huge screen; the public is already constituted and convened at the venue far from the design sites. As the main speaker, the architect delivers his talk seated in a conference room at a distance from the audience, turning his back to a number of panels while facing the screen where a PowerPoint presentation is being projected, and turning his back to the screen while facing the printed images on the wall, the architect barely notices the audience and can hardly react to the moves, and the changing disposition of individual participants in the presentation.

Andrés Perea stands at a distance both from public and visuals. At the same time, the audience is not allowed to come close to the screen and the visuals, to touch or handle any of them. There is a regulated distance, dictated from the conventions of the presentational setting and the whole ritual a public presentation implies. The seated audience can only witness the screen presentation from a distance and eventually see some of the wall panels thus connecting the words of the architect with the images at a closer distance; most of them are able to see the face of Andrés, his reactions, gestures and moves. To ensure that the architect remains visible to the entire audience while speaking, a particular circled-shaped mini-screen transmitting *in vivo* the architect's talk is incorporated into the PowerPoint slides (Figure 7.3). This prank allows the audience to see the projection of the architect talking about the building and to simultaneously contemplate the different aspects of the building-to-come. It is also a way of lessening the distance between architect, public and building: the architect is projected on the PowerPoint slides of his presentation, models and screen images get to share the same presentational space with their designers just as they did in the process of design; the public standing at a distance is finally able to inspect them all on the slides; they are brought closer to design.

Positioned above or behind the models and the images presented on the slides, the architect maintains a privileged speaking position showing the visuals and talking on behalf of the building-to-come. Yet, as the presentation goes, he suddenly stands up and begins to stroll between the screen and the wall panels. Suddenly, we witness Perea taking up the warrior stance reminiscent to that of Koolhaas in the OMA presentation: moving repetitively between screen and printed images, with countless slow and tentative gestures the architect's body progressively connects distant and close visuals, small details and larger landscapes, interiors and exteriors, seen and unseen facets of the same building. As he moves around and about, he makes the *shi* changing by rearranging the positions of objects in the room, recomposing on the spot the configurations of things that need to be connected for the building to emerge before the eyes of the present audience. Moving back and forth Perea mobilizes all 'troops' to increase the efficacy of the presentation and to maximize the potential born from disposition by taking a more active position, recalculating the distance to visuals

Urban Publics: The Fifth Way of Becoming Political   149

Figure 7.3 The public at the presentation of Andrés Perea in Madrid, video snapshot.

and establishing many new dispositions. A quick glance at the iconography of his gestures shows him touching the surface of the visuals and engaging in a more direct, tactile, relationship with them. One can subsequently witness the quick shadow of his profile, hand or back, appearing on a projected image, and then swiftly disappearing as he moves towards the wall panels. Tracing new connections among the visuals on the wall and the screen slides, Andrés succeeds in grabbing the audience attention: they follow his moves, anticipate his gestures and gradually get more involved. From this moment on what we witness are the many tentative movements of an architect 'in attack' strolling between the big screen and the panels behind, seizing details and connecting fragments between the two series of images. As the presentation goes, we witness a bigger degree of corporal engagement in the event: the distances between architect, public and a building-to-come are rearranged according to a new presentational topography. The architect switches between less active and more active presentational disposition, between two ways of getting grasp of the reality; we witness his conviction 'to win the battle' by exploiting strategically the potential born of disposition.

The public reactions to Perea's presentation are expressed after-the-fact of the presentation, while the OMA setting inspired immediate reactions of the participants. And we can go on by enlisting many other differences. The techniques used to enact an architectural event would differ across the settings: the type of arrangements of humans and non-humans that make the building emerge will be different; the designer will be made present in a distinctive way; the techniques to enrol participants and activate engagement will vary; the ways they are chosen and turned into a material public will also alter across the settings.

The two presentational set-ups described so far suggest that the presentation happens in, and according to, a very specific socio-material arrangement, and its participants have a variable ontology. Architects rely on the power of objects to engage and constitute a public (in the OMA case) and to sensibilize an already constituted public (in Perea's case): different types of models, options, different scenarios, project books, panels on the wall, material samples. Presenting, as we witness here both in the case of Koolhaas and Perea, is not about constructing a convincing narrative, it's not a story telling. To present means to re-enact a building, to make it happen in the moment of ambling among objects, turning pages, pointing to different visuals, holding models in hands, evaluating options and scenario, testing material samples. To present, means to activate the dispositions, the *shi*, to get a better grasp of the reality of a building, to render its attachments visible, and to display and demonstrate what it does; but also to provoke, trill and affect. What architects do as they navigate in the complex presentational topography is to trace more attachments between the buildings and clients they design for, the neighbours who might protest against the building, the citizen that would dislike it, the observers that would be bugged by it. As attachments are revealed and built according to the specific material, spatial and cognitive features of the presentational setting an architectural event can 'happen' in time-space.

Scene three: Moshe draws

A different way of presenting architectural projects is exemplified by a short commercial video of the Marina Bay project in Singapore of Mosche Safdie architects. This is a resort comprised of three hotels with a roof park on the top, theatre, casino, museum, shopping and restaurant facilities. I followed this project at an early stage of its development, planning and design (Figure 7.4). As a consultant on the ArtScience museum project, part of the Marina Bay Sands complex, I took part in brainstorming sessions and meetings of the museum Board, and had the possibility to question architects, consultants and representatives of the investors from the Las Vegas Sands working on the project since the competition stage in March 2006 till the beginning of the construction process in the Spring of 2007. I also had access to the archives of Safdie's office in Boston and to some development and programme documents of the investors (i.e. the seven volumes of the 'Executive summary' of the project presented to the Singapore Government in 2006). Using materials, visuals and discussions from the early design and planning process of the Marina Bay, I will analyse the presentation of the project and will compare it with the presentations in Rotterdam and Madrid.

The video presents the Marina Bay Integrated Resort to an imaginary public. The presentation showcases the aspirations of the Marina Bay project to 'transform Singapore into a world-class, iconic destination' and contribute to its transformation into a 'global city'. This world-famous, iconic Integrated Resort was designed in 2006 and was later on completed in 2015. The Singapore Tourism Board had 'visionary plans and ambitious goals to propel Singapore to the forefront of

Figure 7.4 The Marina Bay Sands, Singapore © Courtesy of Safdie Architects.

Asia's tourism future' (*The Marina Bay Sands, The Big Picture, Executive Summary, Singapore 2015: A Truly Global City*, p. 3). Their 'ambitious goals' as well as the ones of the Singapore Government and the Las Vegas Investors resulted in the appointment of the star architect Moshe Safdie and the figure of the architect is key for the understanding of the project and its iconicity. It is a 10 min presentation that starts as follows:

> An anonymous female voice: 'The new integrated resort at Marina Bay, Singapore has inspired a unique joining of forces: an architect known in the world for his vibrant urban space and a development team who reinvented the resort business for 21st century.' The voice is followed by music and images.
>
> Moshe Safdie: 'I am Moshe Safdie. I am an architect. I think Singapore is the best-planned city in the world. It's really the only city in the world that has attempted to do large-scale planning, rethink transportation, build housing at a very large scale for its population. It's the greenest city. There is landscaping everywhere. So, I think of it as "the garden city" of Asia.'
>
> William Eeidner, President and COO, Las Vegas Sands Corporation: 'Singapore is about 21st century. Singapore is about forward looking design.'
>
> Sheldon G. Adelson, Las Vegas Sands: 'We have to create a level of sophistication that is consistent with the Singaporean society.'
>
> (…)
>
> 'We have selected Moshe Safdie because he has the ability to connect the architecture with the surrounding environment.'
>
> > (The Marina Bay Sands. The Vision Realised, presentation 2006)

In the following part of the presentation, the anonymous female voice takes us back to the 1970s and talks us through Moshe Safdie's carrier; a series of slides illustrate his iconic projects. He is named 'visionary architect of urban space'. Then we hear the architect speaking about 'the essence of urbanism', about cities as being primarily defined as the interaction of people; he explains the importance of the agora and the piazza and we are shown iconic images of agora from European and American cities. Then, the presentation discusses the theme of nature and the idea of new urbanism as the Marina Bay project is meant to 'bring nature and city together'. We see pictures of the young Moshe presenting a model of the iconic Habitat project in Montreal in 1967. Then, we hear the architect reflecting on his carrier as being 'an attempt to capture the spirit of garden in architecture'; he explains how this is related to his specific ambitions for the Marina Bay resort to become a garden like Singapore, synonymous to each other.

Subsequently, Moshe Safdie offers more details about the project: the site, the location, the uses, the urban activities and the unique combination of site and programme that the Marina Bay will propose so as to create a new type of urban experience. Impressive slides with watercolours and sketches take us to downtown Singapore and we start imagining the building. Then, from Singapore we travel back to the architect's office in Somerville, Boston, and we see Moshe working on the design – Moshe draws (Figure 7.5). Then, we witness another crucial element of the presentation: we see Moshe explaining an 'Eureka' moment in the design

Figure 7.5 Mosche Safdie draws © Courtesy of Safdie Architects.

process. We follow him drawing again when he talks about the sky garden on the top of the three hotels; the urban plaza, and the ArtScience museum. He concludes by explaining that the hotels and the museum will become the icons of Singapore; this aspiration is reaffirmed by the Las Vegas Sand ambition to make Singapore a big tourist destination. Moshe Safdie is given the final word in the presentation – he explains that 'after satisfying all the requirements, we need to add the magic, and that magic is about 'creating a memorable place which you want to come back to'. The very last sentence we hear reads: 'What we aspire for Marina Bay is to capture that sense of magic.' Music. End.

Tuned in a spirit of anticipation, the presentation follows the pathos of the executive summary and makes specific prognoses about the future of the particular architectural complex designed. The ambition of this project is not just to design facilities for meetings, conventions and exhibitions, but both architect and clients target large-scale, long-term, global objectives that will make the Marina Bay 'unique', 'iconic', 'contemporary', 'the best place to be', and will relate this new architectural ensemble with Singapore and Asia: 'propel Singapore to the forefront of Asia's tourism future'. That is how a particular local project will attempt to reach targets that will make it international, reaching further a 'global' scale.

The Marina Bay is also defined in the designing and planning documents as a *microcosm of a city*. These documents picture the type of actors that are to be mobilized by the resort activities and the types of relations that will be established among them. It possesses all the attributes that make urban cities great such as the waterfront promenades and the Marina Bay Shoppes, which combine civic space, shopping, indoor and outdoor spaces endowed with city skyline views, daylight and greenery. 'It is a place that is vibrant, dynamic and abuzz with activity. It is a place that transforms from hour to hour, from day to night, and is evocative of the signature urban places such as the Champs Elysees in Paris, the Vittorio Emmanuelle Galleria in Milan, Princes Street in Edinburgh, or the seafront promenade in Nice' (*The Marina Bay Sands, The Big Picture, Executive Summary, Singapore 2015: A Truly Global City*, vol. 1, p. 3).

In the presentation, the architect provides his specific answer to the ambitious brief. Designing it does not imply for Safdie to imagine a particular architectural ensemble *in* Singapore. Instead, it means to rethink Asia, and Singapore, their local cosmologies and even the standards of architectural excellence. What we witness in particular, as the architect presents the design moves, is that the context of Singapore does not explain or justify why the building happens in this particular shape and connectivity, with so many water and greenery elements, but it pragmatically implicates in the consequences of choosing one or another material, tree canopy, museum concept or promenade structure, landscape design or gaming culture. Thus, the Marina Bay project redefines its context, and the very meaning of 'localization'. Even if the building happens to be built in a particular situation and according to very specific set of local constraints, requirements and circumstances, client brief and reactions of investors, it never remains *local*, in the sense that it never remains associated to *this* particular site and the local circumstances, which made it possible in a particular time-space. This intention to overcome the local embeddedness and to emerge as global can be witnessed in the initial planning and construction phase of the Marina Bay. As seen here, the Marina Bay has no 'simple location' as *one* major characteristic, which refers equally to both space and time, and other minor characteristics. Although it is designed according to particular circumstances (tropical climate, lack of gaming culture, need of facilities to intensify tourism in Singapore and strengthen it economically, architectural iconicity), it does not remain where it is initially being built, on the site in downtown Singapore, facing the seafront. It does not happen *in* Singapore; it is supposed to *add* something new to Singapore. Therefore, it provides us with a different grasp of reality: it *enriches* and *enhances* Singapore and Asia. Architects have attempted to successfully redo the cosmology of the local people they are designing for, in their attempt to understand Singapore, its micro cosmos, its inhabitants: what they believe in and what they cherish the most.

 The presentation techniques here are very different from the ones witnessed in the office of Koolhaas in Rotterdam or in the public presentation of Perea in Madrid. Powerful men appear on the screen and talk to us. We are part of an imaginary, invisible, anonymous, amorphous and already constituted public, presumably interested in what they have to say about Singapore and this new development. We hear a multitude of voices: the investors, the developers, the architect, the presenter; they all talk about a groundbreaking and iconic development, an ambitious and glorious design venture. They talk. We listen. No interaction, no intervention is possible. The *shi* of the presentation display is carefully set up so as to avoid the constituted public to interfere with the greatness of the concept that is being presented in a theatrical way. The talk is followed by music and images. There is no place for silence, for gaps; no room for faults. The presentational material arrangement is simple: all the major male figures are seated, in a calm dark official décor, peaceful and relaxed body posture, confident. Facing us, the anonymous public, they authoritatively transmit information to us. We see them all the time; they never glance at us. The spaces are void, dark, clinical and empty; the traces of design creativity are missing; the viewers are not invited to have a glimpse at the design process. The only snapshots of design creativity follow the trivial cliché – a star architect working in clinical isolation and solitude is caught in a moment of inspiration, a perfect drawing emerging out of his hands. This set-up has a special impact on the efficacy of the presentation and leads towards the propensity and shaping of specific effects; it says: 'This is the concept; this is the design. We are telling you it's ambitious. We are telling you it is going to be iconic. Just believe it! Do not question or interfere!' The architect is not a general here; he is one of the many warriors that appear on screen. The battle is won before it even started because there will be no battle. If the disposition is effective in the OMA and the Perea presentations and the potential can be renewed as multitude of actors move around tables of models and interact or the architect moves and shifts the patterns of interactions, here, the disposition is fixed and therefore not renewable: it gets a grip on a reality that is known and established. The propensity of architectural things displayed in this presentation allows a definition of power as emanating from the silent display of polished watercolours and the refined authoritative discourse of the established power figures; the lack of creative messiness generates an insurmountable distance that keeps the anonymous imperceptible publics apart, giving them only one chance: 'to agree'. The set-up is handled automatically and so is the power that emerges as we let ourselves follow the images, words and music; cold, anonymous and automatically authoritative is also the discourse about the project. The functional dissymmetry is reproduced and reinvested in a theatrical way: the presenters are visible, yet transparent and predictable; they are placed in the position of the observer but they are incapable of seeing; the public is invisible, yet amorphous and erratic: it sees only what it is being shown. The opacity remains at the level of the set-up.

The architectures of citizenship

The three presentations accounted here display differently the political dimension of architecture. The political, we witness, is not situated on the side of the individual; depending on his subjective, moral or intellectual input. Instead, power is finely distributed in the objective tendency imposed by the situation of presenting. The propensity of architectural things displayed in presentations allow different set of power relations at play; the disposition and specific material arrangement of things give rise to a certain tendency. The *shi* of the presentations denotes the strategic set-up of objects, distances and viewing positions; it exemplifies a configuration of power relations that is played out differently in the three cases. Yet, in the three situations, there is some kind of automatic power that emerges from the set-up; it functions autonomously regardless of the qualities of the person activating the set-up (usually the presenter, the principal architect in a practice) provided it is totally at his disposition; power depends on the technical handling of the set-up. Thus the efficacy of the presentation depends on the totality of the things mobilized in it. There is also a functional dissymmetry: on the one hand, we see the enforced transparency of those who are expected to react in a presentational setting – the guests at OMA, the audience in Madrid, the invisible distant public in the Singapore case; on the other hand, we witness the opacity of the observer (rendered multiple in OMA's case, cut-and-pasted in the PowerPoint of Perea's and glorified in the glossy video display of Safdie's project). The presentational set-up automatizes and dis-individualizes the architectural power. Presentation is about the display and exploitation of the inherent play of forces and its efficacy depends on the dispositional configuration; the more discretely it does so, the more infallible it is.

Simultaneously, in the three scenes of presenting we witnessed three distinctive ontological dynamics of the formation of publics and how they are shaped in problematic mode of issue entanglement. From a pragmatist perspective, the problem faced in these three cases (lighting, internal display, the global culture of Singapore) are not problems of human nature, problems with their epistemic, subjective, emotional or psychological constitutions. They cannot be resolved conceptually by internalization, and therefore having a public that is unable to take these problems seriously would not help addressing them. Nor were these problems simply 'out there' as an objective set of problems that would impact on the human actors of design. Instead, we witnessed how relations of relevance were established as the participants invested themselves accordingly to the degree to which they were intimately affected by the issues at stake. Each setting redistributed differently the issues and the intensity of affectedness among the various entities of the presentational environments: spatial arrangement, technologies and devices, issues, institutions, architectural objects and materials, visuals and so on. Every single detail in the micro dynamics of the presentation mattered: the positioning of the architect, the calculated disposition of all the other participants (investors, developers and potential users), and specific and carefully orchestrated contribution of models, renderings and animations. All these entities enrolled played a role in articulating and addressing the issue.

In all the instances of presenting, the architectural object was never revealed to an abstract and ignorant public 'out there' in an pompous ritual of 'unveiling' a design concept; the public was never fully disengaged, dispersed and ill-prepared to react to design and engage with it. 'Public' rather meant what specific people did in specific situations of engaging with the thorny issues of design; it meant shared concerns, jointly expressed affectedness, togetherness. Presenting meant not revealing *hitherto* hidden properties of a powerful and mysterious architectural object, but unfolding different layers of it, one after another, in a process where the boundaries of inside and outside, design practice and public realm are blurred. In this process of unfolding, materials and objects connect to social, cultural and economic dimensions; big politics, 11th September, American, Spanish or Singaporean context meet columns, greenery, and the special effects of display. None of them comes to explain the other, they all become part of the mix that will contribute to enact a building and affect the participants in presentations. Presenting also makes explicit the attachments of the clients, the investors, the potential users, the critics. Buildings emerge in presentations, not as static entities, but as complex trajectories that are to be performed.

If demonstrations are about showing and experiments are about testing (Collins 1988), is the architectural presentation an experiment whose outcome is not known in advance, or is it a live demonstration of a known and an entirely predictable design entity? Architects know a lot about the building they aim to re-enact in presentations and as such they act as skilful demonstrators. Yet, the presentation is not solely about showcasing knowledge in public; designers do expect to learn something *more* while presenting. Not about their buildings, but about the way their buildings will affect, astonish, strike, disturb, shake, divide, redistribute or reunite the participants; how they will ignite the formation of publics. That is what makes presentations take sometimes the form of public experiments: what is tested is not the quality of the building or any cognitive dimension indeed, but rather the capacity of people to be affected by the architectural objects. What an architect asks while presenting is not 'Is my building good or bad?', but rather 'Is my building able to provoke effects, trigger disagreements, trill the observers, shake communities of neighbours, architects and journalists?' The main concern of architects as experimenters is how to conceive spaces in which the public can be better affected, guided, transformed. And that is what makes the work of architects-presenters gain a political dimension.

Architectural presentations play an active role in 'doing politics' by 'materially refiguring' the practices of designers and affected people, and contributing to the formation of publics through architectural means. Politics is understood as the specific work of constructing collective actors, which would not exist otherwise, such as society, state, publics; democracy is the constant flux of experimentation with different political forms that are spurred by the contestation and which construct different collectives (Dewey 1927). The analysis of architectural presentations demonstrated how the key question shifts from who acts to what acts: how the settings and material arrangements of architectural presentations allow humans to get affected, to get transformed; how the specific practices of presenting shift the trajectories of things and people. That is what made the architectural presentation a site for doing politics.

If political philosophy is right that citizenship begins with a materially achieved issue-affectedness (Marres 2005), such an exploration of the architectural presentation sheds light on the political role of designers in the formation of publics. The analysis of the specific techniques to compel, affect, mobilize and materially engage people in hybrid forums (Callon et al. 2001) can better equip designers to assess how by re-enacting a building in the presence of others, they also make arguments of civic importance. Compelled by architectural objects citizen can become more concerned prospective dwellers of designed environments, and therefore more concerned participants in the democratic process. That is how architectural presentations can succeed in shaping new forms of public engagement and ignite new ways of collective action in urban space.

Conclusion

Dragons and gold

Medieval alchemistry has always enchanted me; at least as long as architecture. One particular book, *The Alchemistry as a Phenomenon of the Culture of Middle Ages* (1979), by Vadim Rabinovitch, has changed profoundly and irreversibly my perception of both natural and cultural sciences. Composed according to Gothic requirements of the written culture of the epoch, alchemistry texts are remarkable memories of alchemist wonders; they remain silent and forgotten in many European museums. Rabinovitch makes them talk. The same alchemist recipe is presented and read at the start of each chapter; slowly and watchfully, over and over again. Yet, through each chapter's narrative a different interpretation of medieval culture is offered. As fragment of a culture that is inherently idiosyncratic, the recipe contains many different ingredients that are to be read, deciphered and interpreted. In one chapter, one can follow the reaction of substances and chemicals, in another the instruments and lab glass; then the objects, then their mixtures, then a dragon emerges out of the fire, but the gold is still to come. The recipe has specific stylistic particularities: it is concrete and it introduces into the world of real objects and things; it follows steps of procedures, all the actions prescribed are operation-based, not mystical. Logical phases, real numbers, measures and proportions, precision of details and strict numbering confer reality to the magic performance. In one reading, one sees the cognitive dimension of alchemistry and in another its symbolic nature and efficiency; in some readings its function is integrative, in others descriptive. In some versions, the practical capacity of the recipe prescription is underlined and in others its symbolic power.

Following the different readings of the same recipe opens up new methodological opportunities to interpret the alchemistry texts in the context of medieval culture thus reaching to the different spheres of life at the epoch. Alchemistry is not self-referential: instead, through the series of readings a careful and multilayered interpretation of the middle ages is offered. Fleeting through the different versions of the same ancient, old fashion and forgotten medieval text, the recipe appears not just as a simple reification of a numb culture; it becomes a real, live material-textual realization. The actions prescribed by the recipe make the reader witness the ecstatic excitation when the oil of the alchemists is thrown in the fire; when different substances are mixed in the experimental ambition to obtain gold. The alchemist himself appears as bestowed with different faces revealed through the recipe: he is a theorist and a theorizing experimenter, a philosopher and a theologist, a mystic and a scholastic, a painter and a poet, a

Christian and a magician. Alchemistry reveals itself as a science, as art, as religion, as philosophy; each of these facets adds to each other. It emerges as a cultural phenomenon, eclectic and contradictory idiosyncratic formation; not a simple precursor of modern chemistry. To treat alchemistry only as symbolic phenomenon, as hermeneutic art, would mean to simplify this unique phenomenon, to fail to see its practical, earthly ambitions.

Similarly, in this book, I took a step from treating architecture as a symbolic phenomenon. To avoid simplifications and purifications, I engaged in describing some complex, often hybrid and multidimensional settings of dwelling, designing, renovating buildings and assembling the city that made me to immerse into the processual, object-centred nitty-gritty reality of architecture. Studying these settings allowed me to unpack what it is to dwell in a material world made by architectural things, to dive into the ontological complexity of architecture and to attend to its political dimensions. Just like alchemistry, architecture has practical earthly ambitions; at the level of the practice of design and dwelling it is an eclectic activity; its beings, settings and arrangements are contradictory, versatile and idiosyncratic formations. They multiply in practice and yet have to come together, to stabilize, to make one world. And that is what makes it political. Designers remain attached to strange creatures such as foam models and chalk sketches, they bestow power to stairs and elevators, they make us delegate agency to elevator buttons and handrails, they dialogue with the obscure forces skulking behind Jesuit frescos and golden leafs; like warriors they activate the potential born from disposition and perform the tricks that will make a building alive in presentational setting, they dialogue with the forces of sun and glare and negotiate with clients and builders; they remain strangely obsessed by the folding repetitive circularity of time and persisting routines where the magic of creativity flares up. Dragons or gold, they remain *in* a world that has never been modern.

From 'who' acts to 'what' acts

In the practitioners' discourses, 'there is no formalism without a certain politics' (Eisenman 1995: 88). In the theoretical and historical conceptualizations too, architecture and politics are believed to be two separate realms that have specific areas of expertise. The literature on architecture and politics still maintains the large divide between the two fields. Architecture may have been recognized as a political actor, but the voice it speaks is predetermined, the issues it affects are fixed and its potential roles are curtailed. Politics may have been relocated into the heart of architecture development and use, but its actual form is often still rather modernist and restrictive. Even though the analysis has shifted towards creating connections between these two realms, the analytical tendency of underlying differentiation between 'politics' and 'architecture' remains the same. Both architects and politicians are believed to have distinct forms of expertise that share different kinds of cultural understandings, skills and embodied competences; the views of publics or politicians differ from the technical competence and skilful artistry of designers. It is assumed that while there are many kinds of design and dwelling cultures, what counts as politics in any given location is obvious; power might intrude in the world of architecture, but in principle it is self-evidently distinct from the authority of architects.

Architectural scholarship revolves around explanations of who, commonly a person or a set of experts, can and should speak about what, how and on behalf of what. Or, else, the questions are: 'Who acts?' 'Who decides?' In this understanding, publics or politicians commonly displace architectural expertise; architects speak on behalf of city governments, city officials speak on behalf of city branding, governments speaks on behalf of the nation. Thus, the answers lead to powerful humans; the approach is critical, revealing who is behind the cold material objectivity of architecture.

Built environment has been long thought of in terms of frames and framing (Dovey 1999); mundane human actions are generally tackled as subjected to planned spaces: rooms, buildings, streets, cities and neighbourhoods set physical boundaries and dictate hierarchical spatial orders. 'Framed' places also have a discursive dimension in which the built environment is seen as generating meanings, thus acknowledging both the material and symbolic dimensions of architecture in the process of framing. Yet, understanding buildings, material settings and cities in terms of 'framing' (Dovey 1999) or 'enframing' (Heidegger 1977[1954]) human activities would mean setting up the world as a stock of 'standing reserve' for preconceived human projects. The interpretative logic of framing and enframing reproduces the asymmetric dualism of nature/culture, subject/object as an ontological attitude to design practice. In this case, as Andrew Pickering demonstrated, 'we have little if any prospect of escape from the world of enframing' (Pickering 2009: 205–206). Engaging in an analysis of built forms as objective, material and cold décors for enframing human, subjective action, as culture imposed on nature, would mean to retain asymmetric dualism as ontological attitude.

However, dualist separations of people and things, of humans and frames are not found ready-made in the world on the ground; they are the products of endless and chancy processes of purification. In a world of epistemological uncertainty and ontological variability, it is hard to decide what lies on the side of politics and what remains on the side of architecture, what is nature and what is culture, what acts as an object and what acts as a subject. If we pay attention to, and remain concerned with determining what there is *in* the world on the one hand, and the work needed for making a common world that includes this on the other, we will reach to a variety of settings where the dichotomy politics/architecture will be rethought. This would mean paying close attention to the characteristics and agency of architectural objects and practices, rather than reducing them down to the interplay of social and political forces. The aim is to escape a view of political determinism according to which what shapes architecture is the social or political system in which it is embedded. At the same time, it is impossible to endorse a view of architectural determinism that would assume that architecture develops as the sole result of an internal dynamic, and then, unmediated by any other influence, moulds society and politics to fit its patterns.

In this book, I have investigated the possibilities that could open when we attempt to reappropriate what has for so long seemed the dark side of a dichotomy. Instead of telling another story of framing, I chose to trace and unpack processes of design and inhabitation that can lead to overcoming the dualisms. Following design-in-action, buildings-in-use, buildings-in-becoming offered complex settings of analysis and socio-material redescription where both the 'frames' and the 'enframed' were seen as redefining their boundaries.

Summary of the argument

I argued here that if we were to understand how the world of architecture is done, we first need to wash away any assumptions about what it contains and how it reflects the world of politics. To do this, as ANT scholars suggest, we need to go and see what is *in* there (Callon 1986). We ought to engage in production of accounts caught in a world of variable ontology, to witness settings that generate contexted truths and relational effects. To avoid the risk this study to become just another apology of power, we made a clear distinction between the highly circumstantial and contexted truths about architectural practice accounted here, and the historical contextualism that dominates architectural theory.

The book made a step forward in materializing the insight that politics are mostly played outside of what is usually called 'the political domain': decision agencies, parliaments (Callon and Law 1995). Moreover, it introduced a radically novel player into the political sphere: buildings-in-transformation, buildings-in becoming. It started with a discussion on how the traditional understandings of politics and architecture can be rethought. Focusing on the consequentiality of design, it recognized that it is not only humans who do politics. Politics is done as seen through the different empirical cases in the book, by stairs, paths and elevators (Chapter 3), experimental devices and glare calculations (Chapter 4), complex images synthesizing and recollecting a city (Chapter 5), gilding techniques and construction drawings (Chapter 6), presentational rhetoric and its material settings (Chapter 7). There are five ways of architecture to become political.

The sites and buildings explored in this book were spread all over the world: design sites in London, Boston and Madrid; renovation sites in Vienna and Moscow; construction sites in Birmingham and Singapore; buildings in Manchester, Vienna and New York; design competitions involving New York and Leon. On numerous occasions I was tempted to speak about big politics and how it varies from Moscow to Singapore, from New York to Vienna and Birmingham. This required scaling up the analysis to reveal the mechanics of Soviet politic behind Bolshoi theatre, of UK politics behind the New Street Train Station or American politics behind the NEWhitney. As tempting as it was to jump up and explain architectural objects with contexts and politics so as to satisfy the curiosity of architectural historians and play the game of mainstream architectural contextualism, I decided to remain at the myopic, microscopic level of the practice; that is, the level of routines and contexted truths. Yet, at any moment in time did these buildings appeared as blatant and purified embodiments of big politics related to governments or ideologies; I rather witnessed *a* kind of politics (politics with small 'p') that was generated by artefacts, devices, material arrangements, settings, technologies and buildings as they connected with many other things in a network. That is, contextual, *relational politics*. Explored through different empirical settings – of design experimentation, architectural presentation, building renovating, inhabitation – architecture emerged as holding implicit political dimensions that can be activated on these sites. Design acted politically.

Making difference

The political dimensions of architecture were presented here in a notoriously descriptive way; and different ways of depicting 'architecture' yielded different political dimensions. I know it, politically radical critics, especially those who argue for the importance of architecture to instigate change, those who believe design should change the world, will worry about this. Yet for me, committing to describe the variable settings, objects and practices that make architecture political means concomitantly stating my willingness to attend both empirically and politically to the disorderly specificities of the world of architecture. If ANT does not encourage us to take sides while describing, this does not mean in any way that our accounts have no political dimensions. Power of description is not won at the expense of any serious attempt at political engagement.

In each setting discussed in the book, I have been confronted with what, following Donna Haraway, we can call 'situated knowledge' or contexted truths about the mechanics of design and inhabitation. Contrary to the epistemology prescriptions of design studies, there is no general methodological due process in design. Design knowledge is specific, it arises out of the practices of architects as they solve problems, sketch or scale models. Architectural knowledge was described and explained here by the same token as produced in a symmetrical way; it emerges in interaction between the natural world, mechanical forces and specialist design cultures related to building sciences and the arts. In practice, design world is irredeemably messy: I witnessed states of instable idiosyncratic relationships, I followed outlandish objects; I saw dragons and gold.

I experienced different architectural settings together with designers and dwellers; I described their more or less unruly specificities and heterogeneity – they are simultaneously material, social, political, technical and architectural in character. I witnessed that politics may vary across settings, but what remains the same is the architectural multiplicity at its heart. There are multiple models on a table that all talk about a building, there are numerous objects in a design presentation that re-enact the-building-to-come, there is a set of experimental practices that all together allow architects to negotiate the glare effects, old buildings have many ways of surprising. Every design process starts with plurality: there are design practices in the plural, design experiments in the plural, buildings-in-becoming in the plural, dwelling experiences in the plural; hence, political dimensions of architecture also in the plural. This is a relational ontology: what there is in the world, social and natural, is an effect of uncertain and provisional relations of representation, political and architectural. The practices vary along with the ways of doing architecture; the question of how we place them together to share a space, to inhabit the world of a building is a question of how they are related, configured, regrouped; this is a question of politics. Thus, after multiplicity a shared space is to be formed, a 'common world' is to be assembled. As Latour has put, 'the provisional result of the progressive unification of external realities (for which we reserve the term "pluriverse"); the world, in the singular, is, precisely, not what is given but what has to be obtained through due process' (Latour 2004a: 239). The common world we share is composed also with architectural means.

If both urban practices differ and the objects of design multiply in practice, how is this multiplicity guiding designers and dwellers towards a decision, towards taking sides: if the city has multiple realities, how are we led to inhabit one of them? How is *this* image of Birmingham able to convey its multiplicity better than *that* image? Which glare angle will offer the best solution? Which path to the lecture theatre in the morning will provide better and more sociable way of guiding me through the university building? All this implies making a decision and taking a side. It also implies treating buildings not so much as objects made of steel and concrete (objects of building science), but as something to do with daily practices: the experiments of designers, the recalcitrance of old buildings, the variability of images, the scalability of models, the hesitations of dwellers. Describing these practices and settings is also about making a difference; it is a form of interference.

Is it possible to attend to specificity and to be political at the same time? Shall we provide prescriptions, recommendations *after* the descriptions are completed? Shall we jump up to another level of analysis? Shall we offer recipes (not alchemistry ones) of how to turn the world into a better place with architectural means, an architecturally sound and just world? To the reader who expected answers to these questions, here is my reply: no, I am not in the position to offer solutions and suggestions of how to make architecture more or less political; more just. While engaging in redescription of design and inhabitation, I do not take any sides. We are all, as Haraway puts it, located in the belly of the monster. The idea that we could climb out and look down to get an overview, and therefore make a judgement, a recommendation, makes no sense. Those who imagine that they can do this are misleading themselves. It simply isn't possible, as she puts it, to see everything from nowhere (Haraway 1991).

Immersing into the world of design, renovation, public presentation and dwelling allowed me to produce descriptions where architecture appears as performative and situated; not a distant and passive formal reality that would project power, styles, national ambitions and identity aspirations. Thus, I have demonstrated that the ontology embedded in and enacted by design and dwelling practices sits poorly with the ontology embedded and enacted in front-line politics. Instead of stepping back to propose a procedure for regulating and sorting out right from wrong, or good from bad, I simply take the side of design here. I describe, I attend to the specificities, the contingency and the uncertainties of the empirical, therefore I take a position. The more I immerse into these worlds of design and describe, the more I understand

and learn. My knowledge practices are performative and so are my descriptions. The more specific they get, the more the difference I can make would be embedded in the specificities and my ability to intrude in the design worlds will increase. Sometimes unpredictably and involuntary, the descriptions start interfering in their object of study. They can disperse it or diffract it, move it on or redo it *according* to the angle they take, the actors they follow, the grain of details, the time-spaces and durations; they make a difference and they make me intervene. I interfere. It is an illusion to believe that these descriptions are neutral. And we have known this since Geertz' *Interpretation of Cultures* (1972); description is never *just* description, it is never innocent. All the descriptions of settings and sites of the political in this book are simultaneously empirical descriptions and interferences. Attending to the specificity of design make us engage in the regime of the political.

In this way of thinking, 'politics is about interfering to make a difference', as John Law has put it, and, perhaps, 'it is about being sufficiently modest to resist the idea that there is a single or explicit mode of ordering the world' (Law 2009). To unravel the political dimension of architecture is to accept in other words that ordering is partial, incomplete, always more or less local, more or less implicit and therefore more or less perplexing. Engaging in empirical explorations of the political dimension of architecture, describing partial local and perplex orderings of the reality is my way of addressing the relationship of politics and architecture. In the slow ethnography of the processes of design, construction, renovation and use, politics appears as a relational phenomenon that could be explored and generated at the level of design practice. Design can have political effects but must not be reduced to a given politics. The interpretations of how architectural settings generate political effects can further inform practice and can instigate a different thinking about design politics among practitioners.

Where is the political?

The question of the political took us back to rethink classic parables of architecture and control: the panopticon and the bridges of Moses. Politics, I argued in this book, is not outside a building or a bridge, projected on their shapes, embodied in their fabrics, imprinted in cities and master plans. A bridge, an atrium, a building are political not because they *embody* politics. Nor are they political *in themselves*. Instead, they are political to the degree to which they can engage people, and make them do things, make then act, group and regroup. Their strength depends on how they are all put in a network with other objects and humans. Here is the political – *in* the various manifestations of the buildings' agency, *in* the many unpredictable alliances traced among the different protagonists in design, construction and renovation, *in* the course of the events that make architects connect with planners, citizens, builders, users and enact the formation of urban publics, *in* the process of accounting for all transformations of the sites of design and construction, *in* the event of recollecting the tentative trajectories of architectural images that grasp the compound reality of a city.

Participating in the ordering of reality, architecture is typically interpreted as negative: architecture segregates, divides or symbolizes at distance. There is an interesting tension here: 'architecture' is tied to negative associations of being 'authoritarian' 'impoverished' and 'mechanistic', 'racist' and 'discriminatory'. Yet 'architecture' is what designers build. And indeed, going back to the classical examples of architecture and social control, we might be tempted to argue that the only proper architecture is no architecture; that built systems should intervene as little as possible in social interactions and ongoing flows of design and inhabitation, since they can only impede and restrain them.

Revising these examples through the lens of contemporary cases is my way of reminding of the limits and dangers of the logic of separating the category of architecture from that of politics. Turning the negative analysis into a positive one I illustrated that through detailed studies of design-in-action, buildings-in-use, buildings-in-becoming (a strangely rare topic in architectural theory) and through careful attention to the precise, practical functioning of buildings, design and dwelling, architecture can become a democratizing force rather than an authoritarian one. Design can facilitate, enable and endorse. The design of buildings and material arrangements are not simply about design; it is about making a difference in how socio-material relations are forged. Focusing on this recursive relation between design techniques, ways of doing architecture and dwelling in a building led us to a new step: architecture becomes itself a *locus* for political action.

On the sites of the political described here, the political teleology was never given; instead, we have seen the architectural objects, techniques, arrangements and artefacts become political. Such an approach leads us to distinguish between critical design and design research that makes difference. It is one thing to explicitly attempt to transform a practice towards a preferred goal, and why not change the world, through the production and implementation of design (critical design); it is another to produce empirical description of rich and messy design worlds that would be performative and will spawn critique 'from within'. The first leads us to achieve 'social change'; the second to rewrite existing relations in a durable way. 'Doing politics' is no longer a procedural attempt to achieve 'consensus', but a substantive move to 'materially refigure' design practices. For political scientists, this is an invitation to explore the possibilities of other ways to do politics. For design practitioners, this offers awareness of the inherent political valence of architecture and insights for a more political kind of practice. Exploring the political dimensions of architecture is a way to affect its development so that more desirable or justly ordered social collectives can be brought into being.

Glossary

Note: All glossary terms are marked with an asterisk (*) in the text when mentioned for the first time.

Actor

An actor is a participant in the process of architectural production and consumption (which can be both a human or a non-human*). The anthropological approach to design helps us to understand how an actor comes into being (rather than taking its properties for granted and fully defined and assuming the world is composed by a number of known entities). We can define an actor on the basis of its behaviour – its performances* – manifested in the process of design making and dwelling.

Affordance

Affordance simultaneously refers to the object and to the environment and the observer. Neither objective nor subjective property, affordance is at the same time matter and mind, physical and phenomenal and it points to the impossibility to separate the cultural environment from the natural one. The term is inspired by the ecological approach (Gibson 1979). Action is viewed as the realization of affordances. Affordances specify the range of possible activities, visible to the users, and therefore, perceived, practiced, experienced.

Collective

A collective is the opposite of society which is an artificial term imposed by the modernist paradigm. Collective refers to the many associations of humans and non-humans*. The division between nature and society occults the political process by which the cosmos is reassembled. The collective plays an important role in this process.

Delegate/delegation

To delegate action to non-humans* means that designers and engineers substitute design objects, environments and devices for the action of people and make them permanently occupy the position of humans so as to be able to shape human action by redistributing competences and prescribing* responsibilities.

Event

This term is borrowed from Whitehead to replace the notion of discovery in an implausible philosophy of history where the objects are commonly static and the human inventors/discoverers are active and usually get all the credits and attention for discovering objects. To define an experience as event, or series of events, means to acknowledge the participation of both humans and non-humans* and all circumstances that shape an experience; this questions the historicity of all the ingredients that shape the circumstances of experience.

Factish

Factish is a neologism that combines fact and fetish showing that both of them have an element of fabrication in common (Latour 2010a). Factish implies a type of activity that does not distinguish between fact and belief. Instead of opposing fact and fetish or criticizing the fact as fetish, this new term suggests taking seriously the role of all actors that take part in their making.

Inscription/script/prescription

Inscription refers to the process of transformations through which an entity materializes as an object, document, trace or archive. The term designates at the same time the vision of the world incorporated in the object and the programme of action it is supposed to accomplish. To quote Madeleine Akrich, who coined the term:

> By defining the characteristics of his object, the conceiver [in our case, the designer] puts forward a number of hypotheses concerning the elements making up the world into which the object is intended to fit. He proposes a 'script,' a 'scenario,' intended as a predetermination of the settings which users are called upon to imagine starting from the technical device and its accompanying prescriptions. (Akrich 1987 and an English version Akrich 1992b)

The delegation* of behaviour onto the humans by non-humans* is termed prescription (Latour 1992). For instance, urban artefacts and environments are seen as authorizing and interdicting, giving permission or holding promises; instead of serving as passive and indifferent frames of subjective passions, they are part of the complex nets that make us part of a city and retain us in its flexible networks. With their specific design they make the user of the urban space blind but connected, partially intelligent, provisionary competent (Latour 1998). Hidden policemen, fences, bicycle shades, fountains, barriers, all these 'objects have two faces: they multiply the possibilities of existences for those they shape; they multiply the possibilities to be absent for those they replace. Anthropogenic on one side, they are sociogenic on the other' (Latour 1998: 107).

Mediation/mediator

The term mediator points to the fact that objects are participants in the course of action that is overtaken by other agencies (Latour 2005b). A mediator can transform, translate, distort and modify meaning; it could act in an unpredictable and surprising way (Latour 2005b: 37–42). If an intermediary* can be defined prior to the process of action, a mediator can only be defined *in* the process of action.

Non-human (as opposed to human)

The term non-human is used by Bruno Latour to replace object as well as to widen its scope. The concept has meaning only in the pair human – non-human* (Latour 1999a: 308). It is also a way to bypass the subject–object dichotomy and to avoid the restricted understanding that suggests that objects are passive things for human subjects to use (Latour 1999a: 303). Latour's view is that non-humans have active role that is often forgotten or denied.

Performance

Performance refers to the specific situation in which an actor* emerges and is defined through the actions, trails, difficulties and experiences. What describes the actor's profile is not a number of qualities or characteristics defined in terms of essence, but rather the results of these events*, trails and experiences – that is performances.

Social (as a noun)

The social does not stand here for a synonym of society; society is often understood as 'the hidden source of causality which could account for the existence and stability of different types of actions or behaviours' (Latour 1990: 113). The social is a way to connect heterogeneous actors* and environments; it is to be composed, made up, constructed, established, maintained and assembled (Latour 2005b).

Thing

Thing stands in opposition to object (Latour and Weibel 2005). A simple object (a building, a door lock, a staircase) can become a thing when it is contested; in the process of contestation it enrols new humans and non-humans*, and gathering many conflicting demands becomes a disputed assemblage. Paradoxically, many design objects often appear as things not as mere objects. In design studies a new design artefact is often a contested territory (Petroski 1993; Molotch 2005); therefore a thing; the study of architectural controversies illustrates the same tendency in architecture and urban design (Yaneva 2012). Things cannot be reduced to simple descriptions of what they are and what they mean; action-based accounts of their contested performances* are needed.

References

Akrich, M. (1987), 'Comment décrire les objets techniques?', *Technique et culture*, 9: 49–64.
Akrich, M. (1992a), 'Beyond Social Construction of Technology: The Shaping of People and Things in the Innovation Process', in M. Dierkes and U. Hoffmann (eds), *New Technology at the Outset: Social Forces in the Shaping of Technological Innovations*, 173–190, Frankfurt/New York: Campus Verlag.
Akrich, M. (1992b), 'The De-scription of Technical Objects', in J. Law and W. E. Bijker (eds), *Shaping Technology/Building Society. Studies in Sociotechnical Change*, 205–224, Cambridge, MA: MIT Press.
Aureli, P. V. (2008), *The Project of Autonomy: Politics and Architecture Within and Against Capitalism*, New York: Princeton Architectural Press.
Barnett, D. and A. Skelton, eds (2008), *Theatre and Performance in Eastern Europe. The Changing Scene*, Lanham, MD, Toronto: The Scarecrow Press.
Barry, A. (2001), *Political Machines: Governing a Technological Society*, London: The Atholone Press.
Barry, A. (2013), *Material Politics: Disputes Along the Pipeline*, Oxford: Wiley-Blackwell.
Barry, E. and S. Kishkovsky (2013), 'Latest Twist at Bolshoi: Director Is Pushed Out', *International New York Times*, 9 July 2013, Available online: http://www.nytimes.com/2013/07/10/world/europe/bolshoi-director-forced-out.html?_r=0 (accessed 13 September 2013).
Bartolini, N. (2015), 'The Politics of Vibrant Matter: Consistency, Containment and the Concrete of Mussolini's Bunker', *Journal of Material Culture*, 20(2): 191–210.
Beaumont, M. and G. Dart, eds (2010), *Restless Cities*, London: Verso Books.
Beck, J. (2011), 'Concrete Ambivalence: Inside the Bunker Complex', *Cultural Politics*, 7(1): 79–102.
Beck, U. (1992), *Risk Society – Towards a New Modernity*, Cambridge: Polity.
Beck, U. (1999), *World Risk Society*, Cambridge: Polity.
Bednar, M. J. (1986), *The New Atrium*, McGraw-Hill Building Types Series, New York: McGraw-Hill.
Bennett, Jane (2010), *Vibrant Matter: A Political Ecology of Things*, Durham, NC: Duke University Press.
Berezin, M. (1991), 'The Organization of Political Ideology: Culture, State, and the Theatre in Fascist Italy', *American Sociological Review*, 56(5): 639–651.
Berglund, E. (2013), 'Design as Activism in Helsinki', *Design and Culture*, 5(2): 195–214.
Blau, J. R. (1976), 'Beautiful Buildings and Breaching the Laws', *International Journal of Sociology*, 12: 110–128.
Blau, J. R. (1984), *Architects and Firms: A Sociological Perspective on Architectural Practice*, Cambridge, MA: MIT Press.
Blundell Jones, P., D. Petrescu and J. Till, eds (2005), *Architecture and Participation*, Abingdon: Spon Press.
Bonetta, L. (2003), 'Lab Architecture: Do You Want to Work Here?', *Nature*, 424: 718–720.
Bonfilio, P. (2000), *Fallingwater. The Model*, New York: Rizzoli.

Boyer, C. (1994), *The City of Collective Memory: Its Historical Imagery and Architectural Entertainments*, Cambridge, MA: MIT Press.
Brand, S. (1994), *How Buildings Learn. What Happens After They're Built*, New York: Viking.
Braun, B. and S. Whatmore (2010), 'The Stuff of Politics, an Introduction', in B. Braun and S. Whatmore (eds), *Political Matter: Technoscience, Democracy and Public Life*, ix–xl, Minneapolis: University of Minnesota Press.
Broudehoux, A. (2010), 'Images of Power: Architectures of the Integrated Spectacle at the Beijing Olympics', *Journal of Architectural Education*, 63(2): 52–62.
Buchli, V. (2013), *An Anthropology of Architecture*, London: Bloomsbury.
Buchli, V. and G. Lucas, eds (2001), *Archaeologies of the Contemporary Past*, London: Routledge.
Busch, A. (1990), *The Art of the Architectural Model*, New York: TMP Design Press.
CABE. (2009), 'CABE letter to the Birmingham City Council', 15 May.
Calame, J. and E. Charlesworth (2016), *Divided Cities. Belfast, Beirut, Jerusalem, Mostar, and Nicosia*, Philadelphia: University of Pennsylvania Press.
Callon, M. (1986), 'Some Elements of a Sociology of Translation: Domestication of the Scallops and the Fishermen of St Brieuc Bay', in J. Law (ed.), *Power, Action and Belief: A New Sociology of Knowledge*, 196–223, London: Routledge.
Callon, M. (1996) 'Le travail de la conception en architecture', *Situations Les Cahiers de la recherche architecturale*, 37 (1er trimestre): 25–35.
Callon, M. and J. Law (1995), 'Agency and the Hybrid Collectif'. *South Atlantic Quarterly*, 94: 481–507.
Callon, M. and F. Muniesa (2005), 'Peripheral Vision. Economic Markets as Calculative Collective Devices', *Organization Studies*, 26(8): 1229–1250.
Callon, M., P. Lascoumes and Y. Barthes (2001), *Agir dans un monde incertain. Essai sur la democratie technique*, Paris: Edition du Seuil.
Champy, F. (2001), *Sociologie de l'architecture*, Paris: La Découverte.
Charney, I. (2007), 'The Politics of Design: Architecture, Tall Buildings and the Skyline of Central London', *Area*, 39(2): 195–205.
Church, A. and S. Penny (2013), 'Power, Space and the New Stadium: The Example of Arsenal Football Club', *Sports in Society*, 16(6): 819–834.
Clarisse, C. (1993), *Ma quete d'architecture. Maquettes d'architectures*, Les mini PA n 18, Editions du Pavillon de l'Arsenal.
Cohen, J. (2000), 'Designer Labs: Architecture and Creativity: Does Beauty Matter?', *Science*, 287: 210–214.
Collins, H. (1988), 'Public Experiments and Displays of Virtuosity: The Core-Set Revisited', *Social Studies of Science*, 18(4): 725–748.
Collins, J. (1999), 'The Design Process for the Human Workplace', in P. Galison and E. Thompson (eds), *The Architecture of Science*, 399–413, Cambridge, MA: MIT Press.
CRL (2004), Chemistry Research Laboratory Building Portfolio, RMJM Architects. Available online: http://rmjm.com/projects/view-bt-detail/39/Research (accessed 16 June 2008).
Cuff, D. (1992), *Architecture: The Story of Practice*, Cambridge, MA: MIT Press.
Cupers, K., ed. (2013), *Use Matters: An Alternative History of Architecture*, London: Routledge.
Daston, L. (1992), 'Objectivity and the Escape from Perspective', *Social Studies of Science*, 22: 597–618.
Daston, L. and P. Galison (2007), *Objectivity*, Cambridge, MA: MIT Press.

De Certeau, M. (1984), *The Practice of Everyday Life*, Berkeley: University of California Press.
Degen, M., G. Rose, and B. Basdas (2010), 'Bodies and Everyday Practices in Designed Urban Environments', *Science Studies*, 23(2): 60–76.
DeHanas, D. and Z. Pieri (2011), 'Olympic Proportions: The Expanding Scalar Politics of the London "Olympics MegaMosque" Controversy', *Sociology*, 45(5): 798–814.
Dehio, G. and A. Riegl (1988), *Konservieren, nicht restaurieren. Streitschriften zur Denkmalpflege um 1900*, Braunschweig: Vieweg.
Delanty, G. and P. Jones (2002), 'European Identity and Architecture', *The European Journal of Social Theory*, 5(4): 449–463.
del Cerro Santamaria, G. (2007), *Bilbao. Basque Pathways to Globalization*, New York: Elsevier.
DeVries, G. (2007), 'What Is Political in Sub-politics? How Aristotle Might Help STS'. *Social Studies of Science*, 37(5): 781–809.
Dewey, John (1927), *The Public and Its Problems*, New York: Holt.
Dixon, T. (2010), *A Tale of Two Cities*, London: Estates Gazette.
Domínguez Rubio, F., and U. Fogué (2015), 'Unfolding the Political Capacities of Design', in A. Yaneva and A. Zaera Polo (eds), *What Is Cosmopolitical Design? Design, Nature and the Built Environment*, 143–160, Farnham: Ashgate.
Doucet, I. (2015), *The Practice Turn in Architecture: Brussels After 1968*, Farnham: Ashgate.
Dovey, K. (1999), *Framing Places: Mediating Power in Built Form*, London: Routledge.
Dovey, K. (2002) 'The Silent Complicity of Architecture', in J. Hillier and E. Rooksby (eds), *Habitus: A Sense of Place*, 267–280, Aldershot: Ashgate.
Dubuisson, S. and A. Hennion (1995), 'Le design industriel, entre création, technique et marché', *Sociologie de l'art*, 8: 9–30.
Dutton, T. A. and L. H. Mann, eds (1996), *Reconstructing Architecture: Critical Discourses and Social Practices*, Minneapolis: University of Minnesota Press.
Dutton, T. A. and L. H. Mann (2000), 'Problems in Theorizing "the Political" in Architectural Discourse', *Rethinking Marxism*, 12(4): 117–129.Edelman, M. (1995), *From Art to Politics: How Artistic Creations Shape Political Conceptions*, Chicago: University of Chicago Press.
Eisenman, P. (1995), 'Eisenman (and Company) Respond', *Progressive Architecture*, 76(2): 88–89.
Elder, M. (2011) 'Bolshoi Rocked by Scandal and Intrigue', *The Guardian*, 22 March 2011. Available online: https://www.theguardian.com/stage/2011/mar/22/bolshoi-rocked-by-scandal (accessed 3 September 2013).
Escobar, M. P. (2014), 'The Power of (Dis)placement: Pigeons and Urban Regeneration in Trafalgar Square', *Cultural Geographies*, 21(3): 363–387.
Evans, G. (2003), 'Hard-Branding the Cultural City – From Prado to Prada', *International Journal of Urban and Regional Research*, 27(2): 417–440.
Evans, R. (1997), *Translations from Drawing to Building*, Cambridge, MA: MIT Press.
Faulconbridge, J. (2009), 'The Regulation of Design in Global Architecture Firms: Embedding and Emplacing Buildings', *Urban Studies*, 46(12): 2537–2554.
Filmer, A. (2013), 'Disrupting the "Silent Complicity" of Parliamentary Architecture', *Performance Research*, 18(3): 19–26.
Foucault, M. (1975), *Surveiller et Punir: Naissance de La Prison*, Paris: Gallimard.
Frampton, K. and S. Kolbowski, eds (1981), *Idea as Model 22 Architects 1976/1980*, New York: Rizzoli.
Freschi, F. (2007), 'Postapartheid Publics and the Politics of Ornament: Nationalism, Identity and the Rhetoric of Community in the Decorative Program of the New Constitutional Court, Johannesburg', *Africa Today*, 54(2): 27–49.

Gale, R. (2004), 'The Multicultural City and the Politics of Religious Architecture: Urban Planning, Mosques and Meaning-Making in Birmingham, UK', *Built Environment*, 30(1): 30–44.
Galison, P. (1997), *Image and Logic: A Material Culture of Microphysics*, Chicago: University of Chicago Press.
Galison, P. and E. Thompson, eds (1999), *The Architecture of Science*, Cambridge, MA: MIT Press.
Garfinkel, H. (1985), *Studies in Ethnomethodology*, Cambridge: Polity Press.
Gateway Project GRIP (2009), 'Birmingham New Street Station', *Gateway Project GRIP 4 Report*, 2(01).
Geertz, C. (1973), *The Interpretation of Cultures: Selected Essays*, New York: Basic Books.
Gibson, J. (1979), *The Ecological Approach to Visual Perception*, Boston: Houghton Mifflin.
Gieryn, T. (1999), 'Two Faces on Science: Building Identities for Molecular Biology and Biotechnology', in P. Galison and E. Thompson (eds), *The Architecture of Science*, 423–459, Cambridge, MA: MIT Press.
Gieryn, T. (2002), 'What Buildings Do', *Theory and Society*, 31: 35–74.
Gieryn, T. (2006), 'City as Truth-Spot: Laboratories and Field-Sites in Urban Studies', *Social Studies of Science*, 36: 5–38.
Gomart, E. and M. Hajer (2003), 'Is *That* Politics? For an Inquiry into Forms of Contemporary Politics', in B. Joerges and H. Nowotny (eds), *Social Studies of Science and Technology: Looking Back Ahead*, 33–61, Dordrecht: Kluwer Academic Publishers.
Goodsell, C. T. (1988), 'The Architecture of Parliaments: Legislative Houses and Political Culture', *British Journal of Political Science*, 18(3): 287–302.
Graham, S. and N. Thrift (2007), 'Out of Order: Understanding Repair and Maintenance', *Theory, Culture and Society*, 24(3): 1–25.
Grubbauer, M. (2014), 'Architecture, Economic Imaginaries and Urban Politics: The Office Tower as Socially Classifying Device', *International Journal of Urban and Regional Research*, 38(1): 336–359.
Guattari, F. (1994), 'Les machines architecturales de Shin Takamatsu', *Chimères*, 21(Hiver), 127–141.
Gurdalli, H. and U. Koldas (2015), 'Architecture of Power and Urban Space in a Divided City: A History of Official Buildings in Nicosia/Lefkosa', *The Design Journal*, 18(1): 135–157.
Hamann, G., K. Mühlberger and F. Skacel, eds (1986), 'Das Alte Universitätsviertel in Wien, 1385–1985', in *Schriftenreihe des Universitätsarchivs*, vol. 2, Wien.
Haraway, D. (1991), 'Situated Knowledges: The Science Question in Feminism and the Privilege of Partial Perspective', in D. Haraway (ed.), *Simians, Cyborgs and Women: The Reinvention of Nature*, 183–201, London: Free Association Books.
Haraway, D. (2003), *The Companion Species Manifesto: Dogs, People, and Significant Otherness*, Chicago: Prickly Paradigm Press.
Harrison, A. L. (2013), *Architectural Theories of the Environment*, London: Routledge.
Harvey, D. (1989), *The Condition of Postmodernity: An Enquiry into the Origins of Cultural Change*, Oxford: Wiley-Blackwell.
Hastings, J. and H. Thomas (2005), 'Accessing the Nation: Disability, Political Inclusion and Built Form', *Urban Studies*, 42(3): 527–544.
Heidegger, M. (1977), 'The Question Concerning Technology', in W. Lovitt (trans.), *The Question Concerning Technology and Other Essays*, 3–35, New York: Harper and Row.
Heise, U. (2008), *Sense of Place and Sense of Planet*, New York: Oxford University Press.

Herbert, B. (2008), 'New Start for New Street Unveiled', 18 September.
Heurtin, J.-P. (1999), *L'espace publique parlamentaire. Essai sur les raisons du législateur*, Paris: Presses Universitaires de France – P.U.F.
Hill, J. (2003), *Actions of Architecture: Architects and Creative Users*, London: Routledge.
Hinchliffe, S., M. Kearnes, M. Degen and S. Whatmore (2005), 'Urban Wild Things: A Cosmopolitical Experiment', *Environment and Planning D: Society and Space*, 23: 643–658.
Hirschauer, S. (2005), 'The Accomplishment of Strangeness and the Minimization of Presence. An Elevator Trip', *Journal for the Theory of Social Behaviour*, 35(1): 41–67.
Holbraad, M. (2009), 'Ontology, Ethnography, Archaeology: An Afterword on the Ontography of Things', *Cambridge Archaeological Journal*, 19: 431–441.
Holleran, M. (2014), '"Mafia Baroque": Post-Socialist Architecture and Urban Planning in Bulgaria', *The British Journal of Sociology*, 65(1): 21–42.
Holston, J. (1989), *The Modernist City: An Anthropological Critique of Brasília*, Chicago: University of Chicago Press.
Houdart, S. (2008), 'Copying, Cutting and Pasting Social Spheres: Computer Designers' Participation in Architectural Projects', *Science Studies: An Interdisciplinary Journal of Science and Technology*, 21(1): 47–64.
Houdart, S. and C. Minato (2009), *Kuma Kengo. An Unconventional Monograph*, Paris: Editions Donner Lieu.
Huyssen, A. (2003), *Present Pasts: Urban Palimpsests and the Politics of Memory*, Stanford: Stanford University Press.
Immerwahr, D. (2007), 'The Politics of Architecture and Urbanism in Postcolonial Lagos, 1960–1986', *Journal of African Cultural Studies*, 19(2): 165–186.
Iveson, K. (2007), *Publics and the City*, London: Blackwell.
Jacobs J. M. and P. Merriman (2011), 'Practising Architecture', *Social and Cultural Geography*, 12(3): 211–222.
Jacobs, J. M., S. Cairns and I. Strebel (2007), 'A Tall Story ... But a Fact Just the Same: The Red Road High-Rise as a Black Box', *Urban Studies*, 44(3): 609–629.
Jarman, T. (2013), Interview in Old School New School Art School, Video, Available online: http://fcbstudios.com/work/view/manchester-school-ofart?sort=highlights (accessed 13 March 2015).
Jencks, C. (2005), *The Iconic Building: The Power of Enigma*, London: Frances Lincoln.
Jessop, B. (2004), 'Critical Semiotic Analysis and Cultural Political Economy', *Critical Discourse Studies*, 1(2): 159–174.
Jones, P. (2006), 'The Sociology of Architecture and the Politics of Building: The Discursive Construction of Ground Zero', *Sociology*, 40(3): 549–565.
Jones, P. (2009), 'Putting Architecture in Its Social Place: A Cultural Political Economy of Architecture', *Urban Studies*, 46(12): 2519–2536.
Jullien, F. (1999), *The Propensity of Things: Toward a History of Efficacy in China*, Translated by Janet Lloyd, New York: Zone Books.
Kaika, M. (2010), 'Architecture and Crisis: Re-inventing the Icon, re-imag(in)ing London and re-branding the City', *Transactions of the Institute of British Geographers*, 35: 453–474.
Kaika, M. (2011), 'Autistic Architecture: The Fall of the Icon and the Rise of the Serial Object of Architecture', *Environment and Planning D: Society and Space*, 29(6): 968–992.
Kaika, M. (2015), 'Architects Are Like Trains ... They Only Go on Rails. The Changing Social Role of Architecture in a Globalised World', in M. Gravari-Barbas and

C. Renard-Delautre (eds), *Icônes globales d'architecture: L'architecture iconique, l'architecte global et l'espace urbain*, 69–81, Paris: L'Harmattan.

Kaika, M. and K. Thielen (2006), 'Form Follows Power: A Genealogy of Urban Shrines', *City*, 10: 59–69.

King, A. D. (1980), *Buildings and Society. Essays on the Social Development of the Built Environment*, London: Routledge.

King, A. D. (2004), *Spaces of Global Cultures. Architecture Urbanism Identity*, London: Routledge.

King, A. D. (2010), 'Notes Towards a Global Historical Sociology of Building Types', in M. Guggenheim and O. Söderström (eds), *Re-shaping Cities: How Global Mobility Transforms Architecture and Urban Form*, London: Routledge.

Knorr-Cetina, K. (1997), 'Sociality with Objects: Social Relations in Postsocial Knowledge Societies', *Theory, Culture and Society*, 14(4): 1–30.

Knorr-Cetina, K. (1999), *Epistemic Cultures: How the Sciences Make Knowledge*, Cambridge, MA: Harvard University Press.

Kostof, S. (1991), *The City Shaped: Urban Patterns and Meanings Throughout History*, Boston, MA: Little, Brown and Company.

Lash, Scott and Celia Lury (2007) *Global Culture Industry: The Mediation of Things*, Polity Press.

Latour, B. (1987), *Science in Action: How to Follow Scientists and Engineers Through Society*, Cambridge, MA: Harvard University Press.

Latour, B. (1990), 'When Things Strike Back: A Possible Contribution of Science Studies to the Social Sciences', *British Journal of Sociology*, 5(1): 105–123.

Latour, B. (1991), *We Have Never been Modern*, Cambridge, MA: Harvard University Press.

Latour, B. (1992), 'Where Are the Missing Masses? The Sociology of a Few Mundane Artifacts', in W. Bijker and J. Law (eds), *Shaping Technology/Building Society: Studies in Sociotechnical Change*, 225–258, Cambridge, MA: MIT Press.

Latour, B. (1996), 'On Interobjectivity', *Mind, Culture and Activity*, 3(4): 228–245.

Latour, B. (1998), 'To Modernize or to Ecologize? That's the Question', in N. Castree and B. Willems-Braun (eds), *Remaking Reality: Nature at the Millennium*, 221–242, London and New York: Routledge.

Latour, B. (1999a), *Pandora's Hope: An Essay on the Reality of Science Studies*, Cambridge, MA: Harvard University Press.

Latour, B. (1999b), 'On Recalling ANT', in J. Law and J. Hassard (eds), *Actor Network Theory and After*, 15–26, Oxford: Blackwell.

Latour, B. (2000), 'The Berlin Key or How to Do Things with Words', in P. M. Graves-Brown (ed.), *Matter, Materiality and Modern Culture*, 10–21, London: Routledge.

Latour, B. (2004a), *Politics of Nature. How to Bring the Sciences into Democracy*, Cambridge, MA: Harvard University Press.

Latour, B. (2004b) 'Whose Cosmos, Which Cosmopolitics? Comments on the Peace Terms of Ulrich Beck', *Common Knowledge*, 10(3): 450–462.

Latour, B. (2005a), 'From Realpolitik to Dingpolitik: How to Make Things Public. An Introduction', in B. Latour and P. Weibel (eds), *Making Things Public. Atmospheres of Democracy*, 1–31, Cambridge, M: MIT Press.

Latour, B. (2005b), *Reassembling the Social: An Introduction to Actor-Network-Theory*, Oxford: Oxford University Press.

Latour, B. (2007a), 'A Plea for Earthly Sciences', Keynote lecture for the annual meeting of the British Sociological Association.

Latour, B. (2007b), 'Is There Cosmopolitically Correct Design? Lecture at the University of Manchester', Manchester Architecture Research Centre, 5 October.
Latour, B. (2010a), *On the Modern Cult of the Factish Gods. Science and Cultural Theory*, Durham, NC: Duke University Press.
Latour, B. (2010b), 'Steps Toward the Writing of a Compositionist Manifesto', *New Literary History*, 41: 471–490.
Latour, B. and A. Yaneva (2008), 'Give Me a Gun and I Will Make All Buildings Move: An ANT's View of Architecture', in R. Geiser (ed.), *Explorations in Architecture: Teaching, Design, Research*, 80–89, Basel: Birkhäuser.
Latour, B. and E. Hermant (1996), *Paris, Invisible City*, Paris: Les empêcheurs de penser en rond.
Latour, B. and P. Weibel (2005), *Making Things Public*, Cambridge, MA: MIT Press.
Latour, B. and S. Woolgar (1979), *Laboratory Life: The Social Construction of Scientific Facts*, Beverly Hills, CA: Sage Publications.
Law, J. (1987), 'Technology and Heterogeneous Engineering: The Case of the Portuguese Expansion', in W. E. Bijker, T. P. Hughes and T. Pinch (eds), *The Social Construction of Technical Systems: New Directions in the Sociology and History of Technology*, 111–134, Cambridge, MA: MIT Press.
Law, J. (2002), *Aircraft Stories: Decentering the Object in Technoscience*, Durham: Duke University Press.
Law, J. (2007), 'Making a Mess with Method', in W. Outhwaite and S. P. Turner (eds), *The Sage Handbook of Social Science Methodology*, 595–606, Beverly Hills and London: Sage.
Law, J. (2009), 'The Greer-Bush Test: On Politics in STS'. Available online: http://www.heterogeneities.net/publications/Law2009TheGreer-BushTest.pdf (accessed 23 December 2009).
Leach, N., ed. (1999), *Architecture and Revolution*, London: Routledge.
Lees, L. (2001), 'Towards a Critical Geography of Architecture: The Case of an Ersatz Colosseum', *Ecumene*, 8: 51–86.
Lefebvre, H. (1991), *The Production of Space*, Oxford: Blackwell.
Lhuillier, M. and L. Quan (2002), 'Quasi-Dense Reconstruction from Image Sequence', *Computer Vision – ECCV, Lecture Notes in Computer Science*, 2351(2002): 470–471.
Loukissas, Y. (2012), *Co-Designers. Cultures of Computer Simulation in Architecture*, London and New York: Routledge.
Lynch, M. (1985), 'Discipline and the Material Form of Image: An Analysis of Scientific Visibility', *Social Studies of Science*, 15(1): 37–66.
Lynch, M. (1993), *Scientific Practice and Ordinary Action: Ethnomethodology and Social Studies of Science*, Cambridge: Cambridge University Press.
Lynch, M. and S. Woolgar (1990), *Representation in Scientific Practice*. Cambridge, MA: MIT Press.
Lynch, M. and S. Y. Edgerton (1988), 'Aesthetics and Digital Image Processing: Representational Craft in Contemporary Astronomy', in G. Fyfe and J. Law (eds), *Picturing Power: Visual Depiction and Social Relations*, 184–220, London and New York: Routledge.
MacKenzie, D. (2009), *Material Markets: How Economic Agents Are Constructed*, Oxford: Oxford University Press.
Maran, J., C. Juwig, H. Schwengel and U. Thaler, eds (2006), *Constructing Power: Architecture Ideology and Social Practice*, Heidelberg: Lit Verlag.
Markus, T. (1993), *Buildings and Power: Freedom and Control in the Origin of Modern Building Types*, Routledge: London and New York.

Marres, N. (2005), 'Issues Spark a Public into Being: A Key but Often Forgotten Point of the Lippmann-Dewey Debate', in B. Latour and P. Weibel (eds), *Making Things Public: Atmospheres of Democracy*, 208–217, Cambridge, MA: MIT Press.

Marres, N. (2012), *Material Participation: Technology, the Environment and Everyday Publics*, Basingstoke: Palgrave Macmillan.

McLean, C. and J. Hassard (2004), 'Symmetrical Absence/Symmetrical Absurdity: Critical Notes on the Production of Actor-Network Accounts', *Journal of Management Studies*, 41(3): 493–519.

McLeod, M. (1989), 'Architecture and Politics in the Reagan Era: From Postmodernism to Deconstructivism', *Assemblag*, 8: 22–59.

McNeill, D. (2008), *The Global Architect: Firms, Fame and Urban Form*, New York: Routledge.

Millon, H. A. and V. M. Lampugnani, eds (1994), *The Renaissance from Brunelleschi to Michelangelo. The Representation of Architecture*, Milan: Bompiani.

Minuchin, L. (2012). 'A Lineal City in the Pampas: Politics, Materialization and Revolution in Wladimiro Acosta's Vision for Buenos Aires'. *Antipode*, 44(3): 911–931.

Minuchin, L. (2016) 'The Politics of Construction: Towards a Theory of Material Articulations'. *Environment and Planning D: Society and Space*, 34(5): 895–914.

Mitchell, W. J. T., ed. (1994), *Landscape and Power*, Chicago: The Chicago University Press.

Mol, A. (1999), 'Ontological Politics. A Word and Some Questions', in J. Law and J. Hassard (eds), *Actor Network Theory and After*, 74–89, London and New York: Routledge.

Mol, A. (2002), *The Body Multiple: Ontology in Medical Practice*, Durham, North Carolina: Duke University Press.

Molnár, V. (2013), *Building the State: Architecture, Politics, and State Formation in Post-war Central Europe*, Abingdon: Routledge.

Molotch, H. (2005), *Where Stuff Comes From: How Toasters, Toilets, Cars, Computers and Many Other Things Come to Be as They Are*, London: Routledge.

Monroe, J. C. (2010), 'Power by Design: Architecture and Politics in Precolonial Dahomey', *Journal of Social Archaeology*, 10(3): 367–397.

Moore, J. D. (1996), *Architecture and Power in the Ancient Andes: The Archaeology of Public Buildings*, New York: Cambridge University Press.

Moore, S. and B. Wilson (2013), *Questioning Architectural Judgement. The Problem of Codes in the United States*, London: Routledge.

Morshed, A. (2002), 'The Cultural Politics of Aerial Vision: Le Corbusier in Brazil (1929)', *Journal of Architectural Education*, 55(5): 201–210.

Morton, T. (2013), *Hyperobjects: Philosophy and Ecology After the End of the World*, Minneapolis: University of Minnesota Press.

Moussavi, F. (2012), 'School Buildings Produce Culture', *The Architectural Review*, 28 September. Available online: http://www.architectural-review.com/view/overview/school-buildings-produce-culture/8636270.article/ (accessed 5 December 2015).

Mühlberger, K., ed. (1993), *Aspekte der Bildungs- und Universitätsgeschichte*, Vienna: Universitäts-Verlag.

Mukerji, C. (1997), *Territorial Ambitions and the Gardens of Versailles*, Cambridge: Cambridge Univ. Press.

Nadaï, A. and O. Labussière (2013), 'Playing with the Line, Channelling Multiplicity: Wind Power Planning in the Narbonnaise (Aude, France)', *Environment and Planning D: Society and Space*, 31(1): 116–139.

'New Bolshoi director Vladimir Urin: "I am no revolutionary"', *BBC News*, 12 July 2013, Available online: http://www.bbc.co.uk/news/world-us-canada-23293677 (accessed 10 September 2013).

Nitzan-Shiftan, A. (2005), 'Capital City or Spiritual Center? The Politics of Architecture in Post-1967 Jerusalem', *Cities*, 22(3): 229–240.

Osborn, A. (2016), Bolshoi Theatre Refit Like Turkish Hotel Says Top Dancer, *The Telegraph*, 27 October 2011, http://www.telegraph.co.uk/culture/theatre/theatre-news/8853730/Bolshoi-Theatre-refit-like-Turkish-hotel-says-top-dancer.html (accessed 3 September 2013).

Parkinson, J. (2012), *Democracy and Public Space: The Physical Sites of Democratic Performance*, Oxford: Oxford University Press.

Pasveer, B. and M. Akrich (1996), *Comment la naissance vient aux femmes. Les techniques de l'accouchement en France et aux Pays-Bas*, Paris: Les Empêcheurs Penser en Rond.

Patterson, M. (2012), 'The Role of the Public Institution in Iconic Architectural Development', *Urban Studies*, 49(15): 3289–3305.

Petroski, H. (1993), *The Evolution of Useful Things*, New York: Knopf.

Pickering, A. (1992), *Science as Practice and Culture*, Chicago: Chicago University Press.

Pickering, A. (1995), *The Mangle of Practice. Time, Agency and Science*, Chicago, Illinois: University of Chicago Press.

Pickering, A. (2009), 'The Politics of Theory', *Journal of Cultural Economy*, 2(1–2): 197–212.

Picon, A. (2013), *Ornament: The Politics of Architecture and Subjectivity*, Chichester: Wiley.

Pikirayi, I. (2013), 'Stone Architecture and the Development of Power in the Zimbabwe Tradition AD1270–1830', *Azania: Archaeological Research in Africa*, 48(2): 282–300.

Ponzini, D. (2011), 'Large Scale Development Projects and Star Architecture in the Absence of Democratic Politics: The Case of Abu Dhabi, UAE', *Cities*, 28(3): 251–259.

Pullan, W. (2011), 'Frontier Urbanism: The Periphery at the Centre of Contested Cities', *The Journal of Architecture*, 16(1): 15–35.

Puwar, N. (2010), 'The Archi-texture of Parliament: Flâneur as Method in Westminster', *The Journal of Legislative Studies*, 16(3): 298–312.

Rabinow, P. (1995), *French Modern: Norms and Forms of the Social Environment*, Chicago: The University of Chicago Press.

Reid, E. (1984), *Understanding Buildings: A Multidisciplinary Approach*, Cambridge, MA: MIT Press.

Ren, X. (2011), *Building Globalization. Transnational Architecture Production in Urban China*, Chicago: The University of Chicago Press.

Rendell, J. (2010), *Site-Writing: The Architecture of Art Criticism*, London: I.B. Tauris.

Rheinberger, H.-J. (1997), *Towards History of Epistemic Things: Synthesizing Proteins in the Test Tube*, Stanford: Stanford University Press.

RIBA Brief (2008), Brief for the Short-listed, Redevelopment of New Street Station Birmingham. RIBA. 14 February.

Rose, G., M. Degen and C. Melhuish (2014), 'Networks, Interfaces and Computer-Generated Images: Learning from Digital Visualisations of Urban Redevelopment Projects', *Environment and Planning D: Society and Space*, 32(3): 386–403.

Rosental, C. (2003), *La trame de l'évidence. Sociologie de la demonstration en logique*, Paris: PUF.

Ruskin, J. (1989), *The Seven Lamps of Architecture*, New York: Dover Publications.

Rydin, Y. and L. Tate, eds (2016), *Actor Networks of Planning. Exploring the Influence of Actor Network Theory*, London: Routledge.

Sandercock, L. and K. Dovey (2002), 'Pleasure, Politics, and the "Public Interest": Melbourne's Riverscape Revitalization', *Journal of the American Planning Association*, 68(2): 151–164.
Sandler, D. (2004), 'Incarnate Politics: The Rhetoric's of German Reunification in the Architecture of Berlin', *Invisible Culture*, 5. Available online: http://www.rochester.edu/in_visible_culture/Issue_5/daniela/daniela3.html (accessed 16 November 2015).
Schön, D. (1983), *The Reflective Practitioner: How Professionals Think in Action*, New York: Basic Books.
Schwanzer, B. (1994), *Architektur-Modelle und Sammlungen*, Wien: Modulverlag.
Sennett, R. (1994), *Flesh and Stone: The Body and the City in Western Civilization*, New York: W.W. Norton.
Sennett, R. (2002), *Respect in a Word of Inequality*, London: Penguin.
Shapin, S. (1998), 'Placing the View from Nowhere: Historical and Sociological Problems in the Location of Science', *Transactions of the Institute British Geographers, New Series*, 23: 5–12.
Shapin, S. and S. Schaffer (1985), *Leviathan and the Air-Pump: Hobbes, Boyle, and the Experimental Life*, Princeton: Princeton University Press.
Sklair, L. (2005), 'The Transnational Capitalist Class and Contemporary Architecture in Globalizing Cities', *International Journal of Urban and Regional Research*, 29(3): 485–500.
Sklair, L. (2006), 'Iconic Architecture and Capitalist Globalization', *City*, 10(1): 21–47.
Sklair, L. (2010), 'Iconic Architecture and the Culture-Ideology of Consumerism', *Theory, Culture and Society*, 27(5): 135–159.
Sloterdijk, P. (2005), *Ecumes: Spheres III, Spherologie plurielle*, Paris: Maren Sell Editeurs.
Sloterdijk, P. (2009), 'Spheres Theory. Talking to Myself About the Poetics of Space', Lecture at the Graduate School of Design, Harvard, 17 February. Available online: http://tirado.wordpress.com/2009/03/02/dasein-ist-design (accessed 16 February 2015).
Sporton, G. (2006), 'Power as Nostalgia: The Bolshoi Ballet in the New Russia', *New Theatre Quarterly*, 22(4): 379–386.
Stark, D. and V. Paravel (2008), 'PowerPoint in Public: Digital Technologies and the New Morphology of Demonstrations', *Theory, Culture and Society*, 25(5): 30–55.
Steadman, R. (2006), 'Why Are Most Buildings Rectangular?', *ARQ*, 10(2): 119–130.
Stengers, I. (1993), *L'invention des sciences modernes*, Paris: La Découverte.
Stengers, I. (2005), 'The Cosmopolitical Proposal', in B. Latour and P. Weibel (eds), *Making Things Public: Atmospheres of Democracy*, 994–1003, Cambridge, MA: MIT Press.
Stengers, I. (2010a), *Cosmopolitics I*, Minneapolis: Minnesota University Press.
Stengers, I. (2010b), *Cosmopolitics II*, Minneapolis: Minnesota University Press.
Stengers, I. (2011), 'Another Science Is Possible! A Plea for Slow Science', Faculté de Philosophie et Lettres, ULB, Inauguratial lecture Chair Willy Calewaert 2011–2012, 13 December.
Stengers, I. and I. Prygogine (1988), *Entre le temps et l'éternité*, Paris: Fayard.
Strebel, I. (2011), 'The Living Building: Towards a Geography of Maintenance Work', *Social and Cultural Geography*, 12(3): 243–226.
Strike, J. (1994), *Architecture in Conservation. Managing Development at Historic Sites*, London and New York: Routledge.
Tafuri, M. (1976), *Architecture and Utopia: Design and Capitalist Development*, Cambridge, MA: MIT Press.
Tarde, G. (1999), *Monadologie et sociologie*, Paris: Les empêcheurs de penser en rond.
Tarde, T. (1895), 'Les Deux éléments de la sociologie', in *Études de psychologie sociale*, 63–94, Paris: Giard et Brière.

Tarde, T. (1898), 'Les Deux éléments de la sociologie', in G. Tarde (ed.), *Études de psychologie sociale*, 63–94, Paris: Giard et Brière.
Tassin, E., ed. (2013), *Architecture in the Anthropocene: Encounters Among Design, Deep Time, Science and Philosophy*, Ann Arbor: Open Humanities Press.
Thomas, N. (1991), *Entangled Objects. Exchange, Material Culture and Colonialism in the Pacific*, Cambridge: Harvard University Press.
Thorpe, A. (2014), 'Applying Protest Event Analysis to Architecture and Design', *Social Movement Studies*, 13(2): 275–295.
Till, J. (1998), 'Architecture of the Impure Community', in *Occupying Architecture*, 62–75, New York: Routledge.
Till, J. (2005), 'The Negotiation of Hope', in P. B. Jones, D. Petrescu, and J. Till (eds), *Architecture and Participation*, 23–41, London: Spon Press.
Till, J. (2009), *Architecture Depends*, Cambridge, MA: MIT Press.
Traska, G. (2006), 'Designing Renovation: The Building as Planning Material', *Building Research & Information*, 35(1): 54–69.
Tufte, E. (2006), 'The Cognitive Style of PowerPoint: Pitching Out Corrupts Within', in E. Tufte (ed.), *Beautiful Evidence*, 156–185, Cheshire: Graphics Press LLC.
Ünaldi, S. (2013), 'On His Majesty's Service: Bangkok's Architects Between Autonomy and Heteronomy', *The Journal of Architecture*, 18(3): 435–448.
Vale, L. J. (1992), *Architecture, Power and National Identity*, New Haven: Yale University Press.
Vale, L. J. (1999), 'Mediated Monuments and National Identity', *Journal of Architecture*, 4(4): 391–408.
Vertesi, J. (2008), 'Mind the Gap The London Underground Map and Users' Representations of Urban Space', *Social Studies of Science*, 38(1): 7–33.
Vincenti, W. (1990), *What Engineers Know and How They Know It: Analytical Studies from Aeronautical History*, Baltimore and London: The Johns Hopkins University Press.
Vinck, D., ed. (2003), *Everyday Engineering: An Ethnography of Design and Innovation*, Cambridge, MA: MIT Press.
Whatmore, S. (2002), *Hybrid Geographies*, London: Sage.
Winner, L. (1980), 'Do Artifacts Have Politics?', *Daedalus*, 109(1): 121–136.
Yacobi, H. (2004), 'Form Follows Metaphors: A Critical Discourse Analysis of the Construction of the Israeli Supreme Court Building in Jerusalem', *The Journal of Architecture*, 9(2): 219–239.
Yaneva, A. (2001), 'L'affluence des objets: pragmatique comparée de l'art contemporain et de l'artisanat d'art', PhD diss, Ecole Nationale Supérieure des Mines de Paris.
Yaneva, A. (2003), 'Chalk Steps on the Museum Floor: The "Pulses" of Objects in Art Installation', *Journal of Material Culture*, 8: 169–188.
Yaneva, A. (2005), 'Scaling Up and Down: Extraction Trials in Architectural Design', *Social Studies of Science*, 35(6): 867–894.
Yaneva, A. (2009a), *The Making of a Building: A Pragmatist Approach to Architecture*, Oxford: Peter Lang Publishers.
Yaneva, A. (2009b), *Made by the Office for Metropolitan Architecture. An Ethnography of Design*, Rotterdam: 010 Publishers.
Yaneva, A. (2012), *Mapping Controversies in Architecture*, Farnham: Ashgate.
Yaneva, A. (2013), 'Actor-Network-Theory Approach to Archaeology of Contemporary Architecture', in P. Graves-Brown, R. Harrison and A. Piccini (eds), *Oxford Handbook of the Archaeology of the Contemporary World*, 121–135, Oxford: Oxford University Press.

Yaneva, A. and A. Zaera-Polo, eds (2015), *What Is Cosmopolitical Design?* Farham: Ashgate.

Zaera-Polo, A. (2008), 'The Politics of the Envelope', Volume 17 (Fall 2008).

Zaff, B. S. (1995), 'Designing with Affordances in Mind', in J. M. Flach, P. A. Hancock, J. Caird and K. J. Vicente (eds), *Global Perspectives on the Ecology of Human–Machine Systems*, 121–156, Mahwah: Lawrence Erlbaum.

Zitouni, B. (2010), *Agglomérer. Une anatomie de l'extension Bruxelloise (1828–1915)*, Bruxelles: Brussels University Press.

Index

activism 4, 15, 19, 171
Actor-Network-Theory (ANT) 2, 8–11, 31, 42, 44–5, 52, 137, 162–3, 176–7, 181
adjustment, adjustments 87, 90, 99, 114, 125–6
Akrich, Madeleine 8–9, 168, 171, 179
Alte Aula 12, 110–12, 114–15, 117–20, 129–31
Anthropocene 75–6, 90, 181
anthropology 8, 42–5, 51, 172
aperspectival objectivity 8, 111, 130
architectural
  design 8, 12, 27, 30, 42–4, 51, 72, 75–7, 90, 96, 98, 181
  firm 8, 43, 142,
  presentation 12, 31, 133–7, 146, 156–7, 163
  visuals 5, 93
architecture in the making 9, 30, 75
assemblage, assemblages 45, 84, 88–9, 104, 141–2, 145, 170
atrium 53, 57–64, 66, 72, 74, 76–7, 95, 165, 171

Barry, Andrew 4–5, 28, 171
Beck, Ulrich 5, 25, 171, 176
Bentham, Jeremy 1, 73
Benzie Art School in Manchester 12, 53–9, 61–5, 69–70, 72–4
Bolshoi theatre 9, 12, 22, 110–11, 120–31, 162, 179
bridge 1–4, 12, 21, 53, 65–6, 73–4, 165
bunker 25, 171

Callon, Michel 8–9, 43, 134, 157, 162, 172
Canadian Centre For Architecture (CCA) 3
causal relation 5, 143–5
causality 15, 114, 120, 169
CCTV 47, 139
coexistence 52, 75–6, 79
cohabitation 88, 104

collective, collectives 10, 54, 62, 76, 119, 157, 166–7
common world 90, 107, 141, 161, 164
composition, compositions 45, 75, 83–4, 88, 90, 93, 101, 103, 105, 108, 146
conservation 109–10, 118, 120, 129–30, 180
controversy 122–6, 128, 173
cosmology 75, 88–9, 104, 154
cosmopolitical
  assemblage 104
  design 84, 173, 182
  ecology 88–9
  perspective 89
  question 104
cosmopolitically correct 90, 177
cosmopolitics 75–6, 90, 92, 176
cosmos 89, 154, 167, 176
Cuff, Dana 8, 33, 43–5, 48, 51, 79, 172

delegate 10, 65–6, 160, 167
Deleuze, Gille 12
democracy 21, 26, 29, 134–5, 157, 172
demonstration, demonstrations 29, 118, 134–5, 146, 156, 179
design experiment, experiments 5, 11, 88, 163
disposition, dispositions 135–7, 139, 147–50, 154–6, 160
divided cities 20, 172
Dominguez, Fernando 4–5, 173
dwelling 7–8, 31–2, 44–5, 65, 109, 160–1, 163–4, 166–7

ecology of practice 33, 51
ecology, ecologies 12, 33, 42, 45, 51, 79, 88–90, 171, 178, 182
envelope, envelopes 67, 77, 80–1, 85–8, 90, 94–7, 101–5, 108, 141, 182
ethnography 11, 34, 36–7, 41–3, 45–52, 104, 165, 175, 181

event, events 4–5, 7, 12, 18, 23, 37–8, 40–1, 43–4, 47, 49, 55, 63, 72, 100, 110, 114, 116, 122, 133, 136, 138, 149–50, 165, 168–9, 181
experiment, experiments 5–6, 11–12, 31, 48, 52, 75, 82, 84–5, 87–90, 100–1, 103, 116, 118, 126, 134, 141, 156, 163–4, 172, 175
experimentation 12, 32, 51, 76, 79, 81–90, 109, 113, 138, 157, 163

Fogué, Uriel 4–5, 173
foundational theories of politics 4, 15

Galison, Peter 8, 30–1, 59, 85, 172, 174
Gateway project 76–7, 79–80, 91, 95–6, 108, 174
Geertz, Clifford 46–7, 165, 174
Gehry, Frank 61, 80,
gilding techniques 111, 128, 130, 162
glare 10, 12, 75–6, 79–90, 92, 104, 160, 162–4
Guattari, Félix 34, 36–8, 174

Haraway, Dona 76, 163–4, 174
Harrison, Ariane Lourie 76, 174
Houdart, Sophie 30, 43–5, 49, 85, 92, 95, 104, 175
hybrid forum 157,

infrastructure, infrastructures 1–5, 6, 13, 18, 29, 53, 62, 99, 101, 103
inhabitation 7, 10, 26, 33, 43–4, 52, 162–4, 166
irreductivist 5–6, 29

Koolhaas, Rem 13, 34, 41, 47, 49–50, 52, 133, 137, 145, 148, 150, 154
Kuma, Kengo 49, 52, 104, 175

Latour, Bruno 5–6, 8, 9, 11, 28, 30, 33, 41–2, 44, 47, 51, 53, 68–9, 76, 84–5, 90, 92, 134–5, 164, 168–70, 176–7, 180
Lynch, Michael 8, 84–5, 177

Marina Bay Sands 150–1, 153
Marres, Noortje 6, 28, 135, 147, 157, 178

material
    arrangement, arrangements 1, 4–5, 10, 12–13, 32, 53–4, 60, 62, 65, 67, 69, 72–4, 135–6, 138, 150, 154–5, 157, 163, 166
    embodiment 23
    public 28, 135, 147, 150
    semiotics 28
materiality, materialities 2, 7, 8–9, 25, 28, 31, 37, 52, 61, 65–6, 74–5, 79, 99, 108, 110, 114, 119, 130, 135, 137, 176
mediating role 16, 109
mediator, mediators 31, 64, 68, 83, 169
model, models 10, 30, 33, 35–6, 41, 44, 46–52, 56, 59, 62, 66, 75, 77, 80, 83, 91, 94, 100, 107–8, 133, 135, 138–48, 150, 152, 154, 156, 160, 163–4, 171–3, 180
model making 49, 50, 140–1
Moses, Robert 1–2, 4, 12, 73, 165
mosque 25, 173–4
multiplicity 8, 48, 96, 107, 117, 122, 129–30, 141, 144, 163–4, 178
multiverse 140, 145
mundane politics 73–4
museum, museums 12, 25, 27, 47, 111, 118, 127, 137, 145–7, 150, 153, 159, 181

negotiation, negotiations 16, 27, 33, 43, 73, 97, 109, 112–13, 118, 181
Network Rail 77, 81–2, 90, 97, 100
new ethnographies 12, 45, 51–2, 85
New Street Station 76–7, 92, 94–5, 102, 105, 174, 179
New Street Train Station 12, 75, 162,

objectivity 6, 8, 31, 111, 126, 130, 161, 172, 176
Office for Metropolitan Architecture 41, 137, 181
office towers 24, 53
OMA 41–2, 45–8, 50–2, 138–41, 144–50, 154–5
ontologically political 91, 107
ontology 12, 26, 29–31, 33–4, 36, 75, 93, 107, 147, 150, 162–4, 175, 178
original substance 110, 113

Palacio de Congresos 12, 137, 147–8
panopticon 1, 4, 73, 165
parliament building, parliament buildings 22, 26
patina of age 110
Perea, Andrés 34, 133, 137, 148–50, 154–5
performance, performances 6, 9–10, 26–7, 29, 43–4, 46, 60, 84–5, 99, 107, 111, 116, 123, 135–6, 159, 167, 169–71, 173
perspectival flexibility 7, 110, 125
perspectivalism 7, 110
persuasive techniques 12, 133–4
pluriverse 164
political
    action 5, 10, 29, 109, 136, 166
    dimension of architecture 8, 109, 155, 165
    philosophy 5–6, 157
    theory 2, 26, 29, 135
    valence of architecture 129, 166
pragmatist 6, 8, 27, 41, 45, 67, 91–2, 147, 155, 181
presentational rhetoric 162
presentational setting 49, 134–6, 146, 148, 150, 155, 160
preservation 109–14, 117–20, 126, 129–30
prison 1, 4, 73, 173
Prohazka, Rudolf 34, 111–16, 118

reassembling 41, 102, 144, 176
relational politics 28, 67, 163
rendering, renderings 11, 22, 33, 44, 49, 51–2, 93, 98–9, 104, 107–8, 156
renovation 4–8, 10–12, 31–2, 109–14, 116–31, 133, 162, 164–5, 181
renovation in the making 109, 111, 130
representation, representations 5, 16, 25–6, 31, 44, 77, 90, 101, 105, 107, 147, 164, 177–8, 181
RIBA 76, 95, 179

Safdie, Mosche 13, 34, 133, 137, 150–3, 155
Schön, Donald 43, 180
Science and Technology Studies (STS) 6
scientific buildings 59

Science studies 31, 33, 43, 92, 173, 175–6
situated knowledge 163, 174
sky-scraper, sky-scrapers 24, 53, 65, 144
Sloterdijk, Peter 76, 89, 180
slowing down 37–8, 61, 87
social
    biography 121
    change 17, 21, 73, 166
    control 1, 166
    life 12, 68, 121
socio-material arrangements 138
stadium, stadia 23, 27, 53, 172
Stengers, Isabelle 28, 31, 37, 42, 76, 89, 119, 180
style, styles 13, 15, 19–20, 23, 36, 41, 96, 123, 134, 138, 164, 181
subpolitical 4–5
surprise, surprises 109, 111–20, 122, 129–30
symmetric anthropology 42, 51
symmetric ontology 26, 31
symmetry 26, 38, 42, 45, 155

Takamatsu, Shin 34–40, 174
tall buildings 24, 172
Tarde, Garbriel 72, 92, 180–1
theatre, theatres 9, 12, 22, 31, 42, 53, 63–4, 69–72, 74, 110–12, 115–16, 118, 120–31, 150, 162, 164, 171, 179–80
Till, Jeremy 7, 12, 17, 171, 181

urban
    artefacts 5, 29, 33, 44, 168
    design 21, 28–9, 91, 94, 170
    publics 28, 174
    studies 2, 26, 76, 173–5, 179

vertical gallery 54–5, 57–8, 61, 63–5
vibrant matter 111, 171

Whitney Museum for American Art in New York 12, 137, 147
Winner, Langdon 1–3, 181

Zaera-Polo, Alejandro 34, 76–7, 79–80, 92–3, 97–8, 101–3, 105, 182

www.ingramcontent.com/pod-product-compliance
Ingram Content Group UK Ltd.
Pitfield, Milton Keynes, MK11 3LW, UK
UKHW021909220326
469204UK00008B/260